MY MIDDLE NAME IS ISRAEL

A Wartime Memoir of Berlin, London and Shanghai

MY MIDDLE NAME IS ISRAEL

A Wartime Memoir of Berlin, London and Shanghai

by

Hans L. Riess

TO ELLIE
WITH BEST WISHES

Hans Riess

ISBN: 1-58820-967-9

This book is printed on acid free paper.

1stBooks – rev. 01/31/01

I dedicate this book to my loving
wife, Joyce, who is my best friend
and has supported me in every way
during the past 30 years.

ACKNOWLEDGMENT

I want to thank my family and friends who have listened to my experiences over the years and encouraged me to put my story down on paper. I also want to thank Kathy and Fred Plotkin without whose support and efforts this book would never have seen the light of day. They are newly found friends whom we shall always treasure.

Finally, I'd like to thank my wife, Joyce. She was there to listen, comment, suggest and read my work. She always said that my story was to be shared and I should "go for it". And so I did.

Chronology of Events – *My Middle Name Is Israel*

1914		My parents marry, two months before the start of WW I
1921	April 10	I am born in Berlin at Augsburgerstrasse 74
1930		The Riess family moves to Augsburgerstrasse 69
1933	January 30	Hitler named Chancellor of Germany
	February 27	Martin van der Lubbe sets the Reichstag on fire. "Uncle" Georg and my cousin Annemarie Hamburger leave Berlin for Israel
1934		Cousin Werner Riess leaves Berlin for Paris. Our number to emigrate to Israel comes up; we don't go
	November 21	My Bar Mitzvah takes place
1935		Nuremberg Race Laws go into effect
1936		Olympic games are held in Berlin
		I begin my studies at the University Engineering School
		The Riess family moves to Augsburgerstrasse 68
1937		Japan begins invasion of China
1938	March 11	Hitler annexes Austria
	November 9	Kristallnacht
		Father (Walter Riess) taken to concentration camp
	December 6	Walter Riess released on condition of leaving Berlin
1939	March	I leave Berlin for London
	April	My mother and father sail for Shanghai on the *Gneiseneau*
	April	The Murrays help me celebrate my 18th birthday in London.

	September	England goes to war with Germany
1940	Spring	I receive a degree in Mechanical Engineering
	June 20	I sail from Liverpool on the *Haruna Maru* for Shanghai
	September	The *Haruna Maru* arrives Shanghai
1941	December 8	Japanese take over Shanghai; Mr. Morrison puts me in charge of Jardine immediately
1943	February 18	Hongkew ghetto is established
	May 18	Stateless refugees, my parents among them, now required to live in the Hongkew area
	November	I am put in charge of "Technical Management" of Shanghai Iron Works
1944	Spring	British nationals are interned on Pootung; Jardine left with no English managers
	June 6	D-Day. Hope comes alive in all the refugees
1945	May 8	Germany surrenders to allies; My grandmother dies in Therisienstad concentration camp
	July 17	American air raid kills and wounds many in Hongkew ghetto
	August 10	Pacific war ends
	August 23	Japanese leave Shanghai
	September 23	Americans land in Shanghai
1947	January	My diploma from ICS arrives
	April 14	The Riess family sails from Shanghai for the U.S.
	May 1	We arrive in San Francisco
	June	We arrive in New York City
1949		Ronnie and I are married
1951		Marc Riess is born

1954	Charles Riess is born
1955	My father dies
1970	Joyce and I are married
1973	My mother dies
1996	I retire for the second time

FOREWORD

The events described in this memoir took place over sixty years ago. Some events I recall clearly as if they occurred only yesterday; others are only vaguely remembered, as one retains a portion of a dream upon awakening.

Writing about some of these long-past events is like picking up a strand of wool that will lead me out of the maze in which, to my surprise, I sometimes find myself.

I know that some who read this account of my life in Hitler's Berlin before the war commenced in earnest will be puzzled. Some will have other reactions, and other feelings, that will surprise you.

I know this will be your reaction, because everyone who has read this account as I have written it down so far has been baffled by my feelings and observations growing up as a young Jew in Nazi Germany.

I have attempted to evoke my unusual Jewish refugee experience without a trace of sentimentality.

Some will find it hard to believe that my parents and I were -- at least outwardly -- so placid and undisturbed -- by the events swirling around us.

Yet I am sure that my story and the story of my parents is not that unusual. It is certainly not unique. There were many Jews like us. You and I haven't read their memoirs, or their accounts of life in Germany before the war, because they haven't written them down.

To be the child of German Jews who escaped from Berlin in 1939 is in itself a special kind of experience which differentiates me from so many other survivors from Eastern Europe. My odyssey was not an "ordeal of civility," to use John Murray Cuddihy's phrase, in moving from ghetto culture to gentility.

There must have been many conversational land mines in my discussions with my parents, of which the Holocaust was only the most obvious. What the other taboo subjects were is so deeply repressed I cannot even recall the topics.

Most of us have read, or know about *Kristallnacht*, the Nuremberg Laws, the deportations, and so on. The horrors we know about, and are familiar to us as our own nightmares. What we don't know too much about is the ignorance, the paralysis, and the helplessness of certain German Jews who did not try to escape until the very end, because they simply could not move.

Our inertia was not so much a paralysis born of fear that endlessly delayed flight from Germany; if anything, it was the inertia of astonishment. We, like so many others, were like deer transfixed in the middle of the road, paralyzed by the headlights of fascism as it speeded up, coming straight for us.

The kind of German Jews I speak of are usually described by one word -- assimilated. The members of my extended family had melted, at least in appearance, culture, and gentility, into German society at least two hundred years before Hitler came to power.

I count myself in that group.

Today in America Jews who count themselves affiliated to some synagogue often speak of their fears about assimilation, and I wonder if they mean anything else but intermarriage.

I do have some misgivings about using this memoir form to tell my story. The anecdotal method is not in the best repute, but perhaps I can make it more respectable by calling it a "testimony."

In a defensive response to anonymous and supposed critics, I have tried to put my story into a larger context of my life in Berlin before the war -- a life that was privileged and cultured.

I am commemorating the positives of pre-war Germany and will let the reprobation of posterity deal with the Holocaust.

Mine is a story of a young man who, though he did not weep nostalgically over the loss of German culture, regretted it nonetheless; nor is my escape from the clutches of Nazism a four-hanky melodrama, though there were a couple of smallish scenes that might qualify for out-takes of a Charles Boyer suspense movie.

I believe that some of my friends -- perhaps even my wife -- feel that the fires of resentment and anger should be still burning bright in my heart after all these years, but they do not.

Besides the sweeping (possibly even mis-remembered) generalities of this memoir, there are also some obvious omissions.

The Holocaust, which radically changed the life of European Jewry for the worse, receives scant notice in this book. The Holocaust, which no doubt affected every Jew in the world at the time for the worse -- whether they lived in the old country or not -- had a measurable impact on my world, in the sense that it turned my family's life, status, profession and resident country topsy turvy.

Of Jews who perished cruelly at the hands of Nazis, I do not here sing a passionate song of elegiac praise; I save those words within my heart for private moments; I do not even lay the laurel gingerly on their grave, then step back weeping into the crowd of mourners. That history has been well documented by others, more competent than I. Moreover, it bears no relationship to my story.

There is a vast and wide-ranging literature of the Holocaust, but there are very few works, if any at all, that tell the story of a thoroughly assimilated family in Nazi Germany that somehow escaped the Holocaust. My story should be a part of that literature, because it is true and it did happen.

In a certain sense, the very phrase "an assimilated Jew in Nazi Germany" is an oxymoron, a contradiction in terms; but this is a subject that has been treated by many others before me and there is little I can add to the story except some color and Berlin atmosphere as my family and I experienced it.

What I can contribute is a different kind of perspective on how denial functions and how being assimilated clouds the mind.

Today, my understanding of Nazism as it pervaded German society is that Hitler's major trick was his use of the reactionary concept of "protecting public order." He appealed to the public's nostalgia for a lost "public order"; he also appealed to that familiar collection of things known in America today as "family values."

In *Mein Kampf*, Hitler wrote almost voluptuously about his passion for a social concept of order and authority that combined religious fervor with soldierly virtues and fierce patriotism. He also wrote of his fanatical hatred of the Jews.

Up to a point, apart from his destruction of European Jewry, there is nothing for me to argue about. Like so many secular people, I happen to believe in a libertarian view of society. And maybe that is today's trap in America just as it was Germany's trap in the thirties.

In today's Germany, of course, the shadow of the Holocaust is still dark, and discussions about patriotism and culture are tinged with fears that any celebration of history will degrade quickly into jackbooted despotism.

I would describe this as a special kind of German dilemma. The dilemma -- how to be interested in German history without falling into the Nazi trap? -- pervades what is referred to (in Germany) as overcoming the past.

Since I am writing a kind of family memoir, I have no problem in that regard; thus, I have been able to follow the dark waters of our escape from Germany back to its source, and to a country where everything was once comprehensible, and then suddenly became incomprehensible.

A brief resume of historical events that occurred just before and contemporaneous with my life in Berlin may provide a useful backdrop to my story.

The Weimar Republic, known today as that period in Germany when a loaf of bread cost a wheelbarrowful of marks, but was Germany's between-the-wars go at democracy -- had failed, and Germany was ready for a new beginning.

The failure of the allied nations to carry out the disarmament provisions of the Treaty of Versailles, was one of the more significant things that made Hitler's rise to power in Germany possible. The treaty had promised that the limitation of German armaments was but the beginning of a general limitation on the arms of all nations; but when the other nations showed no willingness to grant Germany's demand for equality, Hitler, in October, 1933, announced Germany's withdrawal from the League of Nations and the Disarmament Conference.

Shortly thereafter, in March 1935, Hitler introduced conscription. Jewish citizens were of course excluded from this honor.

German troops reoccupied the Rhineland in March of 1936.

Hitler was backed by an almost unanimous vote of confidence in the March elections that year. He had never been more popular.

In his autobiography, *Mein Kampf*, Hitler had declared that all German-speaking people (Jews were of course excluded), wherever they lived, should be united to Germany.

He was particularly interested in Austria, his native country, whose population, from a racial standpoint, was almost entirely German; and so in March, 1938, Hitler annexed Austria in the so-called *Anschluss*.

Every form of propaganda was used to spread the Nazi philosophy and inspire the people with Nazi ideals. A strict censorship of the radio, the newspapers, and all other publications was established. It was not enough that opinions be not opposed to Nazism; they must be definitely pro-Nazi.

The objective search for truth which had made German scholarship famous all over the world was discarded by the Nazis as one of the fallacies of liberalism. The quest for conformity to the party line superseded the search for truth. Schools and universities became mere instruments of Nazi propaganda; and all teachers and professors who were not whole-hearted Nazis were dismissed.

Great bonfires were made in the principal cities of the books of some 150 authors who were charged with being Jewish, socialistic, liberal, pacifist, or in any way un-German. Only Nazis were allowed to produce works of literature or art and a decree of 1935 forbade criticism of Nazi art.

From the time of its origin, the National Socialist party had based a large part of its propaganda on hostility to the Jews. Jews constituted less than one percent of the total population of Germany, but since under the Empire they had been barred by custom and prejudice from high positions in the army and government, they had turned to the professions -- law, medicine, dentistry, teaching, journalism -- and to business. For years they played an important part in the intellectual and business life of Germany. Under the Weimar Republic, which replaced the Empire after World War I, their influence increased.

The desire of the unemployed middle class, which was the backbone of the Nazi party, to get for themselves the positions held by Jews helps explain the bitterness of the feeling against us.

The first months of Hitler's rule were marked by a persecution of the Jews, official and unofficial, unequaled in brutality since the Middle Ages. Thousands were thrown into prison and other thousands driven into exile. There were wholesale removals of Jewish doctors, Jewish judges, Jewish university professors, and Jewish newspaper editors.

If members of my family knew of this, they kept it from me. I know it now, of course.

Jewish proprietors of large businesses were replaced by Nazis, proprietors of small stores were ruined by boycotts. Jews were no longer permitted to be members of trade unions. No secondary school or university might have more than one and a half percent Jews in its total enrollment. Besides these official acts, there were countless instances of unofficial boycotts, assaults, and murders of Jews by mobs often led by Nazi Stormtroopers.

Protests poured in from all over the world. Unofficial boycotts of German goods were established in various countries. These feeble protests had no effect. The German government declared that they were due to Jewish propaganda. The government did restrain some of the mob violence, but propaganda against the Jews continued and their rights were further restricted by law.

The Nuremberg Race Laws of September, 1935, defined Jews as those of seventy-five percent Jewish blood or those of fifty percent Jewish blood who practiced the Jewish religion or were married to Jews. Thus, even unconverted Christians who were simply the spouses of Jews were irrationally labelled as Jews. The crime that stripped them of their Christianity consisted of having sexual relations with a Jew.

Jews were denied the right to be German citizens, to marry Germans, to fly the German flag, to serve in the army, or to hold any office in the state. Jewish children were driven from public schools either by decree or by continued abuse.

The practical effect of all these decrees on the rest of the population was to eliminate all traces of Jewish existence from their daily lives; once Jews had largely disappeared from view, it made their destruction easier to accomplish and more palatable to Christian Germany.

In 1936, all Jews were required to deposit with the treasury twenty-five percent of all their wealth to insure payment of the "flight tax" in case they decided to emigrate.

The annexation of Austria and the Sudetenland in 1938 brought approximately 250,000 more Jews under Nazi control and evidently hastened the movement to eliminate Jews entirely from German life.

The murder of the third secretary in the German embassy at Paris by a half-crazed German Jewish refugee named Herschel Grynszpan was the signal for the outbreak of an orgy of anti-Semitism which amounted to a nationwide pogrom. In every city and town in Germany mobs led by Stormtroopers burned synagogues and smashed and looted Jewish shops. Thousands of defenseless Jews were brutally beaten while the police looked on with indifference or participated.

After a day or so, the pogrom was halted, but decrees were immediately issued which made it seem impossible for Jews to continue to exist in Germany. Jewish owners of buildings damaged in the pogrom were required to restore them at their own expense, but their insurance was confiscated. Furthermore, Jews were prohibited from conducting retail trade, mail-order, commission, or handicraft or folkcraft enterprises; such businesses had to be liquidated or turned over to "Aryans."

A 20 percent capital levy on all Jewish property was imposed to make up a fine of a billion marks as a punishment for the Paris assassination.

In addition, as part of the Nazi *Kulturkampf* against the Jews, all Jews were prohibited from attending theaters, movie houses and concert halls.

Approximately 150,000 refugees, Jews and members of other ethnic and religious groups singled out for Nazi persecution, left Germany between 1933 and 1939. The Assembly of the League of Nations had created a commission headed by an American named James MacDonald to deal with the refugee problem, but it was unable to do anything truly helpful.

At the suggestion of President Roosevelt, an international conference met at Evian in France during July, 1938, to work out some methods of aiding the refugees, some of which proved only marginally useful.

With all countries facing problems of unemployment, no one was willing to accept any large number of refugees. The conference created a permanent committee which discussed various plans of providing a refuge in Africa (a portion of present-day Uganda was a popular suggestion at the time) or South America, but these proved to be impractical.

Although early in 1939 Germany agreed to the plan of this committee which provided for gradual emigration, the "Fatherland" still made it difficult by refusing to allow refugees to take any but a small fraction of their wealth out of the country. No telling of the story of my flight from Berlin can ignore the Holocaust; a crime so vast and methodical must, we feel, have been the work of monsters on whom the mark of Cain is clear. Yet the executioners, those banal administrators of Hitler's "final solution" present us with a blank; they were all very ordinary little men.

By the time I left Berlin, Germany was a land well into decline, without a scrap of honor to its name, part bordello, part reign of terror, and part apocalyptic movie about the end of the world.

In July of 1937, while Europe and the western world were distracted by the Spanish Civil War and wondering what the next move of Hitler and Mussolini would be, Japan began her invasion of China.

With nationalism growing rapidly in Japan and a military clique anxious for prestige in control, a conflict was inevitable. It had been building up since the nineteenth century, ever since Japan began to annex territory belonging to China, and decided that it liked the concept of expansion through military conquest.

The confrontation came in July 1937 over a minor clash between Japanese and Chinese troops at the Marco Polo bridge near Beijing (formerly known as Peiping or Peking). The hostilities quickly escalated, and Japan rushed thousands of troops to China; full-scale war erupted, even though neither side had yet declared war. Japanese battleships bombarded Chinese seaports, and airplanes bombed the interior cities; thousands of civilians were killed.

Though unorganized and poorly equipped, the Chinese offered surprisingly strong resistance, but it was futile. By the end of the year, Japan had overrun most of North China and had possession of the ruins of three great Chinese cities: Peking,

Shanghai (except for the International Settlement and the French Concession), and Nanking.

By December, Japanese troops marched through Shanghai to celebrate the capture of the city from the Chinese.

In the early months of 1938, the Japanese drive slowed up while they tried to strengthen their lines of communication, but in the autumn Canton and Hankow fell. With the capture of Hankow, to which the capital of China had been moved from Nanking, the capital was again moved to Chungking, 600 miles farther west.

Within a year, the Japanese overran east China, virtually severing China's ties to the outside world.

The Japanese ran this occupied territory through an interconnected structure of puppet regimes headed by Chinese collaborators.

The Japanese discovered, however, that the capture of cities did not win the war.

The rural population of the conquered areas remained particularly hostile; economic life was to a very large extent at a standstill; Japan's expenses increased as her armies extended their lines farther from the home base.

After the fall of Nanking, the Chinese leaders changed their tactics. Instead of engaging the invading armies in direct battle, they kept retreating, worrying the Japanese by guerilla warfare.

These were the methods that the Communist armies had used for years to great effect against Chiang Kai-shek and the Nationalists. Now Chiang adopted them and with them the propaganda methods of the Communists for stirring up the peasants against Japan.

As far as life in Shanghai was concerned, most inhabitants of the city did not flee the Japanese; they had not the strength, the resources, nor the will. They saw no great merit in the policies and practices of the rivals Chiang Kai-shek and Mao Tse-Tung, and preferred to face an uncertain future with the Japanese.

This was true of industrial workers in the factories as well as those of other classes. If they left their jobs or their homes and took to the road, they had no guarantees of finding work, unless they were conscripted into the armies fighting the Japanese.

For their part, intellectuals in Shanghai had seen too much of the vindictiveness of the Kuomintang and the Communists, however obscured for the moment by the united front against Japan.

The large International Settlement of Shanghai provided a haven of sorts for many Chinese intellectuals, some of whom wrote anti-collaborationist or anti-Japanese criticisms even though the foreign Municipal Council which governed the International Settlement was subject to continuing pressure applied by the Japanese to suppress all such criticisms.

After Pearl Harbor, the Japanese ended the special privileges of the foreign concessions and international settlements in the Chinese territory that they controlled, although they had allowed Westerners to continue to study and do business -- albeit with restrictions -- in Peking and to a lesser extent in Shanghai.

In March of 1943, the foreign community of Peking (excluding Germans and Italians) was rounded up and transferred by rail to an internment camp in Shandong province where they were obliged to form a "community of survival" without their former privileges and servants.

Americans and Europeans in Shanghai were interned under similar conditions at other camps, but different treatment was meted out to those from Jewish backgrounds.

In mid-May, 1943, the great majority of Shanghai's 16,000 Jews -- refugees from persecution in Europe -- were forcibly moved by the Japanese to the "Designated Area" in the poor Hongkew section of the city.

If I had to guess I would say that the majority of these refugees were either German or Austrian Jews.

This order excluded Ashkenazic Jews, mostly from Russia, who had settled in China prior to 1937. For very special and remarkable reasons, which I shall explain in this book, this order had no effect on me, personally, but it most definitely affected my parents.

Forced to sell their hard-won homes and businesses at short notice for pitifully low prices, the Jews were organized into mutual-security groups for their own policing and protection. Inside the Hongkew ghetto, everyday existence grew more grim day by day.

Many Jews were reduced to performing coolie labor for local Chinese or eating in the soup kitchens that local charities kept going, and nearly all suffered from malnutrition. Some took to begging and others to prostitution as if their earlier lives of hardship were not harsh enough. Many died from lack of medical help in a disease-ridden community. Not a few despaired, and killed themselves.

Let it be said, however, that the Japanese never bowed fully to Nazi proposals that the Shanghai Jews suffer the same terrible program of extermination that had been the fate of their brethren left behind in Europe. It was more like a half bow.

One final word about my story. I am not writing this memoir as a historian might approach a life, determined to see it on its own terms (as opposed to the terms dictated by my milieu, comprehending rather than passing judgment, applying philosophical principles where, before, murky humanistic ones had prevailed -- a methodology summed up in the memorable phrase *wie es eigentlich gewesen*, how it really was (a phrase coined by the great 19th-century German historian Leopold von Ranke).

Getting it all down on paper took priority over figuring out what it all meant.

I do not approach this memoir clinically or impartially. I may have escaped Germany traveling light, but I did not leave bias-free.

Long vendettas don't interest me; on the other hand, I'm neither a forgiver nor a forgetter. In order to forgive or forget, one has to first understand. Yet how can one truly understand what made Germany in the thirties split itself up into lunatics and idiots? I still cannot say I understand.

I present here a running series of free-associative vignettes of events used as touchstones of memory. In retrospect, I think I wrote a very different book from what I originally intended, interweaving descriptions of public events with personal impressions, pushing myself (against my natural inclination) through an unfamiliar process of self-disclosure.

This was not easy for me to do. I'm not very easily given to the confessional style; and, for me, conversation is not confession. Moreover, I have not lived my life exploring my emotions, nor have I lived this long hugging dark memories to my bosom. I have been frugal with tidbits of self-revelatory detail, because I am a reserved and circumspect man and always have been. To this my wife and children will (perhaps ruefully) testify.

But I am not invisible in this memoir, nor am I invincible. You will see flashes of vulnerability all over the memoir, such as how it was to be a boy watching storm troopers with their swastika banners move through my native Berlin.

I deliberately keep this memoir spare and factual for a particular reason. I have always felt that true emotion comes from precision and clarity. I shouldn't have to guide anyone by the hand to the emotion.

I landed in San Francisco in 1947 at the age of 26, a Jewish refugee from Berlin, via Shanghai, and part of the vast tide of upheaval from those days of war. I quickly traded in "Hans" for "Hanley," did my best to master American English quickly, and got a job as a mechanical engineer. I sought to assimilate in America as quickly and as fast as my ancestors had done in Germany three hundred years earlier.

Over the next five decades, I did just that.

Berlin

I was born a German Jew. In 1933, when Hitler and the Nazis came to power, I was 12 years old, and one of only 160,000 Jews in Berlin, a city of 4 million. At that time, there were but 565,000 Jews in all of Germany, a country of 67 million.

Any short description of my family's history in Germany would have to contain the words, "assimilated Jews." Family oral history has it that more than 300 years ago my ancestors left Spain and settled in Posen, which is near Berlin. Longer than has been recorded we lived in Berlin happily and successfully, though not as religiously observant Jews.

Most of my family did not escape the Nazis in time; they were expendable citizens of a country they had called their homeland for over 300 years. Of my immediate family who stayed in Germany until as late as 1939, only my parents and I got out safely.

There is no record of exactly when in the early 19th century we acquired our German-sounding family name, but I do know how we got it. Jews in Germany originally had only first names, "Son of ...." and again, a first name. A decree in the early 19th century, modeled on the Napoleonic code, required that all Jews in Germany must take family names. Some took names which sounded as though they had money, such as Goldfinger or Goldschmidt; others named themselves after cities like Berlin or Wien; still others after their profession. Names like Tischler (carpenter), Schuster (shoemaker), or Schneider (tailor) sprang into existence. One particularly indecisive ancestor of mine, who was living in Bavaria at the time, went to a Bavarian magistrate for advice on this weighty matter and said, "I don't know what name to take." So the magistrate replied, "My best friend has just died. Why don't you take his name?" His name was Riess and from that time forward we were known as the Riess family. I am proud to report that today in Bavaria around

1

Garmisch-Partenkirchen near the Zugspitze, there is a Riessackerstrasse (Riess Field Street) as well as Riessersee (Riess Lake).

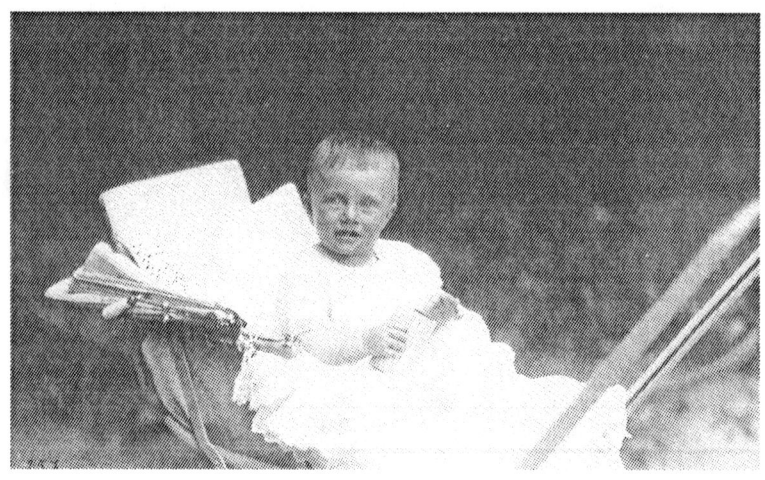

HANS RIESS   (1921)

It is the Berlin of 1931 where my childhood memories begin to emerge and sharpen. I was 10 years old then, living happily as the only child of my dentist father, Dr. Walter Riess, whom I called "Pappi" and my mother, Emmi Anna Riess (nee Loewenthal), whom I called "Mutti." Mutti was not only a homemaker, but also, since their marriage, Pappi's life-long assistant, submerging her own liberal arts college education and fluency in French to aid him in his dental practice. She also handled our family's finances. The experience she'd gained prior to her marriage during the years of 1908 through 1914 as the secretary to the President of the Deutsche Orient Bank stood her in good stead for that duty. (She took pride in the fact that as a girl she could take shorthand in both German and French, though I doubt that she had much use for it as Pappi's assistant.)

My parents were married in 1914, just two months before World War I began. They became engaged at the 1913 wedding of my mother's sister, Lillie Loewenthal (one year older than my mother) to my father's brother, Kurt Riess (one year younger than my father.) My parents' marriage bound our close-knit family even tighter.

Uncle Kurt managed their father Ludwig Riess's wholesale barber supply business; their widowed mother, Margarethe Riess, lived with Lillie and Kurt in a large Berlin suburb apartment. I was a frequent visitor to that home because their only child, my "twice-over" cousin Werner and I enjoyed being together, even though he was seven years my elder.

When World War I broke out, my mother and father, honeymooning in Denmark, immediately returned to Germany to support the Fatherland. It did not occur to them to do otherwise, since they were loyal, patriotic citizens. My father was assigned work in a military dental clinic and my mother was his assistant until he was shipped to Verdun, the frontier of France. Mutti stayed alone in Berlin until the war ended, at which point my father returned and resumed his own fledgling practice.

It was during Pappi's war-time absence that Mutti rented an expensive apartment in the best part of what is now "West" Berlin. This upset my fiscally conservative father, who had begun his practice in a lower middle-class neighborhood. It would take him five years to build up a practice, he worried, at least one large enough to be able to maintain such a grand style. Mutti wasn't concerned about money, however, because she had inherited not only lovely jewelry (platinum, diamonds and pearls) from her Aunt Lisbeth and Uncle Jacob, but also a sum equivalent to about 850,000 present-day German marks, a not inconsiderable inheritance in those days (a similar amount going to Tante Lillie.) During the years of the Weimer Republic (1923-1933), this small fortune was considerably diminished in value due largely to massive inflation that accompanied the global economic depression.

It was Aunt Lisbeth and her husband, Uncle Jacob Eichenwald (a wealthy lace and linens merchant) who took in my mother's mother and helped bring up both my mother and her sister Lillie when their father, Louis Loewenthal, deserted them in 1893. My mother was two years old, and Lillie only three, when he decamped to America, never to be heard from again.

And so it was thanks -- in part -- to the Eichenwald inheritance, that we had an eight-room apartment on the third floor of a red brick four-story house near the center of Berlin. The address was Augsburgerstrasse 74. I was actually born in that very apartment, on Sunday, April 10, 1921, co-delivered by my father and my mother's gynecologist cousin, Georg Hamburger, who arrived for the occasion, I am told, on a bicycle. There was also a midwife in attendance, and I suspect that she performed most of the practical work involved in bringing me into this world. I was promptly named Hans Ludwig Riess. (All of my male cousins bore the same middle name after our Grandfather Ludwig Riess.)

My father's practice thrived, and in 1930 we moved to a ten-room corner apartment just a few doors away: Augsburgerstrasse 69, a gray four-story house. Our apartment served both as our family's residence and my father's dental office. Pappi used the large double-window corner room for his bustling practice; next to it was the waiting room for patients. As you entered the apartment, a corridor -- so long I learned to ride my bicycle in it -- led to the kitchen, past two maids' rooms with their private baths beyond, ending at our family baths and sleeping quarters. (My parents' bedroom held a memorably large black marble sink, I remember). Pappi's dental laboratory was also located at that far end of the apartment. In the front of the apartment were the living room, dining room and the dental office.

The living room was furnished with dark, heavy leather furniture, a leather-covered desk containing a small safe, and a small table with four chairs where we sometimes ate dessert or fruit. A huge bookcase with handsome glass and wooden doors held our family's books, such as the writings of Goethe, Schiller,

Shakespeare, Zweig, Herzl, and Galsworthy, although I believe it was only my mother who actually read them.

A short-wave Telefunken radio stood on an original Biedermeyer cabinet. On the opposite wall was a glass cabinet which held crystal and valuable souvenirs from all over the world, such as a tiny silver gondola from Venice, a bronze of Hans Sachs, the shoemaker from Wagner's opera, Meistersinger, and a hooded beach seat called a *strandkorb* made of silver. A vacationer would sit in a full-size *strandkorb* and admire the sea, well-protected from the sun. The miniatures and other souvenirs were the way my mother's generous Aunt Lisbeth shared the memories of her travels.

On both the living and dining room floors lay elegant Persian rugs, so large they covered the floors entirely. A huge, hand-made iron chandelier hung from the living room ceiling; our dining room table could expand to seat 25 guests. At dinner the maids were summoned by my mother with an electric buzzer to serve the next course.

Hanging on the living room walls were a black and white lithograph of Frederick the Great, an oil painting of the Amsterdam harbor, an oil painting of the bridge over the Spree River, and one of a Berlin castle called the Schloss. There were also pictures in large oval frames of my Grandfather Ludwig Riess and rich Uncle Jacob Eichenwald. Miraculously, my parents managed to bring those two family pictures out of Germany when they left, and I still have them today.

In my own large room I built models of the Berlin radio tower with my Merklien erector set, and played with my electric train, a gift from Uncle Max Wolff (Pappi's baby sister Rosa's husband) made in his factory where he manufactured electric bulbs and electric irons as well as toy trains.

Among my toys were miniature car models in which I placed my long-suffering little turtle, Ilse, as a live passenger. I designed and built a skylighted turtle house surrounded with a fence for her, which I kept on top of my marble-topped dresser. My goldfish collection swam in a large aquarium, and in a separate terrarium, I had a real frog which I was convinced behaved like a barometer. He climbed up a tiny ladder when the weather was good, and down when it was rainy or cold.

As Germany's economic plight worsened, we moved in 1936 to a much smaller apartment (four rooms) in an almost identical house on the same street, Augsburgerstrasse 68. I have a photograph of Augburgerstrasse 68 in front of me as I write today in 1997, the last picture I took of it before I left forever in 1939.

Our building entrance was always locked, so the superintendent would come out only when somebody rang the doorbell. He would direct dental patients to the elevator, thence to my father's office door. Pappi worked from 8 a.m. until 9 p.m. every day, stopping only for long lunch breaks from noon to 3 p.m. I would join him right after school, which let out at 1:30, and we would have serious talks about my studies and how I was doing in school as we ate our main meal of the day. This consisted of an appetizer, meat (except Fridays, when we had fish), potatoes and vegetables. Dessert usually was vanilla or chocolate pudding or rote gruetze, a fruit jello, in the summer.

HANS RIESS IN BERLIN'S TIERGARTEN

At Augsburgerstrasse 68 my father had one room for his office, which was partitioned for his laboratory; there was a large living room, a large smoking room, called a Herrenzimmer -- which means literally, a room for gentlemen -- (in which I kept a little yellow singing canary in a partially glass cage), and a convertible bedroom.

The Herrenzimmer, was not, contrary to what one would think, the only room in which my father smoked. My fastidious mother had a lot of trouble keeping his cold, smelly cigar butts from being parked in ash trays all over the apartment. It was even worse in the old ten-room apartment at number 69, when the laboratory was in the back. My father would smoke in his laboratory, and on his way back to the dental office in the front,

7

make stops in my room, stops in the living room, and sometimes in the kitchen, trailing cigar ashes and depositing butts, before entering his office -- the only place he didn't smoke.

Our convertible bedroom doubled as my father's waiting room, and it connected all the rooms from the main entrance, like a large, central foyer. His office had an alcove with a very large window divided into three sections, one window on each side, making the whole area bright and cheerful. A lamp with a blue glass cover which protected the large bulb hung in front of the dental chair; an electric drill counterbalanced on hanging wheels, was centered over the patient. To the left was a white marble-topped sink; on the right, a large white cabinet which held his instruments. An almost-white linoleum covered the floor of his office as well as the partitioned laboratory.

When she was not assisting my father, my mother sat on a white chair working at a white desk in front of the partitioned laboratory, keeping the books, and typing whatever was necessary, but close at hand should my father need her. The walls of the area where she sat were bare except for a calendar and an illuminated hanging cabinet which contained an assortment of dental drugs.

The practice at Augsburgerstrasse 68 consumed most of our living space, but I don't remember that I minded our smaller quarters, nor indeed, do I recall taking any particular notice of our less palatial life-style. The most important thing to me was that we still had a balcony, which overlooked a wonderfully lively neighborhood. There I spent happy hours, watching a kaleidoscopic world pass by my ever-fascinated eyes.

The corner apartment at Augsbugerstrasse 68 had a famous wine restaurant called Horcher situated on the street level, and faced on to a thoroughfare busy with streetcars and taxis. In front of the restaurant stood a uniformed doorman dressed like an admiral in a comic opera who opened taxi doors and helped elegant customers into and out of expensive automobiles. I admired his impressive gold braid and epaulettes.

Around the corner from our building on Martin Luther Street was the Scala, Berlin's famous variety house and music hall, not unlike New York's Radio City Music Hall, with its velvet curtains and dazzling chandeliers, though without any columns to obstruct the view, and smaller in scale.

The Berlin Scala, named for Italy's premiere opera house in Milan -- built in 1776 -- was built along the Baroque lines of its namesake -- a horseshoe-shaped auditorium, the old-fashioned box-and-tier system, elaborate decor, seats stacked vertically to the ceiling.

The sidewalk in front of the Scala had a curved car lane as a driveway and a huge lighted overhanging canopy at the entrance to protect people from rain as they stepped out of cars and up to the large brass and glass entrance doors. As patrons entered its large foyer they saw broad staircases at each side, leading up to a very deep balcony.

The huge stage of the Scala was able to accommodate almost any kind of entertainment, large or small, from a circus or a symphony orchestra, to a soloist like the famous Italian tenor Beniamino Gilli. One of my father's patients, a Scala regular, a juggler by the name of Rastelli, came to my father every year to have a special denture that he used in his act, either replaced or adjusted. It had two prongs like a fork with which to catch 4-inch cork balls (painted white and which looked heavier than they really were). In the long corridor of our apartment, my father and I would test the special denture by throwing the cork balls from one end of the corridor to the other; the juggler caught them with his mouth, thanks to the special denture.

There were also plenty of pretty girls who lined up in my father's waiting room whenever a variety show was booked -- often free tickets to their performances came our way, thanks to their satisfaction with my father's work.

The Scala exists no more, a West Berlin casualty of a World War II bombing raid.

Across the road were cinemas where I became a life-long fan of Emil Jannings, Greta Garbo, Marlene Dietrich, Willi Fritch

9

and Shirley Temple, not necessarily in that order. First-run American movies as well as German films were shown in very large separate buildings. The German film company was UFA, (the Universal Film Association, which had studios in New Babelsberg near Potsdam at the outskirts of Berlin). UFA showed their new films in a large building called "UFA am Zoo." In a separate building in the same area was the MGM Marbelhaus (Marble House), where the American pictures were shown.

Among the movies I remember best were *It Happened One Night*, with Claudette Claubert and Clark Gable, *Anna Karenina* and *Queen Christina* with Greta Garbo, *Curly Hair* or in German, *Lockenkoepchen* with Shirley Temple, and a German film, *Der Kongress Tanzt* in Wien -- *The Congress Dances* in Vienna starring Lillian Harvey and I think Willi Fritch.

Also across the road from our apartment was a nightclub called *Das Goldene Hufeisen* (The Golden Horseshoe). One of our maids told me that this nightclub had a horse ring in the center where nude girls rode horses. It had, she reported, a reputation for being a wildly wicked place where girls got picked up and prostitutes hung out waiting for clients. Conveniently for their business, next to *Das Goldene Hufeisen* was a "Pension" which rented out rooms by the hour.

I would look out of the window at night, or hang over the balcony and watch the prostitutes on the other side of the street soliciting customers.

When they were successful, I watched them open the apartment house door with a key and disappear inside. They always used the same room each time. Being a normally curious boy, I tried to watch the performance through the poorly closed blinds and timed the duration of each rendezvous with my wrist watch. It usually took twenty minutes for the customer to return to the street, straighten his clothing, make sure his shirt was tucked in, his trousers buttoned or zipped, and then walk briskly away.

10

Ever a source of information not relayed to me by my parents, the same maid divulged the fact that a block away in the opposite direction of our house were two other nightclubs, both called Eldorado. Both catered to homosexual patrons, but one was for women and the other for men. Why this should be, she did not explain, nor did she enlighten me about what homosexuals were.

At the corner directly opposite our apartment was another restaurant, called Schlichter, but it was not so elegant a place as Horcher.

The street one block over from where we lived on Augsburgerstrasse was darker and more quiet. Small bars were on every block. Our milk store was across the street and a large flower store was in our building directly beneath my father's office. Next door was a drug store and a private clinic where my mother's gynecologist cousin (I called him "Uncle" Georg) sent many of his patients.

Five minutes from us was the famous department store KaDeWe, short for Kaufhaus des Westens (Department Store of the West). It was located at a large square, which had a "U" bahn (Underground) station entrance. The major shopping street on which the KaDeWe was located was very wide and had street cars running in the middle of the divided street. At the end of the street was a church, the Kaiser Wilhelm Gedaechnis Kirche. Elegant leather stores, shoe and clothing stores completed the make-up of this street. Beyond the church, another even more elegant shopping street called Kurfuerstendamm began; it was just as wide as the Tauenzienstrasse and not only had beautiful stores, but many cafes with enclosed sections for eating outdoors.

We would walk my Grandmother Riess to the Underground station near the KaDeWe in the evening after her weekly visit, which usually took place on Wednesdays. She would arrive early in the morning, around 8:00 a.m., after walking the short distance from the Underground to our apartment with her usual brisk pace and erect posture. My grandmother traveled to us

11

from Wilmersdorf, another borough of Berlin, where she lived with my Aunt Lillie, Uncle Kurt and their son, my favorite cousin Werner.

Later, around 1934 when my Uncle Kurt's wholesale barber equipment business had all but disappeared because of the dismal economic conditions prevailing in Germany, they could no longer afford their large apartment. As a result, Tante Lillie and Uncle Kurt were forced to move in with my family while we were still in our 10-room flat. Werner had already left home after a particularly heated dispute with his father, and was living in France. My grandmother went to live with one of her daughters, my father's sister and her husband, Aunt Else and Uncle Martin Grünfeld, who also happened to be a dentist.

Although my grandmother never complained, I think she was much happier living with Lillie and Kurt, where she really took charge and ran the household. Aunt Lillie didn't mind that one little bit.

In the earlier, happier days, when Grandmother arrived at our home for her weekly visit, she would immediately ask my mother for all our family mending and head straight for the Singer sewing machine where she spent the morning treadling away.

My tiny grandmother was much beloved by the whole family, and I found her extremely intelligent, able to talk about anything that might come into my young head. She never had to wear glasses or a hearing aid, but she did wear a denture, and I am chagrined to say that I found it quite funny to hide it from her. She also had very thin, gray hair, which she combed carefully over a layer of artificial hair (I think in America they called such a roll a "rat.") Sad to say, I also found it funny to hide that little piece of feminine vanity from her. My teasing notwithstanding, I was allowed to play with a handsome gold watch she always wore on a long gold chain, and when she visited us, that watch and chain were to be found around my young neck.

Not far from our apartment was the famous Zoo and Tiergarten, large, verdant parks right in the middle of Berlin. During spring and summer, I would take my bicycle to the Zoo almost every day mostly in the afternoon, or walk with my parents at night to the outdoor restaurant at the Zoo, where a military orchestra held nightly concerts.

The restaurant was situated on the banks of a beautiful lake; I particularly remember a large flock of live pink flamingos in the lake, all standing on one foot, illuminated by spotlights, and the fountain at the rear of the restaurant which changed its brilliant colors continuously. While taking all this in, I would enjoy my Sahnenbese (whipped cream in two halves of baked meringues) while my parents chatted with Tante Lillie and Uncle Kurt.

In those days our city was still full of life as far as I was concerned. I was barely aware that Berlin and the rest of Germany had a very high unemployment rate, that many people had very little to eat, and that German currency was literally going to hell in a handbasket, worth less and less as each day passed. Like most children, my consciousness barely contained my ego and was basically oblivious to anything that didn't affect me personally. I was living in a privileged upper-middle class setting, with my well-to-do father, successful in his profession, and my even more well-to-do mother whose inherited stock dividends paid for things that pleased her such as vacations, furniture, apartment renovations or made-to-order fashions. In fact, I suspect that my father somewhat resented the fact that his professional success did little to impress my independent mother.

I was a thoroughly spoiled child. My parents denied me nothing. I could tap softly at the glass doors separating my father's practice from the smoking room of our living quarters, and he would come to the door, reach for his wallet and ask me how much money I wanted, never asking the purpose. He would just hand it to me, and say "Have a good time" as he closed the door.

With my easily gained cash I usually went to the KaDeWe to buy toys or something sweet to eat.

I remember the New Year's Eve of 1932 with special fondness. Pappi, in one of his creative moods, decorated the entire apartment like a tent from *The Arabian Nights.* Most of the furniture was removed from the large living room and sheets were draped from the ceiling. On the longest wall, he placed a life-sized three-dimensional mannequin dressed like an Arab sheik wearing a red tapered hat with a black tassel. He draped the figure in a large blue cape; the sheik's yellow trousers were billowing silk, bound at the ankles. A thin moon and some stars -- both colored paper cut-outs -- were affixed to the wall.

Spellbound, I watched the preparation for this fabulous soiree all afternoon. A grand piano was delivered and kitchen help arrived with heavenly smelling dishes prepared by an outside caterer. Sadly, I was not allowed to stay for this wondrous festivity but was shuttled off by bus to usher in the New Year in Wilmersdorf with my Grandmother and my cousin Werner, whose parents were of course attending my parents' gala.

Grandmother greeted me with the consoling news that we three would have our own New Year's Eve party. She had made jelly filled donuts (Pfannkuchen). She did this by dropping raw dough into a huge pot of hot oil; when they'd fried enough, she scooped them out and rolled them in sugar. I do not remember that we ever had doughnuts at any time other than New Year's Eve (which we called Sylvester), so that at the stroke of midnight, when the doughnuts were to be eaten, it seemed a special way of bringing in the New Year.

It was also a German folk tradition shortly after midnight to melt a small quantity of lead, then throw drops of it into cold water. The lead solidified into odd shapes which were interpreted by the participants (like the oracles of Delphi) to predict the future of the New Year. My grandmother could be counted on to foretell only positive events.

My cousin Werner had prepared a complex fireworks display on the balcony that he planned to light at midnight and I was impatient to see it. He had set up "sun displays" which were to ignite one after the other as soon as the first one was lit.

Midnight finally arrived and Werner struck the first match to light the wick, but it didn't ignite, nor did the next, or the next. The reason? He'd left all of the fireworks on the balcony during a rainstorm earlier in the day. Though covered with a canvas, nevertheless they had become damp and soggy. Disappointment and chagrin reigned, until Werner came up with an inspired idea. We would toss lighted colored matches from the balcony and watch them flutter down to the street, four flights below. This entertained us for some little time. At one point we heard muffled screams from below in the street, but didn't connect them with anything we were doing, so on we went, blithely tossing lighted matches off the balcony. Eventually tiring of this amusement, we all went to bed.

Next morning the door bell rang quite early. Our unwelcome callers were a policeman accompanied by an irate lady who claimed that her fur coat had been burned, ruined by the matches she had seen being dropped from the balcony by two young scoundrels the night before.

I was very frightened and blurted out at once that "my father will pay for everything." It was my first encounter with the police, and I hoped that promise would prevent my going to jail. I didn't go to jail, but we did get a summons. My father's lawyer managed to settle the case out of court, and my promise was kept: my father did indeed "pay for everything." I never knew just how much that boyish escapade cost my parents. (The truth is, I was too afraid to ask.)

As I grew older, not too surprisingly I became aware of girls. Sex education not being forthcoming from my parents, I found a worthy mentor for such matters in our young maid, a blonde, blue-eyed country lass of about 28 named Marie, who might be described as a Wagnerian type, with large breasts and full hips. I would go to the kitchen in the afternoons (while my mother was

15

attending patients in my father's practice) to interrogate her about sex.

One day (I was about eleven) during one of her more explicit explanations, suddenly, to my amazement, I had an erection. Marie noticed it and invited me to sit on her lap, an invitation I accepted with alacrity. I was fascinated by her nipples, which I was sure were large and beautiful, like her breasts, and she let me feel them under her uniform. While I was doing that, she opened my fly and massaged my penis. Before I knew what was happening, I came. Acutely embarrassed, I ran to the bathroom to look at the mess. When I had changed my underpants I returned to the kitchen, and she patiently explained what had happened.

Naturally, I thereafter became more and more interested in girls' anatomies and this youthful voyeur climbed up unabashedly to the transom of Marie's bedroom to watch when she undressed. This was assuredly even more interesting than what I could see on the streets peering from the balcony. I am sure she knew I was there watching her, but she never seemed to mind.

When my parents (very occasionally) left without me on Saturdays, I would watch Marie bathing and sometimes even touch her zaftig body. She returned the compliment. Before long, though, she must have decided enough was enough, because she finally suggested that I purchase a book on sex and told me I could buy it at a newspaper kiosk near the Zoo station.

I pedaled fast on my bicycle to that kiosk, but had great difficulty summoning the courage to ask for the book after spotting it. I finally made the embarrassing purchase and dashed home to study this enthralling subject. The book had many illustrations, some of which I tried in vain to understand, though I did get the general principles. I also took my bicycle to second-hand book carts which sold girlie magazines. Since I was never short of money I purchased a lot of them. It seemed wise to bury these educational treasures under piles of clothes in my dresser drawers, and if my parents ever discovered them, they never indicated it to me.

Even with this basic information at my disposal, I was not totally up to speed on the subject of sex. My mother's cousin, the gynecologist Dr. Georg Hamburger, saw his patients in a clinic next to our apartment house and I sometimes played the role of errand boy for him. On occasion he would give me small packages containing aluminum cups to take to my father, which he called "diaphragms," but I did not know what medical purpose they served. (My father added rubber to the rims of the cups, vulcanizing the rubber in his laboratory.) I had seen these cups in a medical store window, along with wheelchair and other appliances, but could not figure out the use of the cups though I eventually suspected they had something to do with sex because neither Uncle Georg nor my father seemed disposed to enlighten me. The girlie magazines I bought on the street did nothing to help my ignorance, either.

When I was 13 years old, my father offered me a package of Russian cigarettes to smoke and any drink I wanted to try. I sampled a cigarette or two and drank some alcohol, though I don't recall what type. At about the same period of time I would often invite my friends whom I had known since I was ten to our home. We all thought we were big shots as we played cards or chess or roulette and now I offered them drags on long Russian cigarettes, which we tried to inhale. Actually, more enjoyable were the tea sandwiches that I would grandly order the maid to serve. That was about the extent of my youthful foray into nicotine and alcohol. In hindsight, I know that my father's strategy of offering cigarettes and alcohol in my own home was an excellent one. As a result, I have never taken up smoking and drink only socially.

In the summer of 1934 my parents sent me to Denmark where a camp counselor rented a house for twenty boys and girls, all around the age of thirteen. Our young group spent four weeks in Revnes near Kalundborg on the coast, not far from Copenhagen. We swam in the North Sea and often visited the

Tivoli Amusement Park and once visited a large radio station in Kalundborg where the Director gave his autograph to a properly awed group of youngsters.

The following summer, I went with a similar camping group to the High Tatra mountains in northeastern Czechoslovakia. It took nearly 24 hours by train to reach our destination, a town named *Tatranska Lomnika* near the Polish border, south of Cracow. We climbed the high mountains, and enjoyed the luxury of a royal castle rented to our group by a former Polish count. We took wooden rafts on the Dunajec river, which divides Czechoslovakia from Poland. Six of us, three boys and three girls, put a song and show together to entertain the group. I performed a creditable version of a dance the Ukrainians call the *gapak*, and Cossacks call the *kazatzki* wherein you cross your arms across your chest, squat low to the floor and alternately stretch out full length first one leg, then the other, as if kicking, while keeping time to a rapid rhythm.

All this was fun, but the main thing I remember from that summer is that I was in love and very happy. I had met my first girlfriend, a charming little blonde girl (quite developed for her age). Lilli and I spent five wonderful weeks in the High Tatra. But as is usually the case with summer romances when you're young (I was all of fourteen, and so was she), when the summer ended so did our romance.

During the winter months following, my parents sent me to a fine dancing school. The class met every Saturday in a different home or apartment of one of the students. Most students' families had pianos, but the school provided the pianist and female dancing instructor, who saw to it that we learned the Lambert Walk, the Fox Trot, the Tango and the Rhumba. I may have been an indifferent dancer, but this was a great way to meet girls so I was an eager pupil and never missed a session.

Sundays at six in the morning, I would take the Underground to "Unter den Linden" to the *Staatsoper* and stand in line for opera tickets for me and my best friend, Herbert Sonnenthal, whose father was the Berlin Director of the Phönix Insurance

Company. Herbert would do the same waiting in line to buy tickets to the classical theater, a block away. Most weekday evenings were spent in the theater or at the opera. It was here that I had my first exposure to *Carmen*, *Margarete* (the German name for Faust), *La Boheme*, *The Flying Dutchman*, *Cavalleria Rusticana*, *Pagliacci*, and of course *Die Fledermaus*.

It was at the Deutsches Schauspielhaus that I also fell in love with the theatre: *Peer Gynt, Hamlet, Faust, Pygmalion, and The Camillean Dame* were perhaps the most memorable plays I saw there.

One night a week I took a class in studio art at the Georg Hausdorf Art School near Kurfürstendamm. My father made a deal with me about those classes. He would allow me to attend for fun if I would agree never to choose art as a profession. I agreed, even though I dearly loved the field. I spent many happy hours at a place called The Museum Island, near *unter den Linden* in East Berlin on the Spree River, which held art exhibits.

My very first class assignment was to sketch a live, nude female model. I loved every minute of that course, though it was far more difficult to draw a nude than to admire it! I designed commercial posters (one for Bosch, the large electrical manufacturing company, featured a sparkplug), and I also painted a few portraits and sketched different parts of Germany on our various vacations.

Although our maid Marie took care of my early sex education, Pappi was in full charge of my academic schooling. Because of the structure of the German school system, which strictly separated academic and vocational studies, when I turned ten, my father was obliged to make a decision about which future profession I would enter.

Since the general economic conditions of the country were poor and the future uncertain, he chose a school which taught modern languages so that I would have greater flexibility in the business world. Thus I was enrolled in the Hohenzollern Gymnasium, a high school for boys only. (Girls went to a

Lyceum, the equivalent of the Gymnasium for boys.) Classes were basically on a half-day program, from 8 a.m. to 1 p.m.

After school I would meet my cousin Annemarie Hamburger (Uncle Georg's daughter) near the city hall in her district (there were city halls in each of the many districts of Berlin) to go ice skating. As it happens, this particular city hall building was very large, and it became the city hall of West Berlin during the cold war, where John Kennedy said, "Ich bin ein Berliner."

At any rate, it was cold enough during the winter to freeze water on the tennis courts near by and we would skate under the lights until 7 p.m. Early in that first semester, Annemarie introduced me to her best girl friend, which spiced up the skating parties considerably, and made up for not meeting girls at my all-boys school.

I had been accepted into the Hohenzollern Gymnasium without an entry examination since my grades were above the basic requirement for admission. The first two years I had a tutorial one hour a day in English grammar and usage, taught by a Dr. Busse, a teacher from London; in my third year, French was added to my curriculum.

The other subjects were mathematics, history, geography and art; all were mandatory, except for religion. Once a week, a pastor and a rabbi would come to the school to teach Christianity and Judaism in a special classroom. Those who chose not to attend either class could go to the school yard. I went to the Judaism classes, but must have had my mind in the school yard for unfortunately all I can remember is that the classes in religion were extremely dull.

The Gymnasium was not a free public school. My father had to pay a fairly high tuition for my studies, but I don't recall how much. Those who could not afford to pay went to public middle schools by default; middle schools prepared students for vocational careers only until they were fourteen.

After a youngster finished middle school, his father would select an apprenticeship for his son, and the boy would continue his vocational schooling with two days a week of study in his chosen field in a trade school while pursuing his apprenticeship. For students on this track, attendance in trade school was mandatory until the age of 18. By that time, it was expected that the apprentice could pass a test which would make him a *Geselle* (a journeyman in his chosen trade or craft). It was an honor to obtain such a diploma just as much as it was an honor to become an engineer. Unlike contemporary America, both academic and trade schools as well as teachers and students in both were well respected.

I was able to advance quickly at the Gymnasium and skipped a number of semesters. The school was associated with a technical university, which made it possible for a student to gain early admission to the university at age sixteen rather than eighteen. That meant that I had finished two years of college study before leaving Germany in 1939.

Studies in German schools were intense, and totally focused on the required courses, although a student was left to his own resources a great deal of the time. Parents were expected to expose their children to culture at home. That is why Germany and most European countries have a definite class system. It is almost impossible to escape the class that a child is born into. That is also the reason why trades are frequently transferred from generation to generation within the same family. In Germany, even today, the status quo is thus maintained.

It had been my father's earlier dream that I should become a dentist, and join his successful practice. His plan had been that he would set up a second dental chair and we would become "Riess & Riess" once I received my dental degree. It was only because he saw how things were going in Germany that he encouraged me to study engineering, a profession where he felt my services would be needed no matter where I might live.

I most probably would have been a dentist if the political picture had not changed, but my father knew that even if I had earned a German dental degree, I would have to begin studies all over again in any other country, to obtain certification under its

21

auspices. Since this was not the case for engineers, he chose engineering for me. In this, he was right, and I never had reason to regret it.

The school year was rugged, but summers were mine to enjoy. My "Uncle" Georg Hamburger, the gynecologist, had a sailboat and most of the members of the immediate family often sailed the Havel River on his boat. The trouble was, many times he was called away to deliver a baby just as we were taking off for our outing. We enjoyed these river trips so much, and were so disappointed when they were aborted, that my father finally bought a small mahogany motor boat so we wouldn't have to rely on Uncle Georg's unpredictable schedule. Pappi kept it stored in a private boating club called the Pichelsdorfer Marina and arranged that every weekend the marina staff would launch the boat and have it ready for our arrival at about 10 a.m. on Saturdays.

Since my father worked such long hours all week, he felt he could afford a two-day weekend without being on call. He and I would leave on Saturday mornings at 8 a.m. on the tandem streetcar (one car pulling two more cars) to the boat marina. We would stop at the club's restaurant, which was built on a stepped terrace at the Havel River, where my father ordered two large steins of Berliner Weisse (White beer with raspberry syrup). We relaxed at a round table under an umbrella and watched boats leave from the club until about 11 a.m. when my mother would arrive with the lunch that she had packed for us.

Often Pappi let me steer the boat, which he called Hase (Rabbit), since "Haeschen" (small rabbit) was my nickname. I loved to be the pilot and especially enjoyed docking the Hase near Peacock Island, our most frequent destination. Tante Lillie and Uncle Kurt would sometimes join us there and we would set up a picnic table and chairs, then swim in the clear river water until evening.

Later we continued on up the river to New Babelsberg, where we rented rooms for the summer in a boarding house with a lovely outdoor restaurant. Sometimes Tante Lillie and Kurt would join us for dinner or lunch here as well. (These family outings were without Werner who had left home when he was 18 after a particularly heated dispute with Uncle Kurt, and was by this time living in Paris.)

Following lunch we would all walk to the New Babelsberg Park where occasionally we caught a glimpse of former Crown Prince Friedrich Wilhelm, the son of Kaiser Wilhelm, astride his horse.

One Saturday night at Babelsberg something traumatic occurred for which I was completely responsible. It also gave new meaning to the term, "butterfingers." Our boat had a small side-mounted motor, usually stored in a workroom overnight. My father had removed the motor from the boat and asked me to hold it upright until he was ready to take it from me. I was standing on the finger slip with the motor, when for no apparent reason, I let go and the motor fell into the water.

After they fished it out of the shallow water, a mechanic and my father were forced to take the entire motor apart in order to dry every part carefully and reassemble it that Saturday night. The next morning, to my enormous relief, the motor started immediately. My father was angry with me for a while, but by the time we went home on Sunday, even he was laughing about the whole incident, like the rest of us.

We returned by streetcar to the Zoo station and dined on Aschinger's famous bratwurst with sauerkraut, and for a treat ate as much bread as we wanted. I was back in Pappi's good graces.

In the background of our quiet but privileged and busy life on Augsburgerstrasse, political events were roiling ominously. My family seemed unaware of the seething volcano that would soon change our lives and the lives of all other German Jews forever. At first we barely took notice of the rumblings, though I remember clearly the democratic elections of March, 1933. They were the last elections held in Germany before the War that were in accordance with the laws of the Weimar Republic.

The coming to power of Hitler marked the end of the Weimar Republic -- the name for the democratic government of

23

Germany between the abdication of Kaiser Wilhelm II and the assumption of power by Adolf Hitler in a new regime he called *das dritte Reich* (the third Empire); Weimar was the city where the Republic's constitution was drawn up. The constitution abolished the several constitutional monarchies that had previously formed the second German Empire.

The week of Hitler's coming to power also marked the flight of 50,000 Jews, one-tenth of the entire Jewish population then living in Germany. Some of the best and the brightest left, including Bertolt Brecht and Kurt Weill. But most of us stayed on.

The Republic was generally unpopular in Germany because of its acceptance of the harsh provisions of the Treaty of Versailles; the large penalties Germany had to pay caused economic chaos in the country, with German money declining daily in value. The Weimar years, however, were a period of political freedom and cultural creativity, both of which were soon to be snuffed out by Hitler.

In the elections of 1933, the Social Democrats' candidate for president was Field Marshall Paul von Hindenburg. Heading up the ticket for the *National Sozialistische Deutsche Arbeiter Partei* (NSDAP, short for the National Social German Workers Party), also known as the Nazi party, was Adolf Hitler.

Two-inch brass medallions with punched-out "H's" for Hindenburg, were distributed before the election, but they were really too large to wear. Although we were not political activists, Pappi belonged to the *Reichsbanner*, the SPD -- *Sozialdemokratische Partei Deutschlands* (Social Democratic Party), an active campaign group, and Uncle Georg Hamburger conspicuously flew the *Reichsbanner* flag on his sailboat until Hitler came into office.

By 1933 Germany had suffered from massive and chronic unemployment for well over a decade and Hitler promised the electorate that he would put Germany back to work. He had an incredibly effective propaganda machine and more and more

24

people started to believe that he could actually improve Germany's economic plight.

Nevertheless Von Hindenburg won the elections, and named von Papen as his chancellor.

By presidential decree, von Hindenburg dismissed von Papen after only fifty seven days in office. Seizing the opportunity for rapid advancement, Hitler insisted that he be the official to replace von Papen as Chancellor of the Democratic Republic, given the fact that he was the leader of the largest political party in Germany. Von Hindenburg bowed to public pressure and finally agreed. On January 30, 1933, von Hindenburg appointed Adolph Hitler Chancellor of Germany.

On February 27 of the same year, a few short weeks after Hitler's appointment, a Dutch national, Martin Van der Lubbe set the Reichstag (the German equivalent of the U.S. Capitol) on fire. The fire raged on all night and half the next day. I rode my bicycle to the Reichstag to witness the enormous flames as they destroyed the large dome. Though I was thoroughly frightened by the terrifying spectacle, I had no premonition of the political consequence that would follow.

Dr. Goebbels, Hitler's Minister of Propaganda, used this incident to create a tremendous hate campaign against the Communists, since Van der Lubbe was a Communist. The Nazis believed that most Jews were liberals and most liberals were Communists, ergo according to Nazi logic, most Jews had to be Communists.

I watched the Nazi Brownshirts (SA -- *Sturm Abteilung*) as they rounded up those they thought were Communists and march them away. The brownshirts became carried away with their work and started singing as they marched through the streets of Berlin. Their song was *Wenn das Judenblut vom Messer spritzt*. It translates to "when Jewish blood splashes from the knife." This was my first taste of real racial hatred.

Dr. Goebbels organized a show trial, following which many Communists were rounded up and placed in hastily constructed concentration camps already awaiting clientele.

25

On the day following the Reichstag fire, von Hindenburg signed a decree suspending a variety of civil liberties, including freedom of the press, and freedom of assembly, among others. This truly marked the end of the Republic and the beginning of the dictatorship.

It was a terrible blow, but life went on; meanwhile, everyone in my family who expressed an opinion said that this could not last long, except Pappi, who was not convinced that this regime would fade away so quickly. Accordingly, he registered an application with the British mandate in Palestine to emigrate with his family; he had even made the required £1,000 pound deposit. He thought that if necessary I could study engineering at the Technion in Haifa and we could all start a new life.

Our number came up in 1934, but Mutti was too comfortable in Berlin and refused to leave. She was afraid of change, and preferred to wait out the Nazi period, which many of our friends and relatives said would pass. (How could this "Nazi madness" survive in a country so cultured as our beloved homeland?)

As always, my father acquiesced to her wishes, and I do not remember that there was ever any friction in our household due to my mother's reluctance to leave Berlin in 1934.

Pappi's careful planning for my education required temporary modification when Nazi laws inaugurating a system of strict apartheid was introduced, requiring that Jewish children attend only Jewish schools.

Luckily, the local Jewish community of Berlin quickly organized a private high school named after the famous Zionist Theodor Herzl, where some of the best teachers in Germany came to teach, and which I attended for two years. Many of our instructors had formerly taught at the technical university of Berlin, but since they were Jews, they were no longer permitted to teach at the University.

One of those was a brilliant mathematics teacher who came to us from the *Technische Hochschule* (technical university) named Franz Ollendorf. Still today, I have a snapshot of him in our schoolyard there in Berlin. Ultimately he emigrated to Israel and taught there at a school of the same name, Theodor Herzl.

All schools, including the Jewish ones, had to follow the prescribed national high school curriculum which included *Mein Kampf*, Hitler's autobiography written in the 1920s while he was in prison.

Like it or not, we Jewish students studied Hitler's plan for the revival of Germany from the humiliating losses of World War I and his blame of Germany's problems on capitalists, communists, and Jews. We learned of his opposition to free intellectual inquiry, which he associated with Jewish science and philosophy. He promised that Germany would become powerful again if it followed him. We discussed it all in class, and even debated many of his arguments, pro and con, as if they were mere philosophical abstractions, instead of being issues directly related to our own life and death.

The anticipated day came when a German inspection team from the Schools Ministry (made up of professors and teachers, not all necessarily Nazis) visited our school to test us on Hitler's autobiography. To the great surprise of the inspection team, each student had his own copy and we proved to be well-versed in the subject. Ironically, we Theodor Herzl school students passed this obnoxious test with flying colors.

I enjoyed the Herzl school much more than the *Hohenzollern Gymnasium* because the students had more freedom. The classes were co-ed, and when the weather was warm enough and sunny, classes were held outside, which was unheard of in other schools. The only disadvantage as far as I was concerned was the fact that the school was located so far from where we lived.

During summer and winter, no matter how bad the weather, I bicycled to school. I don't know the exact distance, but it took me one hour, give or take, to get to and from school, which was located in the suburbs. Berlin's terrain is flat, so the ride was not too onerous, and I was young and strong.

I liked the fact that the school was opposite the Exhibit Hall and the *Funkturm* (radio tower), for I could look out the classroom window and watch as the new cars were being tested during the annual motor car exhibit, then during a lull in the lecturing, take my sketchbook and draw the latest models.

I attended classes at Theodor Herzl for two years before transferring to the University for engineering courses. There I would be the only Jew in my class. I don't know whether I was allowed to enroll because the fact that I was Jewish was never mentioned to the authorities, or because at that time 1 1/2% of the total enrollment was by Nazi law, allowed to be Jewish.

I am sure it is difficult to understand for anybody reading these lines now almost sixty years after the fact, that life in Berlin was good even after Adolf Hitler came to power. Many Germans enjoyed a high standard of living in Berlin, including the Jews, and the city was a clean, sophisticated, and highly cultured metropolis. Generally, the average man in the street was happy with Hitler's new economic program, since those who were formerly unemployed were now engaged in productive work.

Also, Hitler quickly moved to galvanize industrial and military production into high gear. He improved the infrastructure by organizing large work battalions to construct autobahns from one border to the next, which people liked. Actually, these highways were designed to transport military equipment and personnel quickly.

Even though from 1933 to 1939, the political picture changed badly for the Jews, basically, our family's personal life was not torturously affected. At first there were only minor indignities, aggravations, harassments and inconveniences, worsened later by the Nurenberg Race Laws (the *Rassen Gesetze*) enacted in 1935, but we adapted. As late as 1939 when Mutti, Pappi and I finally left, Berlin Jews were not yet required to wear the loathsome yellow star that not too much later served almost as a death sentence. (The yellow star edict did not come until 1941.)

My father continued his practice, although fairly soon after Hitler came to power, he was obliged by Hitler's decree to do work for patients of two insurance companies in addition to his private practice. (The insurance companies, like Medicare today in the U.S., paid less for the work of the doctors than they normally charged. This made little difference to my father, because he frequently did dental work for patients who couldn't pay at all.)

Ironically, soon after Hitler was in control of the government, Pappi was called to the local police station to receive a medal for his military service in France in World War I, awarded by Hitler to all soldiers who had fought on the enemy fronts, and Pappi had served in the medical corps in the front lines.

My father was faced with a great dilemma, for if he did not accept the medal, he would be deemed an enemy of the Reich. Naturally he didn't want the medal, most specifically because it had a swastika in its design. But the police chief of our district, who was a personal friend of my father, said that if my father didn't take it, the chief himself would get into lots of trouble. My father finally accepted it, and the police chief smiled ruefully as he gave him the medal and certificate.

For the time being our lives went on somewhat as usual. During the summer of 1936, for example, we were determined to enjoy our boat and so we nearly always invited a group of friends or relatives to join us for our improvised weekend holidays as we had done the previous summer. Since we would not fly the swastika, we had no flag of any kind on the boat. As far as I could observe, that made our boat unique on the river. But nobody seemed to mind or for that matter, even notice.

It was during one of these boating weekends that I saw an amazing sight. A small car-like vehicle seemed to be bouncing along right through the water towards the beach. It had windshield wipers going and streamlined headlights built into the fenders. As it approached the beach, I recognized that army officers were in the vehicle. They shifted some gears, the vehicle's propeller stopped, its tires gripped the river bottom and started to pull the car out of the water. It turned out that this was one of the first Volkswagens which the army was testing for amphibious operations.

One incident during the early years of the Hitler period should have warned us what was coming. Uncle Kurt, then living with us, was intensely interested in politics as well as classical music, so he wired loudspeakers into our apartment. Although most of the time we listened to concerts transmitted from the Berlin Concert Hall and opera transmitted from the Opera House, nevertheless, often as we were having dinner, Hitler addressed the nation. We listened in the dining room while we ate, then discussed what he'd said among ourselves, our opinions -- understandably -- were not down the party line.

Unbeknownst to us, our maid Marie reported (albeit indirectly) to the Nazi organization that my father made fun of Hitler's speeches. It may have been innocent gossip, but she passed this information on to the doorman of Horcher, the elegant restaurant directly below our apartment, whose best customers were high Nazi party officials like Goering and Udet.

The doorman then regaled the maid's tales to some of his friends, and shortly thereafter, my father was summoned to appear for a hearing in front of a tribunal. It was fortunate that the dental association of which he was a member conducted the hearing, and some of the judges were his friends. The case was dismissed.

Again and again we found that the people in general were not Nazis and wanted to be helpful. When the decree forbidding Jews to purchase butter, milk and eggs was issued, our grocer across the street continued to deliver these products to us as well as bread and rolls. The first morning after the law was in force, my father opened the door and found our groceries and dairy products as usual. He tried to return them to the grocer, saying we hadn't ordered them. The grocer said to Pappi, "This is a gift from us. You are not buying these groceries." His store continued to deliver all "forbidden" items to us until we left Germany.

On the Saturday of November 21, 1934 I was one of 13 boys to be bar-mitzvahed in a reformed Synagogue, *Freedom's Temple*. It was my father who thought I should observe this passage into manhood. He also thought that High Holy Days should be observed, and on occasions such as Passover and Hanukkah he would take me, hand-in-hand, to the Synagogue, wearing his freshly steamed morning coat, a top hat and carrying a prayer book. (Pappi gave me his own interpretation of how the Jews were able to cross the Red Sea when Pharoah's army was chasing them. There was, he said, a high tide and a low tide and the Jews simply crossed at low tide. Suffice it to say, my father took no stock in Biblical miracles.)

The occasion of my Bar Mitzvah was, I think, more a mildly defiant political affirmation of our Jewishness than religious sentiment. It also provided my sociable mother an opportunity to entertain our family and a few other friends. I wasn't hurt, either, by the experience of learning a modicum of Hebrew.

One of the first rabbis to speak out against Nazism and who suffered many arrests by the Gestapo before leaving for the United States in 1937, the famed Zionist, Dr. Joachim Prinz, taught us something about the Jewish religion, and it was he who inscribed a Bible I received as a gift. My mother was so impressed with him as a speaker that even she would occasionlly attend synagogue on a High Holy Day, but only when she knew he would be speaking, planning her arrival to coincide with his address, skipping all the traditional religious preliminaries. Yom Kippur or no, a luncheon at some fine restaurant always followed her visits to the synagogue.

By 1936 the congregation of the synagogue had become so fearful that Dr. Prinz's incendiary talks against the Nazis would bring reprisals upon all of them, that he was no longer allowed to speak there. Those braver souls who wanted to hear him, potential reprisals notwithstanding, rented a concert hall; every seat was filled the day he conducted his last Yom Kippur service in Berlin.

31

Mutti, who really had no religious background whatsoever, chose the elegant Horcher restaurant to cater the luncheon following my Bar Mitzvah, and of course Pappi paid no attention at all to the menu they planned. About 30 guests had been invited, including the Rabbi and his wife (who arrived in a beautiful Mercedes). My Uncle Max Wolff, the toy train manufacturer, was seated next to them at our huge dining room table, which had been expanded to its fullest to accommodate the entire group.

The Rabbi enjoyed the first course enormously, and was obviously looking forward to more of such fine cuisine. Whether out of mischief or real concern, my Uncle Max felt called upon to tell the good Rabbi that the food he was eating wasn't kosher, which ended his partaking further, and caused consternation all around, though I'm not sure that Mutti ever felt she'd done anything wrong. (I'm sure no one mentioned to the good Rabbi that Mutti always provided the family with a Christmas tree!)

In 1935, one of the decrees of the Nuremberg Race Laws forbade intermarriage between Jews and Christians. This was due to Hitler's dream of producing a master race of pure white Aryans that would rule the world. Another decree prohibited Jewish households from employing Aryan female domestics who were younger than 45 years of age, based one must surmise, upon fears that the master of the household might engage in a little social fraternization with the maid.

It was difficult to find maids who were middle-aged, so my resourceful mother went to an employment agency and found a Jewish butler. Mr. Blum was very neat, an able cook and an inspired ironer of shirts. He wore a white jacket when on duty as a butler, and a blue and white striped jacket when he worked in the kitchen. He seemed to love his work.

I thought that he spoke a little oddly, and walked with a little prance, but I didn't know that he was gay. It turned out that he was indeed a homosexual, although I did not learn that from my parents. My mother was quite satisfied with him, but one day on his day off, he just disappeared, never to return. We never heard from him again, nor did we ever learn whether he had been picked up by the homophobic Nazis, or had somehow managed to escape from Germany. We ardently hoped the latter was true.

From 1935 on, life started to change in many other noticeable ways. Germany printed marks without gold backing which made importing goods from abroad virtually impossible. Ersatz goods started to show up. *Leuna* -- a synthetic gasoline made by I.G.Farben, the huge chemical company which, though expensive, came into wide use. Aluminum wire replaced copper. Brass handles were removed from all streetcars and replaced with aluminum. Widespread food shortages became apparent.

A strict apartheid was observed publicly. Certain benches in parks were painted yellow and marked for Jews only. Theatres, opera and concerts were closed to Jews. No one talked freely, knowing they might be reported. We were no longer able to listen to our short-wave radio or read uncensored newspapers, and really did not know what was going on in the rest of the world.

But for all that, Berlin with a population of 4 million, of which only about 160,000 were Jews, was still not so bad a place as for Jews who lived in small towns. We were still comfortable in our apartment and my father's practice was still doing relatively well, though the number of patients who couldn't pay was mounting. He never pressed them for payment, saying, "They need the money more than we do."

We continued on, struggling to live the way we always had, as nearly as possible.

A Jewish cultural organization called *der Jüdische Kultur Bund* (The Jewish Culture Circle) was created, attracting fine performers and excellent musicians. Some of the very best artists in Berlin, who were no longer permitted to perform with the Berlin Symphony Orchestra or the Berlin Opera participated in the Kultur Bund. Tante Lillie and I went regularly, for music was a passion we shared, and her black eyes sparkled whenever we had a concert to attend.

33

Hans Riess

In 1936 Berlin was host to the Olympic games. The city was massively decorated with red German flags with huge black swastikas draped on tall poles all along the *Heerstrasse* (Army Boulevard) leading from the middle of the city to the suburbs where the enormous Olympic Stadium had been built. All the yellow benches "For Jews Only" had been removed, and the billboards for the hate newspaper, *Der Stuermer*, vanished as if by magic, almost overnight. Anti-semitic articles in the newspapers also disappeared. Visitors to the city found it "a wonderful, marvelously clean and well-organized metropolis."

I went to the games by special bus and enjoyed the spectacle and pomp as well as all the events, but the stadium was so large that it was very difficult to see any of the dignitaries at the opening of the games. The colorful staging, the lighting of the Olympic torch at the opening ceremonies, and the representatives of all the countries marching around the oval were thrilling to watch, and quite similar to what we see today on television. Although I did not personally observe Hitler refuse to shake hands with the famous American runner, Jesse Owens, I frequently caught glimpses of Leni Riefenstahl, the famous cinematographer who had been commissioned by Hitler to film the games, as she went about covering the events.

I didn't spot Hitler at the games at all, but I once saw him with Mussolini in an open Mercedes right in front of our apartment window. They were going to the Berlin Scala on one of the nights that the Italian tenor Gilli was to sing. Members of the SS lined the street along the curb, holding their leather shoulder straps between each other, their faces turned toward the car to watch the two make a dramatic entrance to the theatre. Later that night they dined, as many Nazi officials frequently did, at the Horcher, right beneath our apartment.

HANS IS 16 YEARS OLD

In 1936 at Hitler's decree, Jews had to hand in to the authorities all their jewelry. It was very painful for my parents to include their gold wedding bands. Many Jews tried to protect themselves from this unwarranted confiscation, going to a pawn shop to obtain an estimate of the rings' value prior to handing them over to the police. The pawnshops always gave the lowest possible estimate as per instructions from the government. This act of theirs did prove of some value, however. After the end of the war, when Germany was instructed to pay reparations, these

35

receipts served as proof of ownership, and contained a description of the jewelry originally owned by the claimant.

By the summer of 1938 Jews were no longer permitted to hold valid passports and could no longer travel abroad, even though the government wanted us gone.

But we were still there whether the Nazis wanted us or not, and we wanted to take a vacation. My father said, "Let's go to Bavaria near the Zugspitze on Garmisch-Partenkirchen," which is one of the best winter resorts in southern Germany, but beautiful in the summer also. No passport was needed. We stayed in a small hotel and went hiking in the Bavarian Alps, not far from the Austrian border, almost every day.

One day we visited the Eibsee Hotel, but stopped short when we saw one of the all-too-familiar round, yellow signs at the door, which read *Juden unerwünscht* (Jews Not Welcome.) After a brief discussion, (it didn't say Jews were *verboten* (forbidden), so we decided that we were too hungry to hunt farther for a more welcoming restaurant and -- sign or no sign -- we went in anyway. No one questioned our presence.

I remember that the menu listed *Schwarzwalder Kirschtorte* (chocolate cherry cake, one of my favorites), which we all ordered. It was delicious and the service good, the view of the Alps spectacular from the windows around our table. The point of this little interlude is to explain that we still could have an enjoyable outing regardless of the times.

On that same trip we also took the train to Mittenwald where violins were made. We wanted to see the stores and watch the manufacturing process. Again, the station at Mittenwald had a big banner stating that Jews were not welcome. It was not pleasant to see the signs, but we made the best of it, and did not let them ruin the pleasure of our holiday.

Bavaria was something special. Cows walked out of their barn by themselves in the morning, big bells around their necks, and lumbered off to the hillside for a day of grazing and then, bellies full, walked more slowly back to the barn at the end of the day. When we met farmers on the road they would say a traditional German greeting, *Grüss Gott* ("Greet God"), instead of "Heil Hitler" which had become the greeting of choice everywhere in Berlin.

Bavarian food was heavy, but good. When I ordered a sausage, I got two large bratwurst and a large stein of beer, which I did not ask for. This was the custom of the area.

We came back to Berlin and spent much of the rest of the summer on the Havel with our little motor boat, determined to have a good time, in spite of the worsening situation. Although we didn't know it, our trip to Bavaria was our last vacation in Germany, and our last summer in Berlin.

By now, fewer and fewer Jews were able to leave for America or to any country in Europe, and we had missed our chance to go to Israel. The Jews who remained in Germany, though somewhat reduced in numbers, had still not accepted the Nazi message that they were not wanted (nor had they understood their peril); consequently, the Nazis were spurred on to increasingly creative displays of anti-Semitism, even though they had made it now almost impossible for them to leave the country.

Since early 1938 I had been attending the university-level engineering school called *Fachschule für Metalarbeit*. This school taught mechanical engineering (theory) half a day and machine tool operation (practice) the other half. I happened to be the only Jew in the class; my teacher was aware of this but my fellow students were not. If you recall, here in the United States students bought savings bond stamps and pasted them into booklets. When a certain number of booklets were completed, they could be exchanged for a savings bond. This program enabled youngsters to support the war effort.

We also had a similar program in Germany. We bought shiny, silver nails for a penny each. The nails were used to create a Hitler Youth Emblem. The goal was to be the first class to complete the emblem. One student was elected to be in charge of this and I was elected for this chore by my classmates! When this happened, I looked toward my teacher to see how I could get

37

out of it, but he just nodded, indicating that I should accept it. So, for as long as I attended school there, I was in charge of collecting funds and distributing nails to support a war that was being fought against me! Such were the ironies of life as a Jew in Germany.

When Ernst Von Rath, the Third Secretary of the German Embassy, was murdered in Paris by a 17-year-old German Jewish refugee named Herschel Grynszpan, it gave the Nazis a perfect reason to afflict Jews -- not that they needed excuses. They wanted to take it out on the Jews. The result was a night of horror that came to be called *Kristallnacht* (Crystal Night), sending a powerful message that could no longer be ignored. The date was November 9, 1938.

Early on the day of *Kristallnacht,* that same teacher, a Mr. George in the engineering school, spoke to me privately and warned me that "something terrible" might happen that night. Though he knew I was a Jew, he had taken a liking to me, and evidently wished that no harm came to me.

I had known before that he was kindly disposed toward me, ever since the time he took me aside during a class outing to a very large medical exhibit, which was called *Wunder Des Lebens* (The Wonder of Life), explaining the various exhibits to me as though to a private student.

I remember that he showed me an illustration of how Mendel's law of blue versus brown eyes worked. The chart explained that Aryans had primarily blue eyes while non-Aryans had brown eyes. I, however, had blue eyes and both of my parents were non-Aryans. That day, Mr. George and I had a long discussion on this subject, although my doubts and confusions relating to the Nazi interpretation of Mendel's theory of heredity were neither answered nor resolved.

All teachers had to wear some kind of outward symbol of the swastika; most chose the membership pin of the Nazi party, which displayed a swastika. Mr. George, however, preferred to wear an athletic achievement medal which had only a very small swastika as part of the design.

One day as the class was dismissed and I was about to leave with the others, Mr. Georg quietly called me back and said he would like to speak to me. When the others had gone, with a low, worried voice he said, "Something terrible is going to happen tonight." He would not say what that something might be, only warning me. "Please Hans, ride your bicycle past your home this evening. Do not go into your apartment immediately. If anything looks the least bit out of the ordinary, ride by. Do not stop. Instead, go to the home of friends who are not Jewish." That is all he would say, but his eyes were sad and troubled. I thanked him and left, quite troubled myself.

I followed his sound advice and as I passed the house, noticed that my father's office, located on the second floor, did not have his ultra-violet lamp switched on. Since he normally worked until late at night, it struck me as indeed strange that the light was off.

We had many non-Jewish friends who had been alerted already to our danger so it was no problem for me to stop off in a house just two blocks away from ours.

The gentile milkman, who owned a delicatessen across the street, was on good terms with us and all our Jewish friends. He was well aware of the situation. It was he who had told two of my father's patients, the ladies who took me in, that my father had been picked up by the Gestapo. The Gestapo agents had also asked for me, but since I was not home, they left without me.

Kristallnacht would prove to be a horrifying spectacle, but I wanted to see for myself what was happening. Again, with foolhardy indifference to the danger, I left the sanctuary of the ladies who took me in and rode my bicycle to the corner of Kurfuerstendamm and Tauenzienstrasse, (a street similar to Fifth Avenue in New York). The area was full of pedestrians who, like me, had come to see what was going on. The quiet, with the lack of vehicular traffic, was ominous.

I pedaled on towards Fasanenstrasse near Kurfuerstendamm. It was a horrible shock to see the synagogue where I had

39

received my religious instructions burning furiously. The police and fire departments were standing by to make sure that the fire did not spread beyond the synagogue, but did nothing to put out the existing fire. A large crowd watched quietly in disbelief.

Besides the fire, I could see that a large percentage of stores had their windows smashed in; it was clear from the names of the shops they were owned by Jews. Since such a large percentage was affected, shards of window glass were spread over the sidewalks and gutters as far as my eye could see. It was a clear moonlit November night and the broken glass glistened like expensive crystal on the pavement.

Everything was quiet, and the minimal traffic slowed to a crawl. Few cars risked driving over the broken glass; most autos made extraordinary turns and maneuvers to avoid slashing their tires. The shimmering glint of glass and the grim silence of the pedestrians gave that night a very sad, very eerie effect. I will never forget it.

After spending one day away from home, I was told by our non-Jewish friends that arrangements had been made for me; the next day after school I should meet my mother at the restaurant area at the Zoo around 4 p.m. This was a very public area, always crowded with people, so it was a safe place to rendezvous.

As instructed, the next afternoon I bicycled to the Zoo, approximately 20 minutes from where we lived, arriving a little before 4 p.m. I sized up the area. It was peaceful that cold November afternoon, the sky gray and the air somewhat damp. I kept on cycling around until I spotted my mother. She looked worried but well composed. I continued to ride my bicycle slowly, as she walked along beside me so it would appear to be a chance encounter to a casual observer. We had been warned that the Gestapo was roaming the zoo and the Tiergarten.

Calmly, and without crying she said, "Don't worry, we will get Pappi home safely, but he has been picked up by a Gestapo agent, right out of our apartment."

"How can that be?" I protested.

"The Nazi pretended to be a dental patient. His appointment was the last one for the day. When it came his turn, then he revealed what he really was." She spoke softly, but I knew she was angry.

"But we will get him back. I have spoken to our lawyer who knows about these things. He has told me what to do. I must go by myself, not with a lawyer, to the Gestapo Headquarters to find out where Pappi has been taken and what steps should be followed." She didn't mention money, but I am sure that the lawyer told her how to make a discreet offer of cash for his release.

I asked for details of the arrest.

"The agent was oddly solicitous, Pappi should have a good dinner, he said, while he (the agent) waited; he should put on warm clothes and take a warm winter coat with him, since he might not return home that night.

"So did he eat?" I asked. I wanted every detail.

Mutti smiled grimly. "Of course not. Who could eat in such a situation? He picked at his food. Otherwise, he did as advised. He dressed warmly, then accompanied the agent to Gestapo headquarters. The agent suggested they take a taxi cab but Pappi was in no hurry and said drily that on this occasion he would not mind the subway. Even then he could make a joke."

As I listened to my mother's story, I could only hope that my father would be released soon.

"You must stay hiding with our friends for the time being," she said sadly. "I will get word to you what is happening." Accordingly, I left Mutti at the zoo and bicycled back to where I was staying.

The second visit with my mother was arranged for us a few days later in the Tiergarten. I sat on the bicycle while my mother walked alongside on the special bicycle roadway.

"Well, I did it. I actually went to Alexander Platz (Gestapo headquarters.) It was very strange and frightening, and the worst was after I signed in, a door was locked after me."

My frightened imagination caused me to almost hear the clank and the turn of a key, even as she spoke.

Inside, she had learned that my father was being held in Sachsenausen near Oranienburg in the concentration camp approximately thirty miles from Berlin. The Gestapo official she saw said he was willing to release Pappi as soon as he saw proof that my father had booked passage on a ship leaving Germany. For good.

"I cannot tell you how many travel agencies I have been to see, and a Jewish aid organization to locate a safe haven somewhere in the world where we can go."

It had been extremely difficult for Mutti to obtain even an appointment at a travel agency to discuss whatever options existed. Long lines of people had been waiting for days.

Her report was bleak. "The United States and England will not take any more Jewish refugees. Australia is willing, but obtaining a visa and passage would take far too long. Every minute Pappi is in prison he will be suffering agonies we can only imagine."

The only immediate opening, she told me, was Shanghai, China, it being the only available destination that required no entrance visa. In addition, China was the last country left willing to accept Jews. The next ship, which happened to be a North German Lloyd liner, was scheduled to sail from Genoa, Italy on the fifth of December.

"I have booked passage for Pappi and me for that date."

I was not to be included in these plans, because Mutti still hoped there would be a better way out for me.

She did not really believe that both she and my father would in the end actually have to go to Shanghai, but at least the reservation was proof for the Gestapo to release my father. My mother hoped that a better place would somehow turn up, although at the time, I am certain she had no realistic idea of what "better" could be.

The following week, the campaign to round up professional people and their families appeared to subside somewhat. The three lawyers my mother had hired thought it was safe for me to return home to my mother. During the day of my return, we received all kinds of visitors, who offered to help us. Among the visitors were two men who had seen my father in the concentration camp before they themselves had been released. I remember eavesdropping through the sliding doors, heartsick, while they reported to my mother about my father.

They said that his spirits were high and while other prisoners felt hopeless, he encouraged them and told them he knew they would all be released eventually. He was performing heavy labor, such as carrying heavy loads of bricks, and so on. Mutti was advised to try to get him out as fast as possible, for my gentle dentist father was not in physical shape for such demanding exertion. The released prisoners frightened us by saying that each day my father remained in the camp could be his last. Nobody in the camp knew whether they would make it through the day or night, because the weather was below freezing, and prisoners were kept outside the barracks for many hours of the day. Many suffered from severe frostbite.

It was an incredibly anxious three weeks before my mother could acquire all the necessary papers to obtain my father's release. When she finally accumulated them all, she went to Gestapo headquarters where they examined the reservation for the trip to Shanghai and the other required papers, then sent a telegram confirming their findings to the concentration camp. They also "unfroze" enough funds from our bank account to pay for the tickets. I never learned from my mother how much money changed hands to make this miracle happen.

My father was released twenty-four hours later. Remarkably, he was given enough money for the train ride home, a grand total of 4 marks. It was eight p.m. when the doorbell rang that night. My mother rushed to the door. Standing outside was my father with a big smile on his face but no hair on his head, because of course, it had been shaved off, as befitted a Jewish prisoner. Painfully thin, his very fine winter coat, now terribly wrinkled, hung on him loosely.

Under his arm was his wrinkled hat, his bent eyeglass frames barely stayed on his nose. We all were so happy to see him that we did not care what he looked like. He was alive and home. We would take care of him. He had been gone from us in prison from November 11 until December 6, 1938.

As soon as we had closed the door behind him, my father explained that the guards had sent his coat, hat and suit through a de-lousing process which they called dry cleaning as soon as he reached the camp, and when they were ready to release him, returned them, wrapped up in the same package; therefore all his clothes had this terrible appearance. The image of those pathetically wrinkled clothes has stuck in my memory all these years.

Pappi had been forced to swear that he would never talk to anybody about what happened during his stay in the concentration camp. He was so happy to be out of the camp and alive, he had no intention of risking another detention by breaking his oath. His further instructions were to register immediately at the local police station and then board the ship for Shanghai with my mother, as specified on his ticket.

My mother made a special supper for my father but he was far too agitated to eat. Eventually, overcome by exhaustion, he went to bed.

The next morning Pappi hurried to the police station as instructed. The police officer in charge was very happy to see him and though he said it kindly, had to tell him that he must immediately begin to liquidate his practice, and to estimate how long it would take to finish treating the patients who were still in his appointment book.

The police knew that eighty percent of his patients were Aryans, which meant that it was not in the district's interest for my father to leave the country immediately. Subsequent to my father informing them that he would need about two and a half months to take care of all his patients, the police immediately extended my parents' stay for a little over three months. They would not have to leave at the beginning of December but could stay until April, 1939. My mother took the shipping line tickets to the North German Lloyd office and changed the booking accordingly. Pappi's dental profession had bought us a little more time to live in our beloved Germany, time enough to make an organized exit.

**EMMI (MUTTI), WALTER (PAPPI), HANS,
GRANDMOTHER RIESS (AFTER MY FATHER'S
RETURN FROM THE CONCENTRATION CAMP)**

That New Year's Eve, with the bravado of a 17-year-old, I purchased illegally, and more perilously than I might have thought, a ticket for the *Fledermaus* performance at the Charlottenburger Opera House. The *Fledermaus* was traditionally performed every New Year's Eve, but strictly verboten for Jews to attend.

Just before the performance started, it was announced that Hitler and Dr. Goebbels would attend the performance. As they entered, the audience rose and all raised their right arms with a

45

stiff salute. I had no choice; I followed suit in order not to be noticed.

I was not frightened to be there, since I looked like everyone else, and I knew I would love every minute of the performance. The overture was well played and the sets magnificent. No expense had been spared on the production, since the government subsidized the theater heavily. I will never forget the last act, when the prison set split in half and a huge champagne bottle appeared in the middle of the stage. The cork pops out and Frosch, the jailer, climbs from the bottle.

I went home that night, elated by the theatrical experience, wishing I could bring that lift of spirits home to my parents, to share my thrill with them while we saw the New Year in together. Sadly, instead they brought me back to reality. Midnight and 1939 came quietly with Mutti and Pappi, not a celebration so much as a small family uniting that night against the inevitable separation that was coming fast.

Although the extension of three additional months in Berlin had been welcomed by the family, Pappi felt it unwise for me to remain in Germany any longer than absolutely necessary. He was concerned that I would have to interrupt my engineering studies if forced to leave with him and Mutti for Shanghai. After his return from the concentration camp, he had immediately put out feelers for a way of escape for me to one of a number of European countries.

The German Jewish Aid Committee had representation in London at the Bloomsberry House, which in turn worked with the Church of England and other church organizations. These groups were attempting to get as many children and young people as possible out of Germany and placed with private families.

My father was instructed to put together a small dossier consisting of my photograph, a brief description of our family's background and a statement of my educational goals. This was to be sent to the German Aid Committee as fast as possible, for circulation in England. About a month later we heard that a Mr.

46

H.D. Murray, an owner of a machine tool factory in Enfield-Ponders End, Middlesex was willing to take me into his household.

The next step was for all three of us to go to the German Passport Office and apply for passports. After a one-month waiting period, which brought us to February, 1939, those precious booklets became ours.

My passport was not registered in my legal name, which was Hans Ludwig Riess, but rather in the name of Hans Ludwig Israel Riess. All male Jews had to include the name Israel, and all females had to include the name Sarah among their other names. Thus, my mother's name became Emmi Anna Sarah, and my father's, Walter Israel.

Since our legal names contained no Jewish connotation, it was perhaps understandable, though contemptible, that the German government did such a thing. But to solidify the identification, our passports also had the red stamp with a large letter "J," for *Jude* (Jew) stamped on the front page.

Our passports were issued for the duration of one year rather than the customary five years, the end result being that we would be stateless after the first year upon the expiration of our passports. We did not allow ourselves to think about that problem; our first priority and concern was to leave the country. We had come to some kind of terms within ourselves of being stripped of our German citizenship, still thinking it would be only temporary.

Now that we had received our passports, the next step was to set the date of my departure. My father purchased a train ticket for me for March 11, 1939 at 12 midnight to leave Berlin for London.

My parents had no choice but to book passage on the North German Lloyd ship "Gneisenau," destination, Shanghai, scheduled to leave the port of Bremerhaven some time in April, 1939.

Many arrangements were yet to be made between the time of purchasing the tickets and the actual departure date, not to speak

47

of shopping. Although their bank account had been frozen, my parents had enough money to outfit me for London -- in Germany there was something called a postal checking account which was completely independent of bank accounts, and I presume that was how they were able to retain at least a modicum of funds.

My parents went with me to the KaDeWe (Kaufhaus Des Westens), "The Department Store of the West." Here they bought underwear, shirts, ties, socks, handkerchiefs and a very large wardrobe trunk for me. In a men's clothing store my father ordered a heavy winter coat and three suits made to measure for me. At the last moment, I spotted a ready-made tuxedo. The tuxedo required only minor alterations and was not too expensive. Our image of England was that it would be quite formal and a dinner jacket might come in very handy. Therefore, the tuxedo was purchased and I was a very pleased young man.

Our next stop was a shoe store. I bought very light-weight black shoes to go with the tuxedo plus several pairs of brown and black everyday shoes. From there we went to a hat store to buy gloves. I was quite excited about all the purchases, and not terribly aware of the sadness of my parents. They were not worried about the money being spent, since we could not take it with us anyhow. They were far more keenly aware than I of how great was the possibility that we would be parting forever.

On another day my father and I went to buy a good camera and a portable typewriter. I was also to be given the family radio to take with me, since it had a short wave band, and my father thought they probably could not use it in China.

I immediately tested the new camera by making a photographic record of my family, interior shots of our apartment, as well as the house itself. My father's practice and laboratory were also important to me, for it was in these rooms that the Gestapo officer arrested my father. I took pictures of my 83-year-old grandmother, my parents, and aunts and uncles. These small last-minute snapshots have kept my memories green for almost 60 years.

I also wanted to remember the city in which I spent my youth, so once again on my trusty bicycle, I pedaled around Berlin to take pictures of the happy places I had frequented so often.

During all this activity, I was not upset. Perhaps I did not quite realize the finality of it all. I suppose that was it. Of course, at the dinner table, many frightening things were discussed, at which time I realized -- on an intellectual level -- how dangerous the situation actually was. But at an emotional level I was still serene. I had been happy in Berlin. Now I was looking forward to a new life, and believed that it, too, would be happy.

Finally, the fateful day and time arrived for me to depart for England: it was midnight, March 11, 1939, chilly and dark. My parents accompanied me to the *Berlin Schlesischer Bahnhof*. This railroad station was a large covered building with an opening on one end, right in the middle of Berlin. All tracks led in one direction only.

Schlesischer was a very large station with many platforms. We found our platform for the train which would take me to the border at Aachen, where the train would leave Germany and cross the frontier into Belgium and finally to the coast at Ostende. From there, I would take the ferry to Dover in England. A boat train would meet the ferry and bring it and me to Victoria Station in London.

Tante Lillie and Uncle Kurt together with my grandmother, met my parents and me on the platform to say good-bye. Everyone looked quite sad, all except me, I think, and a pall hung in the air; there was very little conversation. I reassured my grandmother that yes, I had packed the darning needles and the darning yarn she had recently given me, after first giving me instructions on how to mend my socks in England. She had even wound different colored yarn on a piece of cardboard, and marked on the needles *stopfnadel* so I would know which needle to use for what purpose.

My mother had made first class reservations for me but did not want the others to know about it, so she and the others waited on the platform rather than accompany me onto the train to see my compartment. She was very circumspect about her spoiling me, not wanting others to know of her extravagance on my behalf.

Lillie and Kurt did not stay until the train left, which surprised me somewhat. I did not know that they were going on ahead to see me again at a later stop in the suburbs for a final wave good-bye. Finally, the conductor raised his signal stick and the train slowly pulled out of the station.

I waved to my parents and grandmother; all of us tried to put on a smiling face through the tears, though my father waited until he got home to weep.

After about 15 minutes, the train made its first stop at a suburban station. Since Uncle Kurt knew the number of my car, he managed to be only a few feet from my window when the engine chugged to a halt. I was happy to see Kurt and Lillie, but disappointed that my parents and grandmother weren't there too. Then again, if they had come to the suburban station the agony of my final farewell would have been prolonged.

When I asked about the absence of my parents, my uncle said that it was due to a lapse in communications: Pappi and Mutti hadn't understood his plan for a second *Auf Wiedersehen*. He hardly had time to explain when the train pulled away from the platform, my family and the suburbs of Berlin quickly receding. I never saw Tante Lillie, Uncle Kurt or my grandmother again.

The train made a few stops during the night and arrived at 9 a.m. at the German/Belgian border, where the police and SS checked everyone's passports. I was told to step off the train and bring my luggage with me. A few other people were told the same thing.

I was directed to a small room in the station building where a customs inspector went through all my luggage at a purposefully slow speed. He took so long that the train left without me and the other passengers who had been ordered to leave the train.

50

There I was, left with my luggage on the station platform with just ten German marks in my pocket, the maximum amount one was allowed to take out of Germany, and no idea when the next train would come by. I had a suspicion that only Jews were kept long enough to miss the train, but of course, couldn't be sure, nor did I bother to determine whether the others were Jewish.

Fortunately another train arrived in about an hour, and I got on, with yet another wait while more members of the SS boarded the train and began to check each compartment. I became concerned that I would be pulled off the train a second time, even though I had already been checked. Fortunately, I was wrong.

A lady passenger whispered to me to be very quiet and not to talk to anybody because the SS would be on the train until we got to Brussels. How she knew this I never found out, and I was too frightened to ask. Needless to say, I did a lot of anxiety breathing until the SS left the train in Brussels.

Apart from my nervousness, and my brushes with the SS, the trip to the Belgium coast was uneventful. When the train reached the port of Ostende, everyone disembarked, each passenger carrying his or her own luggage. Some headed to the terminal -- they were remaining in Belgium -- but most walked onto the ferry boat waiting for passengers to board, ready to depart.

The channel crossing was fairly rough, and the air cold and and bone-chilling damp. It was late in the afternoon and already dark, when the street lights at the Dover coast of England appeared off the ferry's bow. I looked and looked, but could not spot the famed white cliffs of Dover.

The ferry docked with no problem, and the passengers who were continuing on disembarked and walked a short distance to the express boat train, which would carry us the rest of the way to London.

When I boarded, I was concerned about checking my hand luggage, which consisted of the new typewriter and camera, for

51

fear that someone would steal them, but my fellow travelers assured me that it was perfectly safe. They proved to be right.

The train itself was beautiful, with handsome dining tables and chairs in every car. Waiters served food and beverages the whole trip, and I began to appreciate my first experience of British amenities, and the helpfulness and courtesy of the Brits.

The only catch was that since I was now in England, I was obliged to speak English all the time; any last thought I had of speaking German disappeared abruptly. Mine was schoolboy English, and though I supposed my general comprehension was excellent, problems of vernacular usage arose almost immediately. My English teacher had never thought to tell me that on British trains the men's room is called a lavatory, a fact I ultimately learned for myself.

London

From Dover on, the remainder of the trip was smooth and comfortable. Within two hours we arrived at Victoria Station, a huge covered terminal in the southeast section of London.

I peered out the window as we entered the terminal, hoping to catch a glimpse of my cousin Hanna, whom I had not seen for eight long years. Six months younger than I, she was the daughter of Georg Hamburger, my mother's cousin, the gynecologist who helped to deliver me 17 years earlier. Hanna's mother had died in Berlin when Hanna was quite young, and a few years later "Uncle" Georg, with cousin Hanna emigrated to Israel -- as many Berlin Jews we knew had done.

Georg had wisely left Berlin in 1933 primarily because of controversy over his performing abortions, which though not illegal, were much disapproved in Germany. However, he was also outspoken and politically active; he was too visible a member of the community to escape the notice of the Nazis, and he knew it.

Uncle Georg was nothing if not inventive. He managed to avoid the 25% "flight tax" that had been in effect even two years before the Nazis came to power. This he did by putting all of his cash into gold, and having the gold made into hubcaps for his car, which he drove into Budapest, with no problem at the border.

At any rate, when she was old enough, Georg sent Hanna to be educated in England. Hanna had originally been named Annemarie, but when her father re-married in Israel, his new wife's name was also Annemarie. To save confusion, my cousin took the name of Hanna. Before she left Berlin, Hanna and I shared happy times with my grandmother. Once we went to the Children's Theatre to see *Emil und die Detective* (*Emil and the Detective*, adapted for the theatre from a famous children's book of the time). The two of us became so excited that we stood on

53

the back of the theatre chairs, thinking we could see more that way. Hanna stepped into the crack at the rear of the folding seat, which forced the seat to fold upward, pitching her forward with some force. The crash made a tremendous noise, causing a stir in the audience, but my imperturbable grandmother was not upset with us at all; Hanna fortunately, was uninjured.

Hanna had been "conscripted" to meet me at the train station with a gentleman named Reverend Long so she could identify me for him. Reverend Long was a minister of the Church of England who worked with the German Jewish Aid Committee to find homes and shelter with the warm-hearted British for young Jews escaping from Germany. It was he who facilitated the arrangement for me whereby I would live with a family named Murray.

As luck would have it, there were not too many people meeting the train I was on, so it was easy to spot Hanna as soon as we pulled into the station. She was standing in the middle of the platform, waiting for me with a man who had to be Reverend Long.

It was a happy reunion and we embraced warmly. After she introduced me, she explained that Reverend Long had reserved two rooms for us in the Eccleston Hotel right across the road from Victoria station. She also said that Reverend Long had been in direct touch with my sponsors, Mr. and Mrs. Murray and that they were eagerly awaiting me.

I was more than happy that all these arrangements had been made on my behalf; indeed, I was extremely grateful as well, but whether it was from an innate shyness or the rapidity with which my life was changing, I know I certainly failed to express my appreciation adequately.

The pastor was a tall, slender man with gray hair; I guessed him to be about 50. He and I lugged my bags across the street to the hotel, where he assisted in checking us in before leaving. He said that he would pick us up the next morning and then see Hanna off before escorting me to the home of the Murrays. (My cousin had been permitted a short leave from school in order to meet me, but the next morning she was obliged to return to class.)

He then took his leave. Hanna and I parted, too, and settled into our respective rooms.

The Eccleston Hotel, though large, was in its dotage. Although it might once have been a fashionable place, it had settled into a moribund condition of faded elegance. More serious than its lack of glamor was the fact that central heating was non-existent. My room was so cold my teeth started to chatter, quite literally, and I was convinced I'd be frozen solid before the night was over. The windows were of single-pane construction and not insulated or weatherproofed in any way, unlike our cozy apartment in Berlin, so the legendary London cold seeped right in between the cracks. Berlin windows were true storm windows -- doubled-paned with a space in between, making them almost draft free. The London hotel's windows weren't even flush with the sills so that the wind whistled through freely.

I looked all over the room in vain for some indication of how to turn on the steam heat. There was no way, because none existed, but I did discover a gas meter near the ceiling, which to my dismay, required pennies to operate.

I had exactly 10 German marks to my name and certainly no English coins. Desperately I phoned Hanna, who had no pennies either. But she did have the few British pounds Reverend Long had thoughtfully left in case we needed anything. She dashed to the lobby for change and returned triumphantly with six pennies to heat the room for six hours.

Shivering, I climbed a chair to reach the slot to deposit the pennies, and *finally,* about 15 minutes later, the room slowly began to warm, but only minimally. My difficulty in falling asleep that first night in England was due not from being homesick, but from the frigid climatic condition of my room. I even kept my socks and underwear on all night, but was simply too cold to get comfortable.

The following morning the telephone rang to announce the arrival of Reverend Long, who was in the lobby to pick us up for breakfast. Though he wore a wide clerical collar and a black suit, which I found both formidable and intimidating, his manner was affable and compassionate. I recall he had a terrible cold and a somewhat reddish nose that day, doubtless exacerbated by the fiercely cold weather.

As we left the hotel for breakfast, I had my first real view of London in the daylight. The streets were bustling with automobiles and passengers, clogged with a seemingly endless string of red double-decker buses and teeming with London's famous square-backed black taxis, efficiently taking on passengers or dropping them off, then quickly driving on. Bobbies in black uniforms helped to regulate the traffic.

I was enormously impressed with the smoothness of the traffic flow. Red, amber, and green traffic lights were visible at every street corner. It all seemed so much better organized than the traffic system I had grown up with in Berlin. Order has always appealed to me, though whether this is related in some way to the influence of German culture or I am this way by nature, I cannot say for certain, but I have a hunch that both reasons have a large measure of truth in them.

We had breakfast in a Lyons tearoom, one of a large chain of shops of the same name in London, only a few blocks from our hotel, where we savored good coffee, buttered rolls and cereal.

Following breakfast, we walked back to Victoria Station and waited for Hanna's suburban train to take her back to school. After we saw her off, Reverend Long and I took the Underground to meet Mr. Murray.

The clean, quiet and fast-moving Piccadilly line with its comfortable upholstered seats, seemed impeccably efficient to me. Doors opened automatically permitting passengers to leave the train, and others to quickly step on before the doors closed. Each car was equipped with a clear and simple map of all the stations along the Piccadilly line.

Every station platform posted large maps indicating both the position of that station in relation to the overall line, as well as the change-over points to other lines. The different lines were indicated by color coding. It seemed impossible to get lost, yet I imagined it could be done if one tried hard enough, though I had no intention of trying.

Our Underground trip took 45 minutes; we then exited the tubes, and took a Green Line double-decker bus to the "Endfield-Ponders End" Industrial zone. The area was a factory district and had to have been one of the older neighborhoods of greater London since the sidewalks and streets and pavement were uneven and worn.

Several large factory buildings were marked with the name, "H.D. Murray Ltd." The roof of each building was shaped and constructed like a huge skylight in such a way that daylight could help illuminate the entire building.

When we arrived at the office of Mr. Murray, we found him in shirt sleeves, engaged in a business conversation on the telephone. He motioned to us to sit down, as he continued talking; we waited politely for him to complete his call.

Off the phone, he seemed really pleased that I had arrived, welcoming me warmly. Given the circumstances of my departure from Berlin, he had been very concerned about my safety so he was relieved to learn that I had crossed the German border without serious incident. He said that he and his wife had made a room available in their house for me, and if Reverend Long would bring me and my luggage to the factory the next day, the Murrays would take me home in their car.

Reverend Long politely demurred and explained to Mr. Murray that he had arranged for me to visit two elderly spinsters for two weeks in their vacation home in Paignton in Devonshire. They wanted to participate in his program to help German Jewish youth; they felt that I could use some fattening up with Devonshire milk and butter before starting school after Easter break, having heard that Jews in Germany were forbidden such healthy eating. Reverend Long's explanation deflected any possible interpretation by Mr. Murray that my delay in going to his home was rude or ungrateful. At that age and stage of experience, I would not have been able to explain with such tact. It was amicably agreed that Reverend Long would pack me off by train to Devon and pick me up two weeks later to take me to the Murrays.

On the train ride to Paignton, Devonshire moving rapidly down the coast, I observed how red the earth looked. The color reminded me of certain parts of Germany where the earth had a high iron ore content, like the Ruhr valley.

My newly acquired kind-hearted friends met me at the station, and we taxied to their picturesque old three-story row house, similar to most of the houses along the coast of Devonshire. It was a six-step climb up to their large veranda, furnished with sturdy garden chairs from which they could, I supposed, comfortably survey the pounding ocean as well as the neighbors' activities during warmer weather.

From what I recall of the house and its furnishings, it resembled the ladies themselves: old, comfortable, sturdy, bare of ornamentation, and very, very English. They wore long skirts covered with ample layers of aprons and dowdy sweaters to keep them from the cold, a far cry from the stylish women in my own family.

They showed me to an upstairs bedroom where I would sleep for the next two weeks. The walls were freshly painted in a light yellow; a wooden desk looked new, and so did the night table. I wondered if they had done all this just for me. There was just enough space in the room for a chair, a wardrobe and a dresser. The bedspread matched the pretty curtains on the dormer window; the over-all effect was one of country charm.

Stepping into the room, however, I inwardly cringed. The alcove dormer window, which consisted of three sections, gave a beautiful view of the ocean, but the draft howling through the large window warned ominously of cold nights to come. There was absolutely no heat. Not even a miserable metered gas heater like that of the hotel. There was nothing for it but to get used to the English lifestyle, I sighed to myself. This consisted of simply ignoring winter.

The ladies were solicitous; they wanted to know all about "the terrible events in Germany," giving me ample opportunity to practice my English. They were surprised that the picture I painted of my life in Germany was not as grim and frightening as the one they imagined, which puzzled me until I thought, "Well, their information comes from propaganda pieces in the English press circulated by the British government just as Germans have relied on their government propaganda for information." It was only many years later that I learned they had been right, and I so wrong. I had lived in a Berlin which knew nothing of the Nazi death camps.

The first night was so cold that I again slept in my underwear, double socks and shirt. The ladies did provide a hot water bottle, but it turned ice cold in no time at all.

Apart from the cold, my stay in Devon was pleasant, quiet and uneventful. Occasionally, when the wind died down, we took short walks along the water's edge. It was March and the stormy winds were witheringly bitter. Returning from these jaunts, there was tea to be enjoyed in the country kitchen, and toast slathered generously with the butter the ladies thought I so badly needed, retrieved from the toast rack of their English gas stove.

I could picture the coast of Devon as a beautiful place during the summer months when the warm sun would shine down upon the red earth and azure sea. But now it was quiet and so isolated, I couldn't wait to get back to London. In the meantime, I helped the ladies clean house, wash windows, and even did a little carpentry. I was basically happy, or at least not unhappy, during my Devonshire visit, but felt some sadness, having too much time to think. I knew my parents were still in Berlin, but only for the time being.

In the absence of interesting things to do or see, the two weeks in Devon passed slowly; at last the day came for the return trip to London. I thanked my well-meaning hostesses warmly for their hospitality, for I was not ungrateful, as we parted at the small train station, and they in turn expressed pleasure that they could help in some way; they felt that helping me helped in some measure to ameliorate the injustices being perpetrated in Germany by Hitler's government.

The Torqué Express brought me back to London where Reverend Long was waiting for me at the station once again, except this time it was at Euston Station, not Victoria. At the baggage storage area we retrieved the balance of my luggage which completely over-flowed our taxi, including its top luggage rack; finally we managed to squeeze ourselves in, and off we rode.

It took over an hour to reach Mr. Murray's machine tool plant, where we unloaded the taxi and Reverend Long paid the driver. We left the stack of luggage in front of the building and headed to the main office.

Both Mr. Murray and his son Douglas were there to meet me; when they saw us, they beamed. The Murrays brought their green two-door Morris-8 around from the parking lot to the front entrance. They tied my bag containing bedding with several ropes onto the front fender. Douglas then tried to hoist my large wardrobe trunk onto a special luggage rack attached to the rear of the car, but the front wheels of the tiny Morris-8 lifted into the air immediately. The effect was comic, but since no one was in the mood to laugh, no one did.

By pulling the bedding closer to the front, the car became balanced. After we shoved, cajoled and pushed the rest of the luggage inside the car, we bade adieu to the kindly Reverend Long, and Mr. Murray and I squeezed aboard with Douglas at the wheel and off we went.

We drove through the factory district of Ponders End and after five minutes, reached the London city line. As soon as we entered Hartfordshire, Middlesex, the sidewalks disappeared and lovely country roads replaced city streets. We travelled approximately 25 minutes with our heavy load, crossing narrow bridges, and maneuvering up and down small hills.

The country became more and more open and the spring air gave a beautiful welcome. We turned into Halstead Hill and Mr. Murray pointed out the iron gate of their house, "Bonanza." We turned the corner and pulled up the long driveway. "Bonanza" was a small red brick tudor house situated on an extremely large plot of land.

As soon as the car had stopped, a lovely blonde lady with hair parted in the center, came out to greet us. She was, of course, Mrs. Murray. I cannot possibly exaggerate the warmth of her greeting. For some reason I could not fathom, she seemed practically ecstatic, which puzzled me, because after all, I was a complete stranger.

MR. AND MRS. H.D. MURRAY

She did say she felt relieved that I had finally arrived, seemed to feel a sense of personal satisfaction that she was able to help directly in her own way. Thousands of young people had tried to leave Germany, but only a small number had been able to make it; only about 1,000 made it to England. The Murrays

61

were one of the families who made these life-saving miracles possible.

Once again, I felt both happy and sad at the same time to be in the Murrays' home. I was glad because I was safe, but sad because I had no idea when I would see my parents again, if ever. There was a sudden poignant realization that now I could speak only English, but also a sense of satisfaction that I'd studied it for 7 years. Our *Gymnasium* was fortunate in that it had a teacher from London, and I studied with him one hour every day. Consequently, I could make myself understood, although many terms which the Murrays used were unfamiliar to me.

"Fish and chips" were initially a puzzlement, but I found them an agreeable addition to my food lexicon. I also latched on to "blimey" as England's general all-purpose exclamation, and calling girls "birds." But it proved more difficult to adjust to everyday conversational English as opposed to school English than I ever imagined it might be.

We went into the house through the rear entrance and entered the kitchen. It was a cozy, but very small room. We then went through the small sitting room to the staircase, then upstairs to my little room, which had a dormer; it was nicely furnished and spotlessly clean. We carried my smaller luggage upstairs, but the wardrobe trunk was much too heavy to maneuver the steep and narrow staircase. Mrs. Murray and I unpacked the bag containing my bedding downstairs and chose which blanket and which pillow cases and sheets to use. Mrs. Murray had never seen such large down pillows and was surprised that I had not one, but two of them. I also had both a heavy woolen blanket and a down blanket, because my worried mother had heard (oh so correctly) that it was very cold in England in the wintertime.

I had a few minutes to myself in the room which from now on would be mine, but soon I was called for dinner. British food would take some getting used to, I soon learned. I found English meat pretty tough and the vegetables not too palatable, either.

But, I thought, tomorrow is another day and the food might improve. I certainly wasn't going to criticize.

After a few days of English fare, I concluded that the best meal in England was breakfast. The old-fashioned stoves in British kitchens have a special wired fixture for making toast, which I loved. They also sometimes served meat or fish at breakfast as well as hash-brown potatoes. Eggs, too, poached, coddled, scrambled or fried were frequently part of an English breakfast. The English liked a lot of marmalade with their toast, for which I had to acquire a taste, but they also served very good jam, which I liked at once.

The coffee was not brewed to my liking, but I found hot chocolate and justifiably famous English tea to be good substitutes. If I didn't watch it, I got black and white coffee or tea, which means half a cup of milk and half a cup of tea or coffee. Eventually I actually got used to drinking tea with a lot of milk and sugar.

I told myself that eating habits were different in every country, and I would simply adjust to the English diet. Actually, I tried pretty hard. I wanted to adjust. But at the same time, my loneliness did not help the situation. The food was strange, the surroundings new and nobody from my family was around. I hadn't realized how much I had taken for granted the loving concern of my very close-knit family. The sense of a brave adventure was dissipating into homesickness. I wrote long letters to my parents who sensed my loneliness and I knew from their responding letters they felt bad too. I should have tried to hide my true feelings, but just could not manage it.

They tried to write lightly of their trip to Shanghai on the *Gneisenau,* a north German Lloyd ship. They had been required to pay the added expense of going first class, for which my father had to have a tuxedo and my mother evening clothes too. The best part of their trip seemed to be meeting a couple named Blumberg from Breslau, with whom they became fast friends.

My parents had a great deal in common with the Blumbergs, including a very positive attitude towards life and business; they would continue to be friends the rest of their lives. (Mr. Blumberg had been a successful commercial painting contractor in Germany). Their daughter Ursel was about my age and I suppose they compared notes on the subject of rearing an only child. Mr. Blumberg was very tall and slim, my father short and not so slim; when the two walked together they looked like Mutt and Jeff, my short father trying valiantly to keep up with the long-legged Mr. Blumberg.

The Murrays were aware of how much I missed my family. One Sunday morning after breakfast, they asked me to dress in a suit and tie and be ready in half an hour. When I came downstairs, the whole family was dressed up as though for some kind of an event. I got into the car, but had no idea where we were going. Mr. Murray smiled enigmatically behind the wheel and drove toward London.

After a little more than an hour, we parked on Leicester Square in the West End, not too far from Piccadilly Circus. We walked across the square to Lyons Corner House, then took the elevator to a Viennese restaurant where we were shown to a reserved table. We sat down and to my astonishment, a German menu was placed in front of me. My only thought at the time was how very nice of the Murrays to take me to a Viennese restaurant to make me feel more at home. When we finished the main course, our waitress brought a candled birthday cake to the table by the waitress. It was my 18th birthday.

The Murrays had secretly planned for days to make a celebration for me. My homesickness vanished, replaced with a realization of how lovely it was to be free in a country where gentiles welcomed Jews. For the first time in several weeks, I felt extremely happy. This thoughtful family had not only welcomed me to their home, they had shown that I was part of their family.

After the surprise dinner, the Murrays gave me a tour around the West End and pointed out Trafalgar Square, Hyde Park Corner, Buckingham Palace and Piccadilly. It was great to be alive. The city was bustling and I was once more my old curious self, eager to find out how I could get to the West End by public transportation.

Mr. Murray pointed to the Underground, the subway of the "London Transport." He also pointed to the Green Line Coaches, which take passengers nonstop to the London City Line and make stops in the suburbs. I was overwhelmed with the huge number of red double deck buses. They seemed to be everywhere.

Later, on other excursions I took by myself, I eagerly learned more about British transportation. (Transportation in general has held a lifelong fascination for me.) On my early solo forays in England, I found driving on the left hand side of the street disconcerting to say the least.

I was awed by the smoothness of London traffic with English Bobbies directing the flow. Everything seemed so organized. The traffic lights, the poles of which were painted black and white, were placed at every corner. If you walked between the "nails" you were safe. These large, raised metal plates were standard markings all over London. The pedestrians not only had nails for guidance, but black and white posts on which large amber glass balls were affixed; at night they flashed continuously. The English traffic laws on right-of-way were strictly enforced. Any pedestrian walking between the nails and amber lights had the right of way.

As the length of my stay in London grew, I began to observe that British drivers followed the law. I did not see accidents either between cars, buses and trucks, or between pedestrians and vehicles, nor did I see London policemen give parking tickets to anybody. If anyone tried to park illegally, a bobby would mysteriously appear and politely tell the would-be parker to move on since parking was prohibited in that particular spot. He would then point them to a parking area or garage.

Bobbies were gentlemen, proud to be policemen. Their black uniforms, devoid of any brass or shiny buttons, looked like tuxedos. The tall black helmet of the metropolitan police was

65

worn with pride. They did not carry guns; their only protection, a police whistle, was worn on a long band on the lower left sleeve of their tunics. They were always courteous and willing to give information and advice.

The best public transportation in London was the Underground. Though quite old, with wooden escalators and wooden floors in the railroad cars, it was efficient. In particular, the Piccadilly line was very fast and quiet.

The Underground was also called "the Tubes," since the trains moved in tunnels shaped like tubes. The cars had rounded tops to fit the shape of the tubes. You could ride an express train with only a few stops, reaching the suburbs in approximately an hour. The Underground had zoned fares; you surrendered your ticket at your destination. The stations were well marked; maps showing exactly where you were and where that particular line went lined the walls. Each car had a map displayed in the upper part of the car almost as long as the car itself. The Underground was extremely clean, and I did not see any vandalism. Each station had an escalator to transport passengers to and from exits. The Piccadilly line was built so far underground it required a two-level escalator to reach the train platform, which made the Underground a very safe air-raid shelter indeed when the bombs began to fall on London.

The red double-deck buses were just as spotlessly clean as the Underground. The conductor collected zoned fares and in return gave you a ticket. They carried money for change but never seemed to be threatened with hold-ups. Many of the conductors were women, a fact I found surprising, since in Germany, women still lived according to the motto: *Kinder, Kirche, Küche,* (Children, Church and Kitchen.) In Berlin one rarely saw women working outside the home, and especially not as train conductors, which involved contact with the public.

The double-deck buses didn't have entrance and exit doors. They were simply open at the rear, and one could jump on and off whenever the bus stopped.

I had to become familiar quickly with the London Transport since I enrolled immediately at the London Polytechnic Institute on Regent Street. Because my own parents' funds were totally frozen in Berlin, the Murrays paid for all my studies and everything I needed in England. Not only did they finance my education, Mr. Murray also gave me the opportunity to make some pocket money working part-time in his machine tool factory. That experience was to stand me in good stead in the not-too-far distant future.

The courses at the Institute were 50% theoretical and 50% practical. After the theory was taught in the classroom, the rest of the course was in engineering workshops, practicing what we had learned, a method effectively used throughout Europe. By the time I graduated, I was able to operate any and every kind of machine tool needed by a mechanical engineer. I was also gaining practical experience in the design and creation of jigs and fixtures, training I eventually applied in China. My two years of study would go by rapidly.

Meanwhile, the European war had enlarged in scope and severity, becoming a global cataclysm.

It was a warm, sunny September morning in 1939 when at 10 a.m. Prime Minister Chamberlain, who had nervously hoped to avoid any confrontation, addressed the British nation on the radio and announced in ponderous tones that because Germany had invaded Poland, England had declared itself at war with Germany. It was a very sad Sunday for us all.

This news frightened everyone, and me in particular; I was sure German planes would bomb London immediately, but nothing much noticeable happened, except that air raid sirens were tested, and sand bags began to appear, stacked around police stations.

The day after the announcement, all aliens (and I certainly qualified as an alien) were required to go to the nearest police station and hand over all cameras, street maps, radios, etc. It was there that newly printed instructions for "Enemy Aliens" were pasted into my alien registration book.

67

Several days later, elongated silver balloons which looked like blimps suddenly appeared, dotting the skies over London. It turned out that these balloons were the expression of a naively optimistic hope on the part of the government that their presence would assure the British that their country was well prepared to fight Germany, even though they lacked such basics as anti-aircraft guns. I suppose the theory was that if the government could establish a balloon barrier in a few days, Londoners might be lulled into believing that they were prepared to fight the Germans. I wondered how many Englishmen realized that the balloons would not have been very effective as an airborne blockade against German planes, but I knew. Thankfully, the German planes did not come. Not yet, at any rate.

One lone anti-aircraft gun was placed in Hyde Park; then the very same gun was moved to Finsbury Park. Later, it showed up at other locations, hopefully giving the appearance to the enemy agents that the Luftwaffe should beware of England's defense system. The sad truth was that Great Britain was simply not prepared for war.

The Civil Defense Core organized a brigade of taxis for ambulance and other emergency services. Small trailers attached to taxis carried fire hoses. Civil Defense cadres assembled on school playgrounds for assignments. Block wardens patrolled the streets with First World War vintage steel helmets and new gas masks. Everyone was required to pick up gas masks and wear them around their necks at all times. These were simple rubber masks with a simple filter for breathing and a plastic window which covered our eyes to see through.

Now that it was finally at war with Germany, England was frightened. She may have been unprepared for war, but no effort was spared to rush into production of arms, ammunition, and other war materiel required to fight. Overtime was scheduled in most factories. Rationing of certain goods was announced. Full national mobilization was set in motion, and a universal military draft went into immediate effect. Each month that went by, more and more men were called up to military service.

Enemy aliens who were refugees from Germany as well as other countries, were also asked to join the British army voluntarily. Pressure was exerted on us to do so, and many who did not were interned on the Isle of Man.

One day I got a notification to come for a hearing at a tribunal at Bow Street Station, which was a large court facility located in downtown London. I was to bring a person who could vouch for me and guarantee my conduct. Mr. Murray immediately volunteered. I was hopeful that I would not have any difficulty being transformed from an "enemy" alien to a "friendly" one, since I had no contacts with anyone in Germany other than my parents before they left for Shanghai in April, 1939.

On a cloudy morning at 8 o'clock, we started out for London.

Mr. Murray and I arrived at Bow Street station at 8:45. He parked the car and we walked slowly to the courthouse. We found the registration office located in the basement, but were then sent upstairs to wait. At 9:40, my name was called out and Mr. Murray and I went into court.

It was a normal-looking courtroom with a raised bench for the three presiding judges. A young clerk immediately approached me and explained that she was assigned to translate from English to German. I didn't need a translator so I told her I would fend for myself. I was so confident the hearing would go well and I would be accepted as "friendly" that I had absolutely no fear.

The judge sitting in the middle asked for my name and address, which I supplied. He and the other judges checked some papers in front of them, then he asked me if I had corresponded with anybody in Germany. I said I hadn't.

They checked the records again and after some whispered discussion among them, announced that I would henceforth be considered a friendly alien during my stay in the United Kingdom. Then the judges smiled and congratulated me.

I innocently thought this was the standard procedure, but later learned that 98% of all those who passed before this tribunal had been sent to the Isle of Man for internment. I also learned the reason. If an alien whose status was under review denied having corresponded with anyone in Germany, but in reality had, a judge would produce a postcard or a letter the alien had received from Germany or one he had written to Germany which had been intercepted by the postal authorities.

Mr. Murray had written a beautiful letter of recommendation on my behalf, and at the same time, offered the tribunal a personal guarantee that he would watch over me. I have no doubt his efforts were what turned the trick.

My registration book was then altered to display a black label instead of a red label, printed with the words "Friendly Alien." Underneath were pasted instructions for a friendly alien. The more notable benefits of my new status were: I could travel freely throughout the UK, I was permitted to have a camera, a wireless and basically anything else a British subject was permitted to have.

The next day I visited the local police station with my revised registration book as well as the receipt for my wireless and camera then in police custody. Both were promptly returned to me.

Two days after the tribunal, I went to see my girlfriend, Hannie, who had also just turned 18. I had met her early on in my stay with the Murrays at a dance sponsored by the German Jewish Aid group at the Bloomsberry House. I saw beautiful, blond Hannie at least twice a week, enamored as I was of her cheerful mien, her Dresden blue eyes and her charming Rhineland accent.

Like me, Hannie, her parents and her grandmother had also escaped to London in 1939. They lived in a row house apartment at the Underground stop of Finsbury Park on the Piccadilly line halfway between the Murrays and Piccadilly Circus, which was in downtown London. I would meet Hannie either at Piccadilly Circus to see a movie and then go to a restaurant, or visit with her on my way home from the Polytech. Oh how I loved to be with her!

That day, Hannie's grandmother came to the door in tears and told me that Hannie and her parents had been interned on the Isle of Man, escaping that exile herself, perhaps because of her advanced age.

I was desolate. How unfair, that I should be free to come and go while others, equally innocent, were not. Every day I heard of people who had been picked up. Nobody knew the reasons why. Again, I suffered from ambivalence. I knew I was extremely lucky but at the same time I was lonely and missed sweet Hannie terribly.

I wrote to my parents in Shanghai that I had lost my girlfriend and outside of my cousin Hanna and Uncle Georg, (for by now Georg Hamburger had left Israel for England, and was again practicing medicine in London) I really had nobody to talk to. Mr. and Mrs. Murray were more than good to me, but they could not fill all the holes in my heart.

There was another problem I tried to ignore, a situation in the Murray household. Their son Douglas appeared to be a bit jealous of me. Perhaps he felt his parents liked me better than they liked him, because I received so much of their attention. The fact that I was close to his father because of my intense interest in engineering and because I worked in his plant might have had something to do with it.

I knew, too, that Mrs. Murray had become very fond of me. She would come into my room in the morning and kneel down beside my bed. She would take my hands, saying that I had healing hands, and put them to her forehead, as though to cure a headache.

I know she felt happy with me, but I did not quite understand what went on inside her. She, like me, sometimes seemed to be lonely and introspective, though I knew she was a very warm and loving person and could have had many friends if she had been a little more outgoing. She was happy in her greenhouse and when it was warm enough, worked contentedly in her garden. She seemed to be most comfortable around her own home, rarely going in to London at all. That may have been

71

because she did not drive, and was dependent on Mr. Murray to take her any place she wanted to go, their house being quite far from the nearest bus stop.

At any rate, I must have provided some youthful liveliness that appealed to her in an otherwise isolated life.

I, too, was dependent on Mr. Murray to take me by car to the bus stop if I had to go anywhere. Of course, during work days I would leave the house with him in the morning and he would let me off at the bus stop. I would meet him at night at the same stop at a pre-arranged time.

Douglas also used the family car, but did not take his mother (or me) anywhere very often. He seemed to go his own way like the "cat who walked by himself." We never became close, nor did we have any meaningful conversations.

The seasons changed and the war increased in intensity. We lived in constant fear that German bombers would destroy London. At the same time, the war in France and Belgium intensified.

One day I heard that any boat which could float would be loaded up with volunteers to start an invasion in Dunkirk. The boats would leave England at night and get to the mainland at dawn. Many people volunteered, but I did not. In retrospect, I think there were several reasons for this, not the least of which was that since I possessed a valid German passport and no other identification, if I were to be captured by the Germans, they would shoot me immediately for treason.

The Murrays seconded my decision not to volunteer. Mrs. Murray was a pacifist, yet her only son, just one year older than I, had already been drafted. Mr. Murray pointed out that even though I might have liked to become a British subject, I only possessed a student visa; therefore, even if I volunteered to fight for Britain, possibly running the risk of killing my own relatives and friends, I would not be granted citizenship. The government did not guarantee that such service would confer on me the status of a British subject.

Trying to think practically, I realized that although England had offered temporary shelter, England could not offer me a guarantee of security; as a matter of fact, it was also quite conceivable that England would lose the war; in that eventuality, I once again would be at the mercy of the Nazis.

As it turned out, Dunkirk was a disaster. The British forces were overrun by the Wehrmacht and huge numbers were taken prisoner or became casualties. Only a small complement of men survived and managed to return to England.

Soon thereafter, France and the Low Countries were entirely overrun by Germany and surrendered. Hitler made a victorious entrance into Paris and strode down the Champs Elysee, like a latter day Caesar, conqueror of Western Europe. Though France's capitulation did not include its North Africa colonies, the war was over for France, though the French fleet escaped to Casablanca, where free France fought on.

As a result of how the war was going thus far, my parents were intensely worried about my safety, and said so in their letters. They had access to a few scattered newspaper reports, which predicted that England would soon be overrun by Hitler. By 1941, most of Europe was largely occupied by Nazi Germany. To be sure, England was insulated from the Continent by the English Channel, but even British analysts opined that eventually England would also be invaded by Hitler's forces. It was only a matter of time.

My parents wrote that they were comfortable in Shanghai. My father had established himself as a dentist once again and they both found life in the so-called International Settlement more than bearable; they urged me to join them. I too, read ominous newspaper articles, thought about the war situation and in the end, reluctantly made up my mind to join my parents in Shanghai, but not until I completed my studies.

I graduated in the spring of 1940 with a degree in Mechanical Engineering, specializing in machine tools, jigs and fixtures. Degree in hand, I began the search for a position. I searched the Help Wanted ads in the *London Times* and soon found to my great relief and delight that the renowned Jardine Matheson trading company was looking for a British-trained mechanical engineer to work in Shanghai, China.

I wrote a letter to the box number listed, stating my qualifications and expressing my interest and willingness to work in Shanghai. I received a quick reply inviting me for an interview at their headquarters office in London. Jardine Matheson was a privately owned British trading company. One of their divisions was the Jardine Engineering Corporation. The Shanghai branch had as its main responsibility the management of the North China railways.

One of their subsections was a steel window factory in Shanghai, called Hope Crittel, a wholly owned subsidiary of an English steel window manufacturing company. Since skyscrapers were no longer being built in Asia due to the widening war in the Far East between Japan and China, Jardine Matheson had decided to convert the steel window factory to a machine tool manufacturing facility whose product they would export to Australia, New Zealand and India. (Machine tools could no longer be shipped from Europe, but they could be shipped from Asia and were needed for war production.)

I was selected to head up this factory, and I accepted the position with Jardine Engineering Corporation without any hesitation. Soon I would be re-united with my parents, far removed from the war as well, or so I thought. Little did I know at the time how uninformed that idea was.

When I had to tell Mr. and Mrs. Murray of my decision to go to China, it tore their hearts. They both wept. They did everything to persuade me to stay in England and become part of the family factory. That was their hope. For a time, their entreaties made me waver but in the end, my feeling for my parents took precedence.

Between the time of my acceptance of the job and my actual departure, I had a lot of running around to do, and a great many preparations to make. The company had booked passage for me on the Nippon Yusen Kaisya shipping line. I had to go to the line to pick up my ticket, but the ticket could not be handed to me until I had an exit visa. In the meantime, my German passport had expired and I was afraid to go to the German embassy to renew it, fearing the worst.

I therefore went to the British Foreign Office to obtain an exit visa stamped onto a British stateless passport. However, the official at the British Foreign Office explained that since the German Consulate was staffed by the Swiss ligation, I should first petition the Swiss for assistance, and if the Swiss denied both a new passport or a renewal of my existing passport, and I could prove this to the British Foreign Office, only then would the British issue me a British Nansen (stateless) passport.

Well, that left me no choice but to take my brown passport with the big black swastika on it, and head for the German Consulate. I went there more than reluctantly to present my case. The Swiss official who heard my story was extremely polite.

He asked where I was born, asked for the standard renewal service charge of a few pounds and then pasted my passport with Swiss money stamps indicating my payment, and finally stamped it with his official rubber stamp. For those few pounds my German passport was extended five years. All that worry for nothing, I thought at the time. As I was leaving, he gratuitously offered his unsolicited opinion that religion had nothing to do with nationality. He wished me luck, and hoped I would get to Shanghai safely.

I had no idea at the time how important my having that 5-year German passport was going to be for a great many people besides myself, in the not-too-far distant future.

From the German Consulate, I went to Whitehall, where the British Foreign Office was located. I presented my now valid German passport and expected to get the exit visa immediately. This was not to be. The official told me that he would have to get instructions from a special department about what to do about my case and that I should return in a week.

I pleaded with him before I left, pointing out that my ship, the *Haruna Maru* was due to sail from Liverpool in four weeks, that this was a diplomatic ship which was one of three in a special convoy, the Japanese government having made these arrangements with the British government to sail these three ships from the only open port in Britain. They would be marked as diplomatic ships and a diplomatic special boat train would leave Euston station the morning of the departure of the *Haruna Maru* from Liverpool. The consular official dutifully took down the information as I gave it.

When I returned to the Foreign Office a week later, I had to wait approximately one hour. When the same official I had seen the previous week finally saw me, he had a grim expression on his face and a large manila folder in front of him.

To my horror, I saw that the folder was marked "Enemy Alien" in huge black letters. I knew I had been officially designated a "friendly alien," and my registration book so confirmed that status. The thick folder in front of this official was a Scotland Yard dossier and I was alarmed at its size. I had no idea what kind of papers were in it, nor did I ever find out. After the official reviewed the folder, he asked me to come back the following week. I left, worried and discouraged, but decided that I would go to the Foreign Office every day to check the status of my visa application. The same official finally became pleasant and friendly as a result of my daily visits. I learned from this experience that one can make friends with almost anybody, even when they start out hostile.

Two and a half weeks passed and they still did not have my exit visa. By this point the newly friendly official was just as nervous as I was. Finally, 48 hours prior to the scheduled departure, I was told to come back that very afternoon, which I did, whereupon the official happily stamped an exit visa into my passport.

I barely had enough time to retrieve my books, papers, letters, pictures, folders and records, which had been checked by the home office of the British government in London several days before my scheduled departure. One was not allowed to take any written materials out of the country unless approved by the censor and then sealed in a suitcase.

I arrived at the central office by 4 p.m. for inspection. I was amazed at the patience of the inspector, who went through every piece of paper in my suitcase. I'm sure I had a lot of junk mixed in with what I considered valuable material, but he finally let me take everything, though first putting a string around the suitcase and sealing it with red seals. I sighed with relief.

I spent my last day shopping in London department stores for tropical suits and other items I imagined appropriate for the Orient. I was directed to Selfridge Department Store, which had a tropical wear department. There I found a beige tropical suit with removable mother of pearl buttons. It fit quite well, and the minor alterations could be made the same day. I also bought a pair of white and brown shoes plus a Panama straw hat. I was now outfitted with what I hoped was the mufti required for a "foreigner" working in Shanghai.

While the alterations were being made, I made use of the time to do some gift shopping, also in Selfridges, where I found a bracelet for Mrs. Murray and a leather wallet for Mr. Murray. I then picked up my spiffy new wardrobe, and hurried home to pack.

I wrapped my precious radio in a blanket, first removing its tubes and carefully wrapping each tube in my underwear. I then placed the pregnant blanket in the largest drawer of my wardrobe trunk. It fit snugly inside.

The wardrobe trunk filled up fast with shirts, suits and shoes. My large bag held all the bedding; a smaller wardrobe trunk served to pack all the other items, plus the small sealed suitcase, a typewriter and my trusty Voigtländer camera.

As the morning of my departure dawned, I was completely packed and ready when the taxi to take me to Euston Station arrived. Having given the Murrays their farewell gifts the night before, I bade my sad but grateful farewells; it was an emotional parting, leaving my second parents who had become dear to me, but despite my sadness, the thought of seeing my own parents

77

again also filled my heart. Everything in my recent life seemed to contain at the same time great sadness and great joy, all mixed together. It was hard to tell where one ended and the other began.

The taxi pulled up alongside the train I was to take, clearly marked as a diplomatic transport. Most of the passengers waiting to board seemed to be Japanese; I overheard them softly saying their good-byes and observed the formal bows to each other, bobbing up and back almost interminably like automatons.

Finally, as the scheduled departure time arrived, we were allowed to board. I found my seat, and the train left. The trip to Liverpool was uneventful, but that situation changed as soon as I arrived at the dock where the modest-sized 10,000 ton steam vessel, *Haruna Maru*, was waiting to be boarded.

The ship had large letters on each side, which spelled out "Diplomat." Designed to carry half freight and half passengers -- 250 of them, its holds were still open and loading of goods was in progress. As soon as all the passengers had arrived, we had to report to a British Army officer for passport examination. When I presented mine he became very agitated. He had never seen a German passport before and went immediately to his superior and together they made a phone call to London.

After verifying my name, exit visa and the reason for travel, they returned my passport stamped with the departure date. The officer then wanted to see my luggage. After looking around on the dock for a while I spotted it. The luggage had been sorted alphabetically, by last name of the owner, which made it fairly simple to find all the different pieces.

When the officer spotted my large gray wardrobe trunk, he took his gun, removed its sling from around his neck, and placed it on top of my wardrobe trunk. He seemed to me to be very frightened.

He then asked me to open it, which I did. He tried to pull out the large lower drawer on the left hand side of the trunk, but when he was unable to do so, ordered me to do it. After the drawer was open, the only thing visible was a blanket. He tapped the blanket with his knuckles, and discovered something within it was solid.

After I had explained that a wireless set was wrapped inside the blanket, he asked me to remove it, which I did, whereupon he confiscated it forthwith. He also seized my camera, my portable typewriter, and my address book. I had enough presence of mind to request a receipt for the items he confiscated, but he would not comply with my request.

After a brief argument, in which I asserted my right as a Friendly Alien to take the confiscated material with me, the officer cut me off and denied my request. It came down to a simple choice: either leave England on the *Haruna Maru* or stay and fight for my confiscated articles. I wisely chose to leave.

Later that evening, around 8 p.m., a couple of hours after all the passengers had boarded, the ship's whistle blew and its mooring lines were slipped. We were finally underway. It was June 20, 1940.

Hans Riess

The Haruna Maru

The sun had almost set as the *Haruna Maru* eased carefully out of her slip in Liverpool, moving quietly through the English Channel under cover of darkness; the ship was in a complete blackout.

I was more than content that my first ocean voyage should be aboard a Japanese vessel, the *Haruna Maru*, for this signified neutrality to me -- Japan had not yet entered the European war on anyone's side, and I felt safer than if they'd been a combatant.

The porter escorted me to my second class stateroom, an outside starboard cabin whose portholes opened to the sea. I had been told in advance I would share this stateroom with another gentleman, and this was confirmed when I saw an upper and lower berth. I noted that the stateroom did not have a toilet or shower, although a sink was built into the wall which had to be pulled out for use.

I realized suddenly I was very hungry, and decided to find the dining room, leaving the issue of which berth to choose and other little housekeeping details to be worked out later with my as yet unknown cabin-mate.

HARUNA MARU

81

The dining room was impressively clean but not very large so the three passenger classes dined separately at different hours in order to accommodate everyone. With the luck that I was now beginning to take for granted, I arrived just in time for my second-class seating.

A Japanese steward led the way to my assigned table where I found two ladies and a gentleman already seated. I introduced myself and learned that the gentleman was a minister from Germany traveling to Japan. He spoke both German and English, and was on his way to Kobe, Japan, to be a missionary.

One of the ladies was very pretty and quite young, approximately 25 years of age; she was enroute to Lisbon to connect with the Pan American passenger clipper flying to the U.S. The other lady was in her sixties, and like me, traveling to Shanghai.

In the course of conversation I found out that the minister (who appeared to be about forty years old) was to be my cabin-mate, so I focused on him most carefully. I remember well how thin and tall he was, his hairline already receding. He wore glasses and had on a white ecclesiastical collar and a black shirt, but his jacket was an un-clerical light color, which he wore through most of the voyage. We agreed right then and there at dinner that I would take the upper and he would take the lower berth.

That first meal on board came not a moment too soon. I was famished. The cuisine was prepared in continental style and tasted wonderful. I was used to eating in good restaurants and was pleased to note that the service, too, was excellent.

Our vessel was an old and elegant ocean liner. Chattering happily with my new acquaintances, I admired the dining room's beautiful wood paneling with its different colored wood inlaid sections making a decorative pattern along the walls. The massive chairs at the dining room table looked as though they belonged in a castle; they were so heavy they were almost impossible to move. The menu covers were beautiful (Japanese wood cuts and delicate water color scenes). As the voyage continued, the menu itself kept on changing but the artistic covers were repeated from time to time.

With the greedy eyes of a first-time sea-voyager, I noticed everything, for example, the special protective guard on the table. Engineered for rough weather, it could be raised or lowered to enclose the entire table. When the sea was calm, the wine or water in our glasses barely moved.

After that first meal on board, though tired and intending to go to bed early, I walked around the deck for awhile and breathed the salt air. On the way to my cabin, a steward stopped me and asked in perfect English, when I would like to take my bath. Surprised, but not being a person who suffers with indecision even at that early age, I told him "right now" would suit me fine, since I was about ready to go to bed. He immediately went off to fill the tub with hot water and told me to meet him in the bathroom located at the end of the same deck in bathrobe and slippers as soon as I was ready.

The steward was extremely solicitous and even helped me get into the bathtub. It was an odd experience, taking a bath on an ocean liner. I felt the vibration of the engines, heard the heavy chugs and throbs of the engine while the water sloshed up and down in the tub, in perfect rhythm with the roll of the ship.

Fortunately, the sea was calm enough that evening that I didn't get seasick. After bathing, I returned to my stateroom, climbed up a steel ladder to the berth and tried in vain to fall asleep; I tossed restlessly from side to side instead. Everything was strange. The bed was uncomfortable, the engines noisy and soon somebody else, a stranger, would be in my room. Finally exhausted, I fell into an uneasy asleep.

The next morning I woke early to discover that I had slept through rough seas going around France through the Gulf of Biscay. I went into the dining room for breakfast, but found it completely empty. My stomach was seemingly the only one on board to be untroubled by the turbulent movement of the sea.

The waiter showed me to my table and I found that the guards at each table had been raised to prevent dishes from sliding off. My first breakfast order was cereal, eggs, toast and coffee; the waiter brought the cereal right away and as I started to eat, the plate would slide from one end of the table to the other. I learned pretty quickly to hold the plate while I ate.

The waiter removed my water glass, and explained that he would serve the coffee only if I was ready to drink it immediately. He was very polite about it, but he pointed out the peril of spilling it all over the table.

At that point, I decided not to have coffee at all, but only the eggs and toast. The waiter served the rest of my breakfast order as fast as I could manage to eat it. He asked me to leave the dining room as soon as I was through, since the sea had become choppier.

It was so rough that I started to feel an uncomfortable rumble in my stomach. Instead of finishing breakfast completely, I left the dining room abruptly, stopping long enough at my cabin to pick up a raincoat, then headed for the top deck. I thought that breathing fresh air would lessen the nausea.

More than a few passengers were already on deck vomiting over the railing. This was definitely not a good sight, so I hurried to another part of the deck to wait out the storm. When the strong wind and salt water hit my face, I suddenly felt better.

I took shelter underneath one of the covered outdoor areas and remained standing there for quite some time. When the storm subsided a bit, I went into the well-ventilated card room on the top deck, picked out a comfortable chair, and sat down. I was perfectly prepared to do absolutely nothing except recuperate. There were a few people in the room, but neither they nor I felt like socializing.

I ate no lunch that day, but by dinnertime I was once again ravenous. The storm had died down sufficiently so that a trickle of other guests appeared in the dining room, but so few, only the 6 o'clock sitting was served.

Before I went to bed that night I asked the steward to prepare a bath for me again. With a grin on his face, he said that the bath would be ready in ten minutes. It didn't take any time at all to find out why my steward was so amused. As I sat down in the bathtub, the water moved vigorously from one side to the other, splashing out of the tub all over the walls and floor. Suddenly I was nauseated again, and stood up fast, clambering hastily out of the tub.

With only a bath towel wrapped around me, I dashed up the stairs to the top deck. As soon as I breathed fresh air, I was fine once again. For some reason or other, the movement and rocking of the ship while sitting inside the bathtub was worse for seasickness than anywhere else.

I did not sleep too well the second night either. My cabin was located aft near the rudder, and the constant rocking of the ship put pressure on the rudder, which required adjustment of it in the wheel house. The noise of these frequent adjustments sounded like the scraping of steel against steel.

Happily, the next morning was a beautiful sunny day. The air was warm and the sea calm. We had left the bad weather behind while going around France, and we now sailed smoothly on toward Portugal. After breakfast, a number of passengers, me included, played shuffleboard and table tennis.

Lunch was served on deck. A beautiful buffet was set up for us, after which I sunned in a deck chair. I chatted with a number of people who were going to Lisbon. The young woman who was going to take the Pan American clipper was very friendly and it seemed to me, interested in more than just talking, but I played dumb. I watched with detached amusement as she approached several other males, trying to engage them in what I presumed was something other than social chit-chat.

As I was sitting in the sun, another nice looking young lady sat down next to me, accompanied by two attractive boys. The older boy looked to be around sixteen, the younger one, about thirteen. All three spoke good English, though I detected a German accent. They were going to Kobe, Japan, where the boys were to join their parents. It turned out that the young lady was their father's secretary.

My conversation with the secretary, whose name I learned was Ann, led into chatter about the activities of the very sociable young lady who was going to the United States via Lisbon. The lady, Ann reported, was from Vienna, but had lived for some time in England. According to shipboard gossip, she said, the young lady liked to sleep in a different bed every night. Rumor had it that so far she had already taken ample advantage of the ship's opportunities.

That evening, before we were to land in Lisbon, the Captain hosted a farewell dinner and sumptuous after-dinner party in honor of the passengers who would disembark from the vessel there. I spotted Ann and the two boys, who waved me over to their table and invited me to join them. I was pleased, since I did not plan to be completely by myself for a voyage that was originally scheduled to last three and a half weeks. Everybody needs company and I was no exception.

We watched the festivities, which got noisier and more hectic as the evening progressed. Our young Viennese lady, whom we made a special point to observe, danced with every man she could. Her dance partners were of different nationalities; we identified American diplomats, British diplomats, Japanese businessmen, and various Europeans -- all Asia-bound for exotic places like Singapore, Hong Kong, Shanghai or Kobe.

After the party, I went up to the top deck and leaned over the railing, watching the calm sea. Suddenly, in the distance, I saw the horizon practically aglow with light. It had to be Lisbon.

I cannot explain the strong emotional feeling I got from the sight of those lights. After living so long in blackout conditions, I was stunned at the very thought, let alone the sight, of a city totally illuminated at night.

In London, we had lived in constant fear that light from our flat could be seen outside. British bobbies entered homes in the middle of the night to locate and eliminate the source of any errant light. Occasionally, even summonses were issued; repeat offenders could be taken off to the police station for further investigation.

A policeman once knocked at the Murray's door, having seen light coming from my window. The bobby rushed upstairs, looked at the window and saw that I had not drawn the curtain completely. Being a foreigner, I could have ended up in jail, but I was lucky, and my oversight was dismissed as unintentional.

The lights shone all over our ship and city lights radiated from the free port of Lisbon in the distance; I was deeply moved by the sight. We sailed on towards the illuminated city, and as we got closer, I could make out mountains that overlooked the city. They, too, were bright with gleaming light. As our ship approached still closer, I could now make out tandem street cars along the water's edge and identify cars with their headlights on, going up and down winding streets.

We docked at 10 p.m. and shortly thereafter I went to sleep since I planned to go ashore the next morning to do some sightseeing and perhaps some bargain shopping.

The next morning almost every passenger woke up early, especially those who were leaving for America by clipper at 11 a.m. and had to go through certain departure formalities. The rest of us said good-bye to them, then registered our passports with the Lisbon police who had come aboard, prior to our going ashore. I was pleasantly surprised to find the police very accommodating; we did not have to fill out any forms, and there were no restrictions as to where we could go in the city. I had no idea at the time that this would be the last shore trip I would be permitted until the vessel reached China.

I went to the nearest streetcar stop and waited for an open car to arrive. When it came, its bell constantly dinging, I noticed that it had wooden steps along the whole length of it, on which people stood, holding onto steel bars.

As the weather was balmy, I decided to get my first glimpse of the city standing on one of those running boards so I jumped right up onto the car, taking note of its car number as well as its destination to prevent getting lost. I figured if I took the same car going in the opposite direction, I would eventually get back to the *Haruna Maru*.

After the car made several turns, I jumped off at a beautiful square, memorable for a large marble monument in the center, whose significance escaped me. I looked at the beautiful store windows and was amazed to see that most of them had signs in the windows with a swastika saying "German spoken."

Also surprising to me was the large number of German soldiers in uniform walking the streets. Several German officers wore jodhpurs, and rode horseback. This so-called neutral city of Lisbon struck me as something less than neutral. It seemed to favor German military personnel almost exclusively; I did not see any American or British soldiers in uniform.

I walked from store to store, window shopping, looking for some kind of a nautical sailing cap to wear on board, but the prices were very high, and I opted not to buy anything.

I was curious about the mountains so I took another street car that headed towards them. The traffic was heavy on all main thoroughfares, but I was diverted by all the lovely buildings we passed and the vibrant colors throughout the city. Most of the buildings were of sandstone construction covered by quantities of reddish-colored Spanish tiles; beautiful, wrought iron balconies were the rule.

Around lunchtime I made a frugal decision. Since I did not want to spend too much money in Lisbon, I would return to the *Haruna Maru* for all my meals.

My cabin steward was relieved and pleased when he saw me. He had been worried that I might get lost in Lisbon, but I had had no difficulty finding my way back to the harbor, since I could actually see it from where I had been, high in the hills overlooking the city. (The city was surrounded by hills which rose higher and higher the farther one travelled from the harbor area.)

None of the passengers had any idea when we would set sail for the next port because our ship's officers had been told to wait for a number of refugees from France who were trying to get through southern France into Portugal. The captain had instructions to wait as long as necessary.

While we waited, day after day I left the ship each morning, sometimes returning for lunch and other times just for dinner, but always glad to be back on board. The ship had become my home and I felt secure there. It also was extremely clean, which was more than I could say about Lisbon.

Finally, after about one week in port, a notice was posted on the bulletin board advising the passengers that the *Haruna Maru* would sail at 5 p.m. that day. Accordingly, we had to be back on board by 3 p.m. In a way, I was sorry we had to leave, but the trip from Liverpool to Shanghai had been scheduled to take about four weeks, and already 10 days had passed and we were still in Portugal.

At 5 p.m., the ship's whistle blew sharply three times, the mooring ropes dropped into the water, and the *Haruna Maru* maneuvered slowly away from the dock. I was on the top stern deck together with a group of others, positioned to watch Lisbon disappear in the distance.

Later there was a lot to talk about with Ann when she and the two boys sat down on a deck chair next to me. She was excited about her impressions collected in Lisbon, and she wanted to share them.

The French refugees we had been waiting for were now on board, and many of them wanted to tell anyone who would listen about their horrible experiences in France, and how they managed to escape. They were stopped countless times by the Germans and had to fabricate countless scenarios to explain why they were traveling.

Ann, the two boys and I became more and more friendly. We were all native Berliners and had a lot in common; in addition, many of their experiences in England were similar to mine. Ann was also Jewish, and we talked frankly about the situation in Germany and why we were going to Shanghai. (Ann thought Kobe was a better place to go, but at that point the die was cast for the Riess's -- we were committed to Shanghai.)

89

Hans Riess

On the outdoor recreational front, as a group the four of us played shuffleboard; inside the ship we borrowed board games from the ship's library which we played in the card room.

All of us expected that our ship would pass through the Straits of Gibraltar, sail eastward across the Mediterranean and through the Suez Canal and onward to the Far East, but we were mistaken.

A day or so after we left Lisbon, the Captain posted a notice to the passengers on the library bulletin board, which indicated that our next port of call would be Casablanca.

The explanation for the detour came via the usual channel -- the ship's grapevine. It turned out that the Italian authorities were responsible; they would not permit our ship to go through Gibraltar. (Italy was refusing passage for any ship regardless of nationality, and saw no need to give a reason.)

Casablanca would be a new experience for both the Captain and his crew since none of them had ever sailed around the Cape of Good Hope. No crewman or passenger we spoke to knew exactly how long the trip would take. If the Captain knew, he wasn't telling.

That night at dinner everybody was buzzing with excitement about the news. As we cruised towards Casablanca, German, British, and other fighter planes regularly overflew the ship presumably to check our ship's name, flag, and other identifying marks. What they saw was a large symbol of the rising sun and the letters "Diplomat" on both sides of the ship. The name and mark were illuminated at night to make it easy for planes to identify us.

At first these flyovers were exciting; the fighter planes would suddenly appear overhead, as if from thin air, then disappear in a flash, as if never there. After a while, the flights became so routine, we ceased to pay any attention to them.

Everything else on board also gradually became routine. We got so used to the ship that we could hardly think of ever being any place else. We had the feeling that as long as we remained on board we were safe. At least that's how it appeared to us. We would not go hungry or thirsty or be killed. Still, it was incredible to think that our existence was bound to this floating island of neutrality in the middle of a sea of world conflict.

The next day, the North African coast came into view. Our ship slowed in a fairly rough sea. After breakfast, we spotted the harbor of Casablanca in the distance. As we came closer to the coast line, we saw many ships at anchor in and around the harbor.

We found out pretty soon that the harbor was overloaded with ships and the cargo-laden merchant ships outside the harbor were lying to, waiting their turn to enter. When we heard our anchor chains and the anchor lowered into the water, we realized that we would also have to wait our turn. It took us five days before we slowly edged into the harbor.

We noticed several French war ships, each chained to another, instead of tied up to a conventional mooring. At first, no one could understand why this method had been used. After our ship docked, so-called Free French soldiers came on board and shouted instructions to both our passengers and crew. We later learned that the French fleet had refused to surrender to the British navy, choosing instead, to take refuge in Casablanca. Since there were so many ships, the only way to dock them was side by side.

These Free French soldiers were angry at everyone, the British, the French, and from what we could tell, all other nationalities as well. Consequently, they permitted no one to go ashore.

Although we did not know why we had docked at Casablanca in the first place, we assumed that many of the ship's stores and provisions were being replenished. Then somebody circulated a rumor, which turned out to be true: our Japanese captain had been instructed by his government to load gunpowder into the holds.

Accordingly, a large vacuum pump delivery system was installed on board, and soon bright yellow gunpowder began to be sucked into the ship from trucks on the pier. This process was not terribly neat, however. Very quickly the ship became an unsightly mess; it, together with any person unwise enough to be on deck, was soon engulfed in a yellow cloud of dust.

It took two days for the crew to load the gunpowder. During the loading, a few British planes suddenly appeared and circled the harbor. As usual, I was on the highest deck and watched the British systematically drop a hundred or so spiked explosive mines arranged in the shape of an arc, effectively sealing off the harbor. When I saw that, I wondered whether we would ever leave the harbor.

The Captain of the *Haruna Maru* had received instructions from Tokyo to take any and all reasonable risks to leave Casablanca at his earliest opportunity, and that's exactly what he did.

In the process of taking every possible precaution to prevent our vessel from hitting the mines, he lowered most of the life boats into the sea, manned by crew members, so they could more effectively function as lookouts, directing the ship away from the ominously bobbing mines. Using this prudent method, it took a long and anxious 24 hours for the ship to crawl out of the harbor.

After the ship was finally outside of the mine barrier, the Captain continued to follow the coastline of Africa very closely, sailing south.

The weather continued sunny and warm. One morning as I leaned over the port railing trying to spot animals on shore, I saw a few giraffes and elephants approach the water's edge. I was sure that there had to be more animals in the vicinity, but without field glasses I couldn't spot them. I stood peering out from the railing all morning in beautiful sunshine under a crystal clear blue sky, getting browner by the minute. I enjoyed every minute of the cruise around Africa.

Again, we had no idea how long this portion of the trip would take. We only knew that the next port of call was Capetown without any intermediate stops. The crew checked the knot indicator every hour and posted the knots covered on the bulletin board in the library. Our cruising speed was 20 knots, and the seas, calm. Occasionally we saw flying fish and shark fins.

If another ship passed us sailing in the opposite direction, going north, they passed on our starboard side and the crew blew our whistle and dipped the Japanese flag from the mast which was the protocol of courtesy at sea. Some days the cruise was so bland and uneventful, a passing ship would be the only excitement.

The Captain returned to his previous state of calm equilibrium and began to plan some shipboard activities for the passengers. Many had become restless, or bored, or depressed; activities offering passenger amusement and distraction were defnitely called for. One afternoon, he organized a tea party. He wore his immaculate white officer's uniform and white cap. Everybody else got dressed up, too, for the occasion, which offered an opportunity for the first time to really converse with the captain, whose full name and title were Commander K.T. Torii.

He was a short, thin man, approximately 60 years old, who spoke quite acceptable English. He became very friendly with me because I was German. (I think he did not understand what the J on my passport meant, and probably thought all Germans were Christians.)

For the first time, we learned from him that on this voyage the *Haruna Maru* was the middle ship in a Japanese convoy consisting of three ships of the same class. We never saw the other two ships, but were told that they had gone through the same procedure we had.

It was only now, after cruising four days down the coast of West Africa that the Captain admitted that the trip would take considerably longer than originally scheduled. Consequently, I went to the radio officer and sent a radiogram to my parents saying I was enroute to Shanghai on board the *Haruna Maru*, but did not know its exact arrival date. I found out later that the radiogram that my parents received actually read as follows: "Late arrival on *Haruna Maru*. Missed date."

93

Until I actually arrived in Shanghai, my parents were never sure that I had even left England, even though I had been sending radiograms all along, nor did they receive my letters. Mail from our ship was picked up at every port but for some reason or other was never delivered to Shanghai.

We had a large complement of Indians on board whose destination was Bombay. Since we had plenty of time, the Captain suggested that one night the Indians might want to invite the rest of the passengers to a typical Indian dinner. They were happy to comply and showed us their quarters in the third class section, and where they prepared their food. They shared their living space with their livestock, which consisted of goats (for their milk), chickens and rabbits.

They cooked all their meals on charcoal stoves; entire families helped to prepare the food. It did not look very clean to me but to be polite I sat down with the Indians at dinner time and followed their instructions. I can't be said to have enjoyed the meal, but I managed to down a few morsels and somehow survived the experience without being rude.

On another night, the dinner meal was organized by our Japanese contingent -- both crew and passengers. They called it "Sukiyaki Night" and it was exciting. Despite the fact that I prided myself on being somewhat worldly, having grown up in cosmopolitan Berlin, I felt rather provincial when it came to certain things that I considered quite exotic, such as sushi, raw fish and red caviar.

The crew of the second class dressed in native Japanese costumes. I had never eaten Japanese food, and I enjoyed the raw fish cooked on hibachi stoves, and watching the waiters prepare the food right at the table. Since we were not used to sitting and eating in the Japanese style, the Captain suggested that we occupy our regular chairs at the tables. After dinner, a band played and my friend Ann -- the lady with the two boys -- made a valiant effort to dance to the strange rhythms.

Because of the ship's proximity to the equator, the nights were now becoming quite warm, and the cabin far too sticky to sleep comfortably. We slept with our port holes wide open; the stewards supplied each cabin with a gadget which could be placed into the port hole to increase the flow of air from the outside. Nevertheless, it became so unbearably hot in the cabin, I took to sleeping out in the open in a deck chair at the stern of our deck.

The night sky was beautiful and so crystal clear it seemed as though I could see every star in the Milky Way. Night after night, the ocean was calm; a wake of white foam gently trailed the ship. It being that time of year, shooting stars fell every evening at roughly the same time. I assumed these meteor showers were associated with the Pleiades.

My friend Ann decided that her cabin was also too hot and she placed her deck chair outside next to mine. Before falling asleep, we had long conversations on a broad range of subjects -- life experiences, books, history, geography. Ann was easy to talk to and highly intelligent. We really liked each other, and though she was young and pretty, we did not have an affair. We just enjoyed each other's company.

Black-haired Ann was quite attractive, deeply tanned, with a petite (5-feet-2) perfect figure. Her voice was soft and her poise and general manner exceptional. To me she seemed a paragon of femininity. She had no trouble in getting the attention of the officers, but even so, I do not remember being jealous.

I spent more and more time with her and less with anybody else. Together, we checked the position of the ship daily, taking several different compass readings. The vessel moved inexorably towards that imaginary line around the earth called the equator.

Our friendship made the time pass very quickly and we did not even notice that weeks had passed since we boarded the *Haruna Maru* in Liverpool.

Apart from the increasing warmth due to approaching the equator, the days were just as lovely as the nights. The crew decided to set up a temporary swimming pool on top of the hold at the bow. A heavy canvas tarpaulin, normally used to cover the hold in case of rain, was pulled up to the deck by loading cranes and held in place by cables. Then salt water from the ocean was pumped into the raised canvas, until a deep pool was formed where many of us spent almost whole days. I think the captain and his officers on the bridge had great fun watching us, and eventually some of the crew also frolicked in our improvised pool.

We had thought it would be extremely hot at the equator when we crossed the line sailing south, but when the day we reached the equator finally arrived, we did not notice any unusual difference in temperature from previous days.

To celebrate this crossing of zero latitude, a mock ceremony was held ending with the passengers dunking several crew members in the swimming pool. Some of the guests also chose to celebrate by jumping into the pool with all their clothes on. After this frolic, a special afternoon tea party was held where special delicacies were served. That night a screen was set up on deck behind the pool and we were treated to a movie. Who would have thought we were all escaping a war?

Again, I could not help but be overwhelmed by the seemingly ever-increasing number of glittering stars in the sky at night. Our on-board schedule settled down to a predictable routine: we watched movies twice a week and went swimming every day; there was shuffleboard, card playing and dancing. Our lives revolved around our ship and our little society on board; the microcosm of the *Haruna Maru* became our entire world, our personal "ship of fools."

Every morning after breakfast, I checked the position of the ship on the library bulletin board, and noted the temperature, speed, the number of nautical miles covered and our current distance from Cape Town. At that point, I don't believe any of us realized that it would take us 16 more days to reach our next port, but it did.

The weather was pleasant, but as we approached Cape Town the days became shorter and shorter. After all, though it was June, and summertime in Europe, it was winter where we were, south of the Equator.

With so much time on my hands, I began a journal about my stay in England. I sat at the typewriter every afternoon, and when I got tired of typing, I made pen and ink sketches of Westminster Abbey, Westminster Bridge and other sites of London from memory.

By the fourteenth day out, our drinking water turned brownish, because our water reserves were running out. The ugly color was caused by rust at the bottom of the water tank. Prior to our departure from England, no one could have foreseen that our voyage would take this many weeks. Provision had not been made for steaming so long a distance between ports as we were now forced to do.

Another discomfort related to the hot water, which was becoming colder and colder. The ship was running extremely low on coal, so low in fact, that the ship's engineers were concerned we might not have enough coal to reach port. This made everyone more than a little edgy, and we could not wait to arrive at Cape Town.

As we approached the Cape of Good Hope, the weather changed again; now it rained most of the time, and by 4:00 p.m. every day, the sky was completely dark, although the temperature was in the 50 degree Fahrenheit range. We didn't know it at the time, but we were experiencing the rainy season in Southern Africa. All we knew was that it was hardly our idea of wintry.

The actual trip around the Cape of Good Hope proved to be quite stormy, as I had expected it to be. It was common knowledge even in Germany that the sea is always rough in that area.

On the fifteenth day, we arrived at the entrance to the harbor of Cape Town, though we did not go into port until the morning of the sixteenth day, and thus spent the night at anchor in a stormy sea.

When we finally got under way the next morning, the vessel proceeded slowly. In order to pass through the harbor and get to port, we had to traverse another mine barrier. From my usual look-out point at the railing I could see it was a steel net, mined with explosives, which could be opened or closed on one side by a tug boat to permit the passage of vessels like ours.

We were told that the barrier was a wartime precaution in case of attack; South Africa was a British Crown Colony and so it was fair game for Germany.

Table Mountain was visible just beyond the city, as well as beautiful white skyscrapers making Cape Town a modern-looking city.

As soon as the *Haruna Maru* had docked, tall men in black uniforms boarded the vessel. At that time, I couldn't tell whether they were policemen or military personnel, but the distinction made little difference. Whichever, I instinctively knew they represented potential trouble for me.

We were informed that the dining room would be used for passport control so with trepidation I took my passport and lined up with the rest of the passengers. All in front of me on line were given landing passes and told they could go ashore on an unrestricted basis.

When my turn came, the officer took his time examining my passport, which had a prominent black eagle and swastika on its cover together with the designation, "Passport of the German Reich" printed in large letters.

The officer went carefully through every page, expressing surprise that my passport had an expiration date five-years hence, contained a British exit visa, and a notation that I was going to work for a British company in Shanghai.

He then said I would not be permitted to leave the ship while in port. He added that my passport would be kept at the Cape Town police station until the ship was ready to continue its voyage. Summoning one of his colleagues, he instructed him to take me to the smoking room and guard me carefully. It was as if I were a fugitive from justice, instead of the fugitive from *injustice,* as I really was.

The guard escorted me to the ship's stern, where he picked up two of his companions. All of us then proceeded to the smoking room.

Once there, the only bizarre and unsettling experience of my trip began to unfold. The guards secured the doors of the lounge, and tip-toeing about surreptitiously, tried to make sure that nobody was in the area. I found their behavior mystifying, suspicious, and extremely intimidating.

Once they were sure no one was eavesdropping, they greeted me in German with a vigorous "Heil Hitler" and threw in a few gratuitous patriotic slogans, ending with "Deutschland über alles."

They "confided" to me that they were pro-German, and claimed they were members of the Nazi Party, showing their membership cards (with photo I.D.'s) which identified them as Nazis. They certainly looked the part of SS men in their black uniforms.

I did not know what to make of all this, but something told me that performance of theirs might have been just that -- a charade designed to entrap Nazi sympathizers. In any event, I had no intention of asking any questions, or, for that matter, answering any. My instinct for self-preservation was too strong to reveal my true feelings to these men so I simply listened to them and put an interested but passive expression on my face.

One of them spoke to me as if I were thoroughly familiar with the history of South Africa, which I was not. He told me that he had not forgotten what the Boers had done to the white South Africans. I think I grunted at that point; I had no idea what he was referring to. He also said that all South Africans of German extraction hated the British with a bloody passion. At that moment, it actually crossed my mind that they were waiting for a signal from Germany to began an insurrection in South Africa.

That idea never went beyond the level of conjecture, for I was never able to find out for sure. I never found out whether they really meant what they said, or whether they were trying to trick me into making some kind of absurd admission. In any event, they were intensely interested in why I was going to Shanghai and why I traveled with a German passport.

Of course, the answers to these questions were quite straightforward and I didn't mind laying them out, but my interrogators were not the slightest bit satisfied with the truth.

In a way, I could understand their suspicion, but at the same time it was very unfair of them to prevent me from going ashore. I was enroute to Shanghai to work for a British company; I had a British exit visa, and we were docked in a British Crown Colony port.

For the first time I resented the restriction, but there was nothing I could do about it. Gazing wistfully through the large picture window of the smoking room, I watched as my fellow passengers disembarked and went into town.

During our 24-hour stay in Cape Town we took on drinking water, but only a limited amount of coal. Scuttlebutt had it that we must sail on to Durban, located just around the Cape, in order to buy enough coal for the remainder of our trip.

When the ship was ready to sail, the guards said good-bye to me and left the ship without returning my passport. I reported this to Captain Torii at once and he wired the Cape Town police station requesting the urgent return of the passport.

The Cape Town harbor pilot who would steer us out of the harbor was still on board. When the Captain told me that my passport would be returned to me by the small boat which came to pick up the pilot, I felt a trifle less anxious, but I still remained quite nervous waiting for the boat to arrive, which took about a half-hour longer.

The boat came to a stop alongside our ship; a police officer on board the small boat reached up and handed my passport to a Japanese crewman, who had climbed down the ladder from the *Haruna Maru* to retrieve it. Most of the passengers were hanging over the railing to witness the passport brought on board our ship.

Then, at last, we were ready to sail again.

100

The trip from Cape Town to Durban on the southeast coast of South Africa was uneventful and the seas were calm.

Durban was a much smaller city than Cape Town, the streets unpaved in many areas, and the buildings smaller. I guessed that in the world of international commerce, it was a port of minor importance.

When it came to wild monkeys, however, Durban was formidably first in rank. The piers, the loading platform, and the harbor equipment, were all teeming with agile monkeys; they were everywhere and it was almost impossible to keep them from taking over the ship.

They kept on coming in large packs, climbing nimbly up the thick mooring ropes which held the ship fast to the dock. They were hungry and tried to steal the food being loaded onto the ship. Sailors were stationed at each rope to deter them from boarding, which so angered the monkeys they hurled small pieces of coal at the ship and anyone who ventured close to them. Apart from this expression of frustration, the mischief-makers were otherwise harmless. They lingered, hoping to find a way to get onto the ship.

The *Haruna Maru* needed coal badly, and Durban had plenty of it. Piles of different types of coal were heaped all around the dock area. Our crew loaded coal as fast as possible. At the same time they took on fresh water, since the next leg of our voyage along the east coast of Africa would take approximately 14 days. Our next destination was Bombay, India.

Since the departure time from Durban had not been posted, all passengers stayed fairly close to the *Haruna Maru*. Later that day, we learned the ship would sail before dark. At 4 p.m., the crew did a final check of all decks and corridors for monkey stowaways, and finding none, the ship's moorings were slipped and once again we were underway.

As soon as we had moved away from the dock, the deck crew attached hoses to the water valves and started to scrub all decks and walls. Although the ship was quite old, it was kept spotless. The Japanese would not only clean the ship every day,

101

but continuously paint the metal, masts and wooden railings. They went from one end of the ship to the other. When they were done with the front they started again at the back.

The east coast of Africa was not too interesting. Hardly any animals were visible on shore, and as the ship proceeded north, we lost sight of the coast completely.

Our shipboard activities remained unchanged. We swam daily, played shuffleboard and ping pong, saw movies and occasionally ate too much rich food, on our self-contained floating island home. We had not unloaded any passengers since Lisbon nor had we taken on any new passengers, either.

So far we had been on board five weeks, which meant that most of the 250 people were at least acquainted, and many knew each other quite well. I myself knew a large number by name, as well as many members of the crew who were friendly with all of us. It was nice to say hello to a lot of people and try to pass the time by getting involved in all the shipboard activities on the schedule, but I craved a real friendship.

The relationship between Ann and me came closest to satisfying that need. We spent many hours talking about many things. I certainly needed somebody to talk to, and so did she. I cannot explain it, but my companionship with Ann never progressed beyond a platonic friendship to something sexual.

Usually, a ship is a hot house for the germination and spread of rumors. The gossip mill had it that Ann and I were having a physical relationship, and she and I eventually heard about it; we concluded there was no sense in trying to convince anybody that the rumor was false so we mutually decided to ignore it and simply enjoy being together.

Just before we got to Bombay, the Indian passengers prepared a farewell dinner for all the passengers, which I attended, though not too fond of the food (as usual). The adjective "exotic" was taking on a somewhat negative connotation in my traveler's vocabulary.

We neared Bombay on a very hot July day, slowly moving up the Ganges River. One of the very first sights coming into

102

view was a large group of Indians in white garments, bathing in the river. The knowledge that the river was holy to millions of Indians did not alter the fact that it was filthy. Somebody on board came up with a theory that the Ganges looked dirty because the limestone bottom was reflected in the water, but I didn't buy that for a minute.

As we advanced further up river, one could see scrawny trees and shrubs along both banks, and white-fenced stone mansions could be spotted from time to time. Little vehicular traffic moved along the paths and roads on either side of the river.

As we got closer to the harbor, we spotted cattle walking freely along the quays and loading areas. Since cows were deemed sacred in India, nobody restrained or obstructed their wanderings. They ambled freely among bicycles and pedestrians.

The ship moved slowly into the harbor and began the docking process. Ann and I were stationed as usual on the top deck, leaning over the railing, watching the procedure.

Confusion reigned supreme among the Indians on the pier who were supposed to help us dock. The whole operation looked like a flock of chickens darting about randomly from one corner of the barnyard to the other, with orders cackled from different corners.

As a result of the commotion, the crew had difficulties getting the *Haruna Maru* docked. As soon as one line was in place at the bow, the ship would drift away from the dock at the stern. The dockworkers couldn't seem to pull both ends of the ship at the same time. The whole performance was extremely inefficient, extremely noisy and extremely funny. Almost an hour elapsed before the ship was securely docked.

Even getting the gangway in place seemed more difficult here than other ports. Several approaches failed, but finally one Indian on the moving gangway was able to securely fasten one end of it to the ship and lower its other end to the ground.

103

Once again I was informed by the port authorities that I would not be allowed to go ashore since Bombay was a British Commonwealth port. I was not sure whether the passengers who went ashore were luckier than I or vice versa, because the weather was incredibly hot and humid. Shorts, white linen shirts and sheer summer dresses were the apparel of the day. From what I could see from the ship, both public transportation and taxicabs were at a premium; from our vantage point, there were none in sight. I overheard discussions among the passengers, debating whether they should walk to the heart of the city.

I was not disheartened in the slightest for having to stay on board. I could see a good part of the city from the top deck and it looked to me like chaos. All I could see of the natives were hordes of filthy beggars.

While I hung over the railing trying to get a good view of the city, a swarm of large flies attacked me. Their persistence, plus the unbearable heat, hastened my withdrawal to the library of the ship, for there it was quiet and clean. For a while, I read a book; after that, I continued to write my story about England. The time passed pretty quickly and before I knew it, some of the passengers returned to the ship, it being lunchtime. (Ann kept me company and did not go ashore because, she said, Bombay was too dirty for her.)

She was right. The others reported that the city was so dirty they were afraid to eat in any of the restaurants. Lunch was served as usual in the dining room, but the service was minimal because some of the crew had shore leave themselves. Of course, the number of diners were few as well, since not all the passengers had returned for lunch.

Only the most adventurous of those who had gone ashore wanted to return to the city. The rest complained about the lack of sightseeing opportunities. (I myself found the report of some that on certain streets prostitutes were kept in cages for viewing by customers to be definitely intriguing.) But even the British passengers, who of course were allowed to go ashore, had no

104

desire to do so during the last two days in port -- despite the allure of the reported tourist attraction!

In all, we spent four unbearable days in Bombay, the dirtiest of all the ports we called on. The ship was at first unloaded, then reloaded with a lot of new cargo.

We were all glad when the ship sailed on the fourth morning at 10 a.m. I was leaning over the railing to watch departure when suddenly, in typical Bombay confusion, a passenger appeared on the quay in the midst of a large crowd of natives. He was waving and shouting to stop the ship, which, of course, was difficult to do under the circumstances.

A loading crane manned by inspired dock personnel came to his rescue. The passenger was told to hold firm to the gangway, which he did. While it was lifted off the ground by the crane, the dilatory passenger hanging on for dear life, the gangway was quickly turned 90 degrees. The crane then moved forward until the gangway was positioned over the ship, and promptly dumped it and the passenger unceremoniously on to the *Haruna Maru*, none the worse for his tardiness. Thus ended our unpleasant experience in Bombay.

The distinguished French anthropologist Claude Levi-Strauss of *Tristes Tropiques*, once summed up India as a place of filth, chaos, congestion, ruins, huts, mud, dirt, dung, urine, and pus. From my brief encounter with India, I can certainly carry on the tradition of a disgusted observer.

As our ship slowly retraced its way down the Ganges River to the Indian Ocean, we again passed the perpetually bathing Indians. Gratefully, we felt once more the cooling breezes of the ocean.

The sailors couldn't wait to flush the decks with water and scrub the ship sparkling clean again. Almost immediately, shipboard activities returned to normal. The dining room was filled with chattering passengers for lunch, the outdoor activities followed the normal schedule, and one could take a quiet nap in the afternoon on the sun deck.

105

Later that day, I went to the library to check the future course of the *Haruna Maru*, and saw that our next call would be Columbo, the capital of Ceylon, and yet another British port.

Evenings on the calm seas of the Indian Ocean were beautiful. Ann and I had great fun studying the stars, which seemed to have returned to their original position. The Southern Cross had disappeared, since we had long ago crossed the equator for the second time. Romantic though the evening atmosphere might be, our relationship remained platonic.

From time to time, the Captain scheduled a Captain's Tea Party to give us a change of pace. For days we saw no land nor even another ship. Only an occasional flying fish or shark fin riffled the surface of the water.

The harbor of Columbo hove into view one evening just after dark. I will never forget the huge red neon sign on top of the highest mountain ringing the city. It read "Ceylon For Good Tea."

We slowly moved towards the harbor, and again did not enter it that night. Instead, we anchored, and a police boat came out to meet us. We went to sleep that night with difficulty as the ship riding at anchor made it rock back and forth without let up.

We awoke to a warm and clear morning, the ship still anchored in the same place. After breakfast, Ann and I went to the top deck to see if we could find out what was happening, and watched a boat moving between two towers. We found out that the boat was pulling a steel net which, when closed between the two towers, prevented submarines from entering the harbor.

After the small boat had reached the opposite tower, the *Haruna Maru* raised its anchor and proceeded past the net into harbor, which was slightly "U" shaped, with only one opening for entrance, another safeguard. Our ship was still not permitted to dock, but instead was sent to the middle of the harbor where we dropped anchor. Here the waters were well sheltered, and the ship hardly rocked or swayed after the anchor was lowered.

Small boats surrounded the *Haruna Maru* by now, their eager owners offering all sorts of wares for sale, ranging from hand carved elephants to straw baskets and blankets. A police boat remained tied up to the ship, to control the exit for passengers disembarking. British passengers and a few other nationalities were ferried between the *Haruna Maru* and the port of Columbo.

Once again, I was told by the British officials that I was not permitted to leave the ship. I was used to this by now, and so it didn't bother me too much. I had learned to swallow my disappointment and accept the inevitable.

I could see the hilly terrain, and fairly high mountains in the background. In contrast to Bombay, Columbo appeared pleasant. The pier workers looked Malaysian, but they apparently spoke English and looked well fed and much cleaner than the Indians, as well as more industrious and organized in their work of unloading and loading the ship.

We spent three uneventful days in port, then raised anchor. The anti-submarine net opened, the ship moved slowly out to sea. Next stop: Singapore.

By now we had been on board seven weeks, and still had no idea when we would reach Shanghai. My main concern was for my parents, who were undoubtedly desperately worried about my late arrival.

The voyage from Columbo to Singapore was uneventful. Two days prior to our arrival in Singapore, the British executives on board gave a farewell party. It was a typically British affair, stiff and formal. The Japanese Captain and his officers were polite as usual, but I don't think anyone had any real fun except the British.

One memorable passenger, a Japanese bank official from the Mitsui-Mitsubishi Bank, was particularly unhappy. He had established a very close friendship with a British secretary who was returning to her firm in Singapore, while he was returning to Japan. The man was extremely handsome, had a moustache and a beautiful suntan. An ardent movie fan, I thought he looked quite like Clark Gable, and in my imagination, acted like Gable in the movies I had seen.

107

Hans Riess

ON HARUNA MARU
(Hans, third row from bottom, second from left)

As we saw the green covered hills of beautiful Singapore, we slowly neared the entrance of a passageway which would take us into port. One Japanese officer, in his sparkling clean white uniform, pointed out to me the large black guns facing directly towards us. As we entered the river, we saw more and more of those ominous reminders of the war.

He bragged that Japan would occupy the British Crown Colony within the next six months. I was extremely surprised to hear this kind of confidence expressed out loud, considering the reserve of the Japanese I had met. The officer further declared that Hong Kong would also soon fly the flag of the Emperor. I was stunned and speechless.

A large crowd waited at the dock. Well-dressed British gentlemen seemed to be expecting a great number of people and the dock was loaded with Chinese workmen as well as with spectators. The docking procedure went smoothly. Thirty

108

minutes later, the first British passenger disembarked. As usual, I was not permitted to go ashore, and once again, I went to the top deck to get a better glimpse of Singapore.

The city was situated upon rolling hills overlooking the harbor. Green shrubs and lawns were visible everywhere. I could see British Navy personnel on the piers below in their white shorts and white short-sleeved open shirts. A number of British Army personnel were visible as well; they wore khaki shorts, open khaki shirts and tropical helmets. They looked smart, efficient, and authoritative.

The harbor seemed to be well-managed and the Chinese coolies followed instructions very carefully.

Singapore had a large Chinese community. In fact, the labor force consisted almost entirely of Malayans and Chinese. If I had been British, I might have found Singapore a pleasant area to work. British colonial rule could be sensed everywhere; and, of course, colonial rule meant plenty of servants and conveniences for the British colonialists and their bureaucrats. The weather was hot, but not uncomfortably humid. The climate was certainly bearable if one were properly dressed for it.

A good portion of our remaining passengers disembarked in Singapore, and the ship never seemed the same afterward. After being together on the *Haruna Maru* for such a long time it was sad to lose so many from our floating sanctuary all at once.

After only one and a half days in port, we left Singapore, taking the same route down the river to the Pacific Ocean as we had entering the harbor.

We knew that we would be in Hong Kong in approximately two days, and that made me happy, because after Hong Kong, Shanghai was the next port of call. The Japanese crew was happy because they would be on native soil in Kobe, Japan before long. The long voyage was nearing an end. We all, passengers and crew, seemed to share a feeling of accomplishment, finishing an astonishing ten weeks at sea, unharmed by the war.

I was fascinated when the Japanese crew talked to us about the exciting city of Shanghai -- which they called the "Paris of

109

the East," offering anecdotes which focused on one exotic aspect of the city or another. However, they warned us not to drink the water, nor eat the fresh fruit or vegetables and to be very careful about everything else in general. What "everything else" was left ominously unspoken, and I found myself growing a little apprehensive.

They said Shanghai was a "nice place to visit" but that Japan was a much better place to live. Since we had no Chinese passengers on board, we could not compare notes with them about Shanghai, vs. Kobe or Yokohama.

The two-day cruise to Hong Kong was uneventful except for the pre-docking informational travelogues. During the day we sunned ourselves on deck chairs and watched the peaceful waters of the Pacific, as if mesmerized, while the *Haruna Maru* steamed towards Hong Kong at top speed.

I became so excited about reaching the first Chinese port that was a British Crown Colony, I started checking the ship's position on the map in the smoking room three times a day. I had a pretty good idea that again I would not be permitted to go ashore, but that didn't dampen my exhilaration one bit. I would see for myself this famous island and a half called "Kaulun," leased by Britain from China for 99 years.

At the end of the second day around dusk, the rocky hillsides of Hong Kong appeared on the horizon and soon the silhouette of the city's highrise buildings came into view. The Captain had explained the layout of the city at dinner the night before. The British residents lived on the top of the hill overlooking the busy business district below. A ferry connected the main island of Hong Kong with the mainland section of the city, called Kowloon; it was the main method of transporting Chinese workers into the downtown district.

As the *Haruna Maru* approached the harbor, I could identify large blocks of buildings at the flat bases of land below the hills. On top of the hills I saw the smaller houses and I could also make out buses and cars climbing up the highways that rimmed the perimeter of the mountains.

110

The port was visibly busy, with almost as many ships leaving the harbor as entering. As we laid anchor just outside the harbor, a number of Chinese junks approached the *Haruna Maru* selling all sorts of local handicrafts. They offered redwood hand-carved Buddhas with big stomachs for good luck, metal necklaces, glass bead necklaces, glass vases, folding paper fans with hand-colored designs, and most desirable of all, green jade. They had baskets of all sizes made of hemp or bamboo (some of them painted bright colors) and funniest of all, sandals made from old automobile tires.

We remained in Hong Kong for 24 hours, just long enough to load cargo bound for Japan and take on enough provisions for the balance of the voyage. As expected I was not permitted to go ashore, but no one else was interested in lingering either, neither the few passengers still on board going to Shanghai or Kobe, and especially not the younger members of the crew who were increasingly eager to get home.

We sailed from the harbor of Hong Kong on a bright and sunny morning on a China Sea that was especially calm. It took us a day and a half to reach Shanghai, during which I mentally reviewed everything I had learned about the city, aside from the unflattering things heard via the Japanese crew. The Captain had reiterated the same warnings about avoiding all food and water in Shanghai because of contamination, and I tried to put the resulting images conjured up out of my mind.

I thought instead about Shanghai being the largest city in China and the most populous one in Asia. It was in the eastern part of China on the Pacific Ocean and was known to be one of the world's great seaports. I knew that originally it was opened to foreign trade by the Treaty of Nanking in 1842, and over the years a prosperous International Settlement of foreign business people grew up, making it a very sophisticated city. After World War I, it became a treaty port administered by Britain, the U.S. and France until occupied by Japan in the Second Sino-Japanese War which had begun only about 10 years earlier.

111

The best fact as far as I was concerned though, was that it was a port, indeed, the *last* port, open to refugees like me and my parents. Surely that fact bespoke something positive. I desperately wanted to believe it did, for Shanghai was going to be my home -- and who knew for how long?

Shanghai, Part I

As the *Haruna Maru* moved slowly up the Yangtze River into Shanghai harbor, I peered down from the top deck at the dirty river, an ugly brownish yellow, and watched the small sampans and junks all around us, bobbing like toy boats.

A magnificent skyline began to dominate the horizon as we moved steadily closer to Shanghai. Ships of all types and sizes, in addition to ocean liners, were docked in the harbor; deep-ruddered small junks with red fishtailed sails dancing from high-poled masts wove adroitly in and out among the larger vessels. I could hardly identify all the kinds of boats there were: tramp steamers, dredgers, scows, tankers, barges, canal boats, liners, launches, tugs, tows, sampans, houseboats and fishing ferries, all mixed together.

On one side of the harbor was a large area where scores of the Chinese junks were docked; families with children lived on these tiny boats, beehives of activity with laundry hung up to dry, mothers cooking food, and live chickens and crabs scurrying about amid countless toddlers.

Finally the *Haruna Maru* eased carefully into its mooring, and we lost sight of the skyline and the main part of the city. We were in a cargo docking area located in an outlying suburb of the city, with freighters surrounding our ship. Many passengers (me included of course) were leaning over the railing to watch the docking procedure.

An electric jolt of emotion surged through me when I was able to make out a number of Europeans standing on the dock waiting to greet disembarking friends or relatives. The thrill passed quickly, for I did not see my parents among them. In vain I scanned the faces of those waiting. My diminutive father and mother were not in view.

While waiting for the luggage to be unloaded, I ate my last breakfast on board alone. By approximately 11 o'clock, we were

113

able to disembark and I quickly retrieved my luggage on the dock, but still no one emerged from the crowd to embrace me.

At last! There they were! Pappi, impeccably attired in a white tailored summer suit, custom-made shirt and handsome tie, seemed unchanged except for his face which was a little more lined. His familiar rimmed spectacles could not hide his brilliant blue eyes, glittering brightly with joy and perhaps a tear or two; a yellow straw hat protected him from the hot sun and hid his slightly grayer hair and slightly more receding hairline. My lovely mother appeared equally unchanged, and impeccably turned out as my father in a bright print cotton dress, with matching shoes and handbag. Her hair was still a rich brown, her generous smile just as I remembered it. My heart turned over with relief to find them well, and if appearances meant anything at all, that Shanghai had not been unkind to them.

My small parents hadn't been able to push forward through the press of the crowd to the front which is why they were not visible to me from the ship. Needless to say, they were extremely happy to see me; I wish I could say my excitement matched theirs. I was happy to see them, but not only was I unaccustomed to dealing with such emotional exuberance from them, I was not entirely certain I was ready to leave the protective home that the *Haruna Maru* had provided me for almost ten idyllic weeks.

After our initial poignant greetings, before anything else, Mutti and Pappi wanted to show off my father's dental office in the downtown district of Shanghai; they planned a celebration lunch afterward. (I was eager to see the office, but not so eager to eat in Shanghai, after the warnings I'd heard on the *Haruna Maru!*)

We took a taxi from the dock to my father's office by a route that led through the harbor district along East Broadway, which housed British-owned buildings where both incoming freight and outgoing cargo was stored. My father said these were called *godowns* -- the Chinese expression for warehouse. To unload goods from a ship, the Chinese laborers had to "go down" into the holds, thus *godown,* he explained.

114

As we proceeded on Broadway, I gawked at the *godowns* and cargo ships on the left hand side of the street and souvenir stores on the right. We also passed a lot of bars and a red light district. Though still fairly early in the morning, streetwalkers were already out in significant numbers, some trolling for customers, others, merely patrolling. The girls represented every nationality of the world it seemed to me, and so did the uniformed sailors as they slowly strolled along the sidewalk, sizing up the "merchandise."

As our cab approached the Garden Bridge which spans the Soochow Creek, I noticed European-style apartment houses and office buildings dominating what was called the International Settlement where most foreigners lived and worked. Shanghai was known as an "open" city, meaning that it was one of five port cities that xenophobic China opened up to Britain in 1842 by the Treaty of Nanjing for "the purpose of carrying on their mercantile pursuits." The treaty also permitted the establishment of consulates. Shanghai was the only one of the five (the others being Canton, Fuzhou, Xamen, Ningbo) to become a boom town, because "concession" areas were made available for the French and other foreign settlements to wheel and deal in practically everything.

As soon as we crossed the bridge, we were on an unusually broad street. It was the Bund, that celebrated drive along the shore. I was astonished by the area's European-like landscaping, and an impressive mansion that we passed, surrounded by a wrought iron gate with two golden lions on top of each post, encasing a coat of arms, which I recognized as the House of Windsor. This was the British Embassy.

Its beautiful green lawn, edged with shrubs and flowers, was divided by a diagonal black-top road leading to a large, wide, colonial-style building. At both the gate and the entrance door, two British soldiers were posted, standing at attention. A black Rolls Royce limousine was parked in front of the building. I was beginning to feel more comfortable now that I'd seen a few familiar symbols of Britain.

115

Along the Bund stood monoliths of architecture testifying to global wealth and industry: insurance and oil companies, banks, the stock exchange, publishers, hotels, shipping lines, and textile companies. Almost all the buildings displayed a highly polished brass plate at the entrance door. I spotted the *Shanghai Hong Kong Bank, Jardine-Matheson, British General Consulate*, and some well-known steamship lines. The Shanghai Hong Kong Bank had two impressive sandstone lions guarding both sides of the entrance.

After five blocks we turned into Nanking Road at the corner of the Cathay Hotel, which faced the Palace Hotel. At this corner the Bund overlooked the harbor, where numerous ferries were docked and merchants displayed gaudy merchandise for sale right on the pavement.

The whole area along Nanking Road was teeming with rickshaws, pedicycles, taxi cabs, British double-deck buses (painted light yellow, not the familiar red I knew and loved) as well as bright green street cars.

We drove along Nanking Road for two more blocks, then turned left into Kianze Road. At the corner of Kianze and Kukiang Road we arrived at my father's office in the large corner office building that was unofficially known as the American Express Building because that company occupied so much of its space.

A Chinese doorman greeted my father as we walked into the lobby. Pappi proudly led the way to the elevator. He had pointed to a white and black sign affixed to the outside wall of the building, which read *Dr. Walter Riess, Dentist*. He now pointed to another sign before we entered the elevator indicating that Dr. Riess was located on the fourth floor.

The uniformed operator opened the elevator's old-fashioned chain-link door and greeted my father with grave courtesy as he brought us to the proper floor, where my father again pointed to a directional sign printed with his name. We walked to the end of a long corridor where there was yet another sign, pointing left. As we approached his office, again a black and white sign with

116

his name on it was visible at right angles to the door. He had made quite sure no patient would be unable to find Dr. Walter Riess!

Underneath that last sign sat a young Chinese boy dressed in a white jacket, head in his lap, fast asleep. My father opened the door to the foyer, which was used as a waiting room and we entered. Since it was lunch time, no patients were waiting. My father had to wake the boy to ask him whether there were any messages. The boy sleepily said in English he did not know of any. When he wasn't sleeping, this same boy ran errands for my parents, including bringing lunch from one of the near-by restaurants; he also kept the office immaculate.

My father opened the door to his office with a flourish, and to my surprise there was the same dental chair with the electric drill as well as the desk and cabinets, set up exactly as I remembered from Berlin. Even the ultra violet light hanging over the chair was the one from Berlin.

For a moment, I experienced a temporal and spatial displacement of some kind; I could hardly grasp the fact that I was not actually standing in my father's old office, back in Berlin. After a moment of re-adjustment, I began to see differences. This office was considerably smaller than the one in Berlin, and a large double window faced the dental chair instead of a windowless wall, but overall it looked the same, even down to the same upholstered black, curved chairs with their colorful flower design.

Pappi, still beaming proudly, then led me into the hall and through a separate entrance, into the laboratory where again, I was surprised. The identical large wooden work-table was there, flush with the wall. Three cutouts with room for my father and two technicians to sit, each had a wooden support for holding dental plates. Even the bunsen burners were the same. Gas, electricity and hot water were supplied just as they were in Berlin. A Shanghai office building being so much like a European one? Remarkable!

Everything looked immaculate and efficient. The laboratory had a vulcanizing oven, denture-making equipment and a porcelain oven to make porcelain crowns. The work currently underway was for his primary patients, who, for the most part were British officials in the Shanghai Health Department or other British-related offices. In general, the Chinese did not visit European dentists, except for wealthy merchants, for whom a European dentist was a sign of prestige.

I was relieved to notice a drinking water stand upon which sat a five gallon glass jar of purified water, delivered regularly by Aquarius, an American company. An ice box below cooled the jug. I was beginning to feel better about Shanghai, not so barren of what I considered "essentials" as I'd feared -- specifically, water that was safe to drink.

At the large double window was a beautiful view of the waterfront and the modern surrounding buildings comprising the International Settlement. The whole scene was reassuringly European. The only differences were the rickshaws pulled by coolies, and curbside vendors selling unfamiliar kinds of food and goods. I watched curiously as coolies queued up to purchase hot lunch from the vendors, then plunk themselves down on a rickshaw crossbar to eat. I could understand their fatigue, for I learned they were able to bear enormous weights of such disparate items as drums of oil, bales of cotton, trunks of silk, bags of coal, kegs of tea and blocks of cinder.

My father suggested lunch in one of the nice restaurants in the downtown business area, but I begged off, remembering the dire warnings given by the Japanese crew on the *Haruna Maru*. I suggested instead that we return to the dock and have lunch on board the *Haruna Maru*. I also had a hidden agenda; I wanted my parents to meet Ann and the two boys she was escorting to Kobe. It would be the last chance for me to say good-bye to them all, but especially to beautiful Ann.

My parents had to be a little puzzled that I insisted on returning to the ship, but nevertheless politely acquiesced. We took a 30-minute street car ride to the waterfront area in

Hongkew (a very, very poor district), crossing the same garden bridge we crossed earlier, and left the handsome International Settlement.

We found the *Haruna Maru* dining room almost empty, most of the remaining passengers having gone ashore; Ann was nowhere to be found either, for she and the boys were among them. After introducing my parents to a few of the remaining passengers, we sat down to eat by ourselves. I recall that I was somewhat depressed and did not talk very much.

Ann and the boys finally returned about 3 p.m. and we all visited for over an hour, then said our final good-byes. All the hellos and good-byes that day were almost too much for me. I suspected I would never see or hear from Ann again, and subsequent years proved me right.

We returned to my father's office where Mutti had taken up her old post as Pappi's assistant. While they finished a few workday chores, I telephoned my new boss, Mr. R.G. Morrison, manager of Jardine Engineering Corporation, who was extremely relieved to hear that I had finally arrived. We made an appointment for 10 a.m. at his office the next morning.

Pappi locked the office promptly at 6:00 p.m., and we boarded a street car to my parents' apartment, located on Bubblingwell Road in the International Settlement, an area which looked generally not unlike Fifth Avenue in New York City. It had elegant jewelry and fur stores, restaurants and movie houses. The Seymour Road Synagogue (built by emigré White Russian Jews who were now jewelry and fur store owners) was only a block away from where my parents lived. Eventually I would meet their new friends who lived in the area, as well as some who lived in the French Concession on Avenue Foch, an even more elegant area.

My parent's apartment house was in a cluster of buildings two stories high, organized around a "U" shape with an inviting courtyard in the center. The entrance from the courtyard, protected by an iron gate, had a private driveway. Old trees provided cooling shade to the entire area.

119

My parents' European-style garden apartment had only two rooms besides a kitchen and a bathroom, but since I was to be housed by my new employer, Jardine, I would be staying only one night with my parents. We made the most of it, catching up on the highlights of the past two years.

Mutti had finally adjusted to what was not so terrible a life as she had feared, although I later learned that for a brief period after their exodus from her beloved Berlin, she suffered what was called in those days a "nervous breakdown." In a deep depression she took to her bed, unable for several months to carry out the simplest household details. Alone, Pappi had shouldered setting up his new practice, and maintaining meals and cleaning until she was on her feet again.

That night I heard about how they had urged my grandmother to come with them to Shanghai, and she had almost agreed. In the end, the rest of the family prevailed upon her to stay, to ride out the Nazi regime, as they were attempting to do. My parents had sent her the money from the balance of the rebate of their round-trip tickets the steamship company had required them to buy (a supposed guarantee against the possibility of their not being accepted in Shanghai). The money could only be collected by the family remaining in Germany if the request was sent to the authorities in writing from Shanghai. My parents had been able to ascertain its safe arrival to my grandmother.

So far, they said, they believed our family in Berlin was still alive and well, though it was hard to read between the lines of the family letters -- which they knew were censored by the Nazis -- as to what was really going on. As far as they knew, no one else in the family had been arrested. Uncle Kurt, though, had been dragooned into working for the garbage detail as a street cleaner by the German authorities (my parents assumed this was in lieu of taking him to a concentration camp the way they had taken my father).

I wanted to hear all the details of how they had settled into their new life. They had sold the handsome Persian rugs from our Berlin home after arriving in Shanghai for enough money to live on until Pappi could establish a practice. Their financial situation had also been buffered by help from a couple named Blumberg from Breslau, Germany, whom they'd met on board the liner *Gneisenau.* By the time they arrived in Shanghai, the two couples were fast friends, and the Blumbergs offered to loan them money until they were able to get established.

As soon as they arrived, my father had taken his credentials to the German Ambassador who then certified to the International Settlement Board that his papers were in order and thus was eligible to practice. He was now in business again, though not nearly at the level of his Berlin practice, and certainly not as lucrative.

First Pappi, then Mutti, told about their new friends, their enjoyment of Viennese restaurants (managed by European refugees) and the cabarets featuring German and Austrian entertainers. I could hardly believe my ears at all this good news. We did not know that night how badly things would disintegrate in the not distant future, but for that night we were a happy family, together once more.

****

The morning after my arrival I presented myself at the very impressive headquarters of Jardine Engineering Corporation at precisely 10 a.m. The sandstone building was a whole city block long, and a large well-polished brass plate was placed on each side of the entrance. One plate read "Jardine, Matheson, Co., Ltd." and the other, "British General Consulate." The juxaposition reassured me that Jardine couldn't have been better positioned vis a vis the British authorities than they in fact were.

Two Sikh watchmen in khaki uniforms stood guard in front of the entrance. Each wore a turban and a long beard, and both had large revolvers hanging by a cord around their necks. As I walked by them through the entrance, they nodded politely; I

121

nodded back with as much pomposity as I could safely manage to convey. I don't know why I was feeling so cheeky, but I was.

Once inside the building, I asked a Chinese boy at the information desk where I could find Mr. Morrison, and was directed to an office on the second floor, where a sign said "Mr. R.G. Morrison, Head, Manufacturing Section, Railway Division." I knocked lightly at the door, and entered, hoping I looked appropriately professional. A British secretary asked whether I had an appointment; I introduced myself and displayed my contract.

She remarked tartly they had been expecting me a lot sooner and had wondered what had happened to me. When I explained that it had taken 10 unscheduled weeks for the ship to reach Shanghai, she became more cordial, and magically in less than a minute Mr. Morrison emerged from his office.

A man in his late thirties, of medium height and build, and typically British, reserved but friendly, he was wearing a neatly pressed white suit and a broad smile. We entered his old-fashioned office where I watched a large fan fastened to the ceiling turning far too slowly to do much cooling of the heat that was already becoming oppressive. My own freshly pressed look was wilting fast.

Mr. Morrison sat down in a comfortable chair behind a huge desk and I sat meekly before him. He wanted to know all about the long detour of the *Haruna Maru;* he was a good listener, but after about 45 minutes of my tale, he asked whether I cared for tea. He pressed a button beneath his desktop and like a Chinese genie, a boy in a white jacket appeared from nowhere. Did we prefer Chinese or English tea? Chinese, thank you, we both said.

Not five minutes later, the boy returned with green tea, the leaves still swirling in tall clear glasses, so hot, I had to wait before risking a sip. No ice for the British! Later I learned that in Asian countries hot tea is considered helpful in cooling one off.

We were also offered English-type biscuits and the *North China Daily News*, which I learned was the only English language newspaper printed in the entire region.

As we chatted, Mr. Morrison took a moment to comment on my "excellent English," which was important, he said, because English was the primary language at Jardine, even for Chinese personnel; no one was hired without fluency in English.

Office hours were 9 to 12 and 2 to 5 he told me, but only 9 to 12 on Saturday. A small chauffeured limousine, an English Vauxhall, would pick me up and take me home each day; I would be joined by two other Jardine employees. Curiously, this "perk" came about because foreigners working for Jardine were not permitted to drive in Shanghai. The reason was simple: the company rule prevented local Chinese from trumping up negligence cases against foreign individuals or companies by willfully throwing themselves in front of a (presumably wealthy) foreigner's automobile and trying to collect on the insurance. Chinese drivers employed by Jardine, however, were not subject to the rule because the Chinese settled disputes among themselves out of court.

I learned that foreigners who lived and worked in the International Settlement were not subject to local laws. We had extra-territorial rights virtually identical to those of diplomatic personnel, and could not be tried by a Chinese court. The worst fate that could befall us legally was to be deported to our country of origin. As far as I was concerned that would be a pretty bad fate. I mentally vowed to stay out of legal trouble.

Mr. Morrison also explained that my living arrangements would consist of a fully-furnished duplex apartment, for which I would pay the company the equivalent of two American dollars a month as rent. I would have the services of a "cook boy" and an "Amah" (maid) at my personal disposal, which would cost the equivalent of an additional five American dollars a month.

The chauffeur would pick me up from the office for lunch and bring me back after lunch. The number of restaurants in the downtown area was limited, and there would be too much time

123

to kill for the 2-hour lunch period if I stayed downtown, so Mr. Morrison suggested other restaurants outside the district.

Other perks he mentioned included access at cost to many items of luxury such as Scotch whiskey, Carnation milk, Australian butter, Remington typewriters, and Monarch calculators. The cost of what I purchased would be deducted automatically from my salary each month. Employees could also have dinner in night clubs or restaurants in the Bubblingwell (uptown) area and simply charge the amount, using business cards printed in English on one side and Chinese on the other, indicating name and company affiliation. By signing a bill and presenting the card, the amount of the bill would be automatically deducted from my monthly salary.

I thought this a very efficient arrangement, especially because it eliminated the need for me to carry any significant amount of cash. (Mr. Morrison warned that expert pickpockets were an ever-present epidemic, and that I should wear a money bag around my neck if I were carrying anything valuable.)

Only one third of my salary, which I was assured would be more than sufficient to cover daily expenses, would be paid me directly. Two thirds of it would be deposited in my name with the Bank of England in London, to assure a nice nest egg when I returned to the UK; equally important, this payroll system would keep the Chinese government from blocking any transfer of money at the time of my leaving Shanghai. About the disposition of my salary, I had no choice. These arrangements had been company policy for years, but when it came time to leave, I appreciated it more than a little.

Mr. Morrison further suggested that I open a bank account with the Shanghai Hong Kong Bank, a bank influenced by British interests. With these instructions and advice, he ushered me out of his office and led me to my desk in the Railway Division. There he introduced the Jardine staff of whom only about 10% were not Chinese. These Caucasians were white Russian engineers who were experts on boilers, a few other

Europeans who were experts on elevator systems, and a healthy sprinkling of English of course.

After this brief orientation, it was already lunch time and I was invited to be Mr. Morrison's guest at the British Club. While we descended one flight of stairs to the Peking Road entrance of the building, he said that as an employee with the Engineering Division, I would be using the rear entrance of the building. This was because the building, which took up the entire block from the Bund to Peking Road, had several entrances. The Jardine Matheson entrance was on the Bund; the Engineering Division entrance was in the rear.

We walked a short distance along Peking Road to Nanking Road, and soon reached the British Club. Foreigners, he told me, ate primarily at their clubs rather than at local restaurants; indeed, life -- both personal and professional -- revolved around one's club. I learned that the French Settlement, which was to a great extent a residential area, had the finest clubs and buildings in Shanghai. The British clubs were located in the International Settlement.

Inside the club, the maitre d' greeted Mr. Morrison by name and after we were seated, were shown an impressive English menu, but first we ordered Scotch and soda. My new boss stressed the importance for managers (like ourselves) of keeping within the framework of the normal office hour schedule because it set a good example for the staff. I preened inwardly -- now I was a manager!

It was customary, he said, on Saturday afternoons after work, for new managers to be invited as a guest to one of the country clubs, for tennis or swimming, and that I should expect such an invitation from other managers in Jardine (as well as their friends) and that I should plan accordingly. He was certainly painting a rosy picture for me.

I could already see that life for a Jardine employee in Shanghai was going to be formal. No one was permitted to remove jackets in the office regardless of the temperature, or whether or not the office had a ceiling fan, and of course ties and white shirts were worn at all times.

The Jardine plant was located outside the geographic boundaries of the International Settlement; I would tour there the next day. The plant still manufactured steel windows, but would soon be converted to other purposes after I took charge and installed appropriate equipment. It already had general machine tools, but would require additional manufacturing equipment to convert its production line. The castings for the various new machine tools had been imported and were ready to be machined as soon as the instructions arrived from the home office in England.

Mr. Morrison and I discussed all of these facets of the company and company life at our first lunch together, and time passed quickly. I spent the afternoon back at the office reading company handbooks on various administrative policies and procedures. I was also introduced to the chief cashier and signed several forms, which effectively put me on the payroll. It was comforting to learn that the chief cashier himself would personally hand me my paycheck each month.

I felt very comfortable after my first day in the Shanghai office; everyone had been more than friendly and helpful. Now it was time to go home with the two gentlemen who would share the company limo with me. A uniformed chauffeur opened the car doors for us, and I stepped in thinking I could adapt to this life-style in Shanghai quite easily!

The trip home took us through the very crowded Nanking Road, home to many department stores and office buildings, large movie houses which showed the latest American and British films, around the very large Race Course (a British horse race club) and on into Bubblingwell Road where my parents lived.

The middle of the road had tracks for street cars. Double-deck buses, rickshaws and bicycles, as well as cars and streetcars, all jockeyed for advantage on the traffic-clogged road. Traffic police with white arm bands, wearing shorts, regulated the traffic as best they could, but the general picture was total mayhem. After about an hour we finally arrived at the edge of the International Settlement, where Jardine's employee housing was located.

Inside the residence to which I was assigned, the houseboy took my jacket and asked if he could serve tea or a cold drink. I was ready to decompress with a whiskey and a comfortable chair. Dinner -- prepared in typical English fashion with an elegant spread of silverware and china on which I was offered an array of English food -- was served in the dining room. (My meals for the next few years consisted typically of meat pies, mutton, goulash, and fish and chips. All of these for the most part were overcooked, except for the vegetables sauteed in soyabean oil in a wok.)

After dinner that first night I listened to the radio for a bit, then retired early after an exciting first full day in Shanghai.

****

I woke the next morning without an alarm promptly at seven. The houseboy had laid out my newly washed and pressed white linen suit and matching white shoes, socks and shirt. I ate breakfast while reading the *North China Daily News,* which helped to get acquainted with Shanghai life. I was adapting to the life of a fledgling executive quite nicely, I thought, as I dashed out to meet the company car with the other two managers already in it.

Our trip to the downtown office was slowed by the same rampant traffic confusion as the night before. We arrived at Jardine at 8:45 a.m. and I found it necessary to re-discover my office. After several wrong turns, I finally located it and settled down behind my desk, intending to review the material received the day before, but almost immediately the phone rang. It was Mr. Morrison asking me to join him and others in the conference room to discuss future plans with the various department heads -- Planning, Financial, Personnel and Engineering. We paused only

127

once at 10 a.m. for the customary tea and biscuits served by white-coated Chinese boys.

My boss again invited me to lunch with him, this time at the Palace Hotel, for him to give me a preview of our afternoon tour of the plant. The elegant dining room in the Palace reminded me of the Hyde Park Hotel in London, with very formal British service. Getting down to business, Mr. Morrison explained the delicate matter of my position with the company. He said it would be difficult for the Chinese *compradore* (Vice President), a Mr. Wu, to accept me as his boss (who was in fact, boss of the entire factory) basically because of my age and lack of any experience. However, it was company policy that a Chinese manager must report to a European manager from the home office in all cases. Mr. Wu knew this, he said, and would have to adjust to the situation, but I knew the sub-text to all this explanation, was that I was to make it easy for the vice president to "keep face." I got the message. I would never "pull rank" on Mr. Wu!

We settled down in Mr. Morrison's comfortable car after lunch, and the chauffeur cruised along the Bund to the Garden Bridge which he crossed into the industrial district of Hongkew. The Soochow Creek divided the International Settlement from the rest of the city which was under the control of the Japanese occupying army. (In 1937 a war between China and Japan broke out, resulting in the Japanese Navy occupying Shanghai except for the International Settlement and the French Concession.

Across the bridge, the landscape changed dramatically. The streets were lined with low, cheap houses and large *godowns* along the waterfront. We passed a great number of two story brick and stucco houses with open store fronts and shutters which could slide shut at night. Old paint and poor construction combined to give the area the look of extreme poverty. The store fronts had no windows, and only rickety counters from which the owners plied their wares. Upstairs were their living quarters, with washing hung out on bamboo sticks to dry.

After driving a half hour we arrived at the modern, walled facility which bore the name "Hope-Crittal" on a large sign outside. A watchman opened the iron gate and we drove into the circular driveway.

Mr. Wu, the compradore, was waiting in the courtyard to greet us. (A "compradore" was a Chinese agent engaged by a foreign establishment in China to have charge of its Chinese employees and to act as an intermediary in business affairs.) Mr. Wu was a tall, heavy-set, good looking gentleman, about 45 years old. His English was excellent, possibly even more fluent than mine. He shook hands and politely invited me into the building for a look around.

Mr. Wu explained what the employees in the various offices did and introduced his operations staff, each one shaking my hand and smiling politely. After the tour, because the manufacturing plant was several blocks away and completely separated from the administration facility where we then were, Mr. Wu suggested that we drive to the factory so I could see for myself what equipment was currently available, and accordingly he called for the car.

After only a five minute drive -- apparently "managers" never walked anywhere -- we arrived at an old looking plant marked "Shanghai Iron Works." Mr. Morrison explained that for political reasons this plant was "officially" owned by Mr. Wu, but was directly connected with Jardine Engineering Corporation.

We entered the factory by crossing over an earth-covered driveway and walked onto the large, loud, dirty and dusty factory floor, abuzz with countershaft pulleys and belts driving various machine tools which stood on a dirt floor.

Raw materials for production were stacked all over, but the machines used to manufacture steel window frames were standing idle. Walking at a normal pace, Mr. Wu led us around the factory area and then into an adjoining building which housed the pattern shop where skilled pattern makers did the important pattern work by hand.

129

This building was connected to a foundry on the same side of the factory. Workers sitting on the sand floor were carefully preparing the shapes to be cast. The foundry was casting its own bronze bearings and cast iron parts, and from what I could see in the short time I was there, the type of work these workers produced was impressive.

After the tour, which was all too brief from my perspective, Mr. Wu invited us into his large, well-furnished office where a Chinese houseboy immediately placed glasses of steaming green tea on small, dark brown tables made of wood I would soon recognize as standard for most Chinese furniture.

I saw that I had to quickly get used to drinking hot tea at 80 degrees Fahrenheit with the large green tea leaves swimming unstrained in the tall glass, since this was the beverage of choice in Shanghai.

After English cigarettes were passed around, Mr. Morrison explained the new company objectives to both Mr. Wu and me since we would be working together very closely.

Hope-Crittal was to cease manufacturing steel windows immediately, and gear up to manufacture radial boring machines, milling machines and planers designed in the London office, per the drawings I had carried with me from England. I would be in complete charge of the machine tool manufacturing plant, but as far as chain of command was concerned, all personnel would report to Mr. Wu, who in turn would report to me. I was to visit the plant at least once a week to discuss progress and problems, and have a field office at the factory as well as my office back at headquarters in the International Settlement.

Inscrutable Mr. Wu listened politely, but offered no direct comment on the marching orders laid out by Mr. Morrison. I hoped that he found the directives acceptable and that he would be cooperative.

I asked a few questions, and he offered additional information about the workers. The work day was from 7 a.m. to 7 p.m. Many workers slept on the machines, he said. (Mats were placed on the large machines, which had wide enough flat areas for a man to stretch out full length. Sometimes they slept on the floor.)

Mr. Wu said that three meals were provided all workers by an outside kitchen at Jardine's expense; raw rice was also stored in the plant. Family members often stayed with the workers on weekends, though only the workers were allowed to sleep on the machines.

On the way back to the home office my boss said he wanted to convert the factory to making machine tools as fast as possible since the supply of these machines from England had stopped, and that I was to submit a plan of action to him in two days; after it was approved, I was to implement the changes.

I spent the next morning trying to understand the company's procedures better, before embarking on a plan. I had to phase out old methods and phase in new, while maximizing use of the existing equipment and current personnel. It took me two full days to come up with a workable plan, no small challenge for a young man just out of school, who was feeling greener than Shanghai tea.

Mr. Morrison reviewed the plan and suggested certain changes. After an additional day, my ideas were approved. I invited Mr. Wu to the Jardine Engineering Division office to review the details. I had a lot to learn, and knew that I needed Mr. Wu a lot more than he needed me. He was experienced; I was not. He knew his workers (who spoke only Chinese); I did not.

As we reviewed the plan, Mr. Wu was helpful and made useful suggestions. He seemed to be going along with the changes with a positive attitude, and took a copy of the plan with him to discuss with his staff. I promised to visit him in two days.

In the meantime, I collected as much information about the company's operations as I could at Headquarters. I had more than a hunch that the plan would be far easier to develop than to implement. The Chinese would probably say yes to everything, because of their extraordinary politeness, but would then do

131

whatever they were accustomed to do. After all, was this not the nature of most human behavior?

It was three years before I really began to understand the Chinese mentality. It was far more complex than I ever imagined, and far more stubborn and hard-headed than even the German mentality, which is saying a mouthful.

Two days later, I was to spend the day at Hope-Crittal. Mr. Wu was waiting for me outside, but we quickly moved to his office for a glass of the ubiquitous green tea. Formalities occupied the better part of an hour before we got down to business; then he called his foreman in to discuss the implementation plan.

Two hours later houseboys began to set up a large round bamboo table in the middle of Mr. Wu's office. Mr. Wu had invited the staff of six for lunch, so six bowls and six place settings with chopsticks had been set up Chinese-style, with steaming fish, vegetables and rice in large bowls and bamboo containers placed in the middle of the table. All six of us picked up our chopsticks, then paused. No one wanted to be the first to start. In an extraordinary tableau, each member of the staff gestured to all the others with his chopsticks, pantomiming that someone else should begin first, a marvelous illustration of how excessive politeness can paralyze action.

After at least three minutes passed, Mr. Wu broke the ice (with a little smile) and served himself some fish from the center dish. The fish bones were placed on the table in a pile; to this pile the guests added any leftover food that remained uneaten.

Noisy discussions in Chinese went on during the entire meal, of which I understood not a word of course, but every now and then Mr. Wu would translate something that he wanted me to know, although he needn't have bothered. I remained utterly confused with or without the translations. My culture shock was deepening, but in general, I managed to keep myself on an even keel.

After lunch we visited the factory, foundry and pattern shop. We discussed the drawings for the pattern shop, since it was to be the area re-tooled in the factory conversion process. We agreed on a reasonable schedule to create and finish the castings, a time-consuming process because each casting would have to age several months before the actual machining of cast parts could begin.

The gear cutting and drilling, however, could start as soon as fixtures were available. Therefore, the production of jigs and fixtures had the highest immediate priority. I had to schedule drawings for the design office as soon as I could.

I was well satisfied with the progress at the end of the day, though the responsibilities at Jardine were still so overwhelming to me, I had no interest in going out for nights on the town. I had my dinner and read the newspaper, simply too excited and focused on the work ahead of me to be interested in any frivolity. I wanted to get going as soon as possible, but I could already foresee that getting things done in China would take a lot longer than they would in Germany or even England. I would leave visiting my parents for the week-end.

Over time, I learned to appreciate the fuller meaning of the word "minsu," used so often in Shanghai conversations. It literally meant "tomorrow." Everything would be done "minsu." I privately compared China to Mexico, even though I had never been there. I thought of them as both "mañana" cultures, but China was Mexico with manners.

For example, when I asked why work assigned had not been done, the answer was: "minsu, minsu," which meant that it would be done the day after tomorrow. Checking two days later and discovering it was not yet done, I would be told: "minsu, minsu, minsu," which meant that it would now take an additional three days. For someone like me, reared with a strong German work ethic, it was frustrating to deal with the slow pace and relaxed attitude.

On my next trip to the Shanghai Iron Works a week later, I went straight to the pattern shop to see what progress had been made since my last visit. Very little.

133

I also found out that a 12-hour work day actually translated to a 6-hour work day, since three meals and multiple rest periods were taken between 7 a.m. and 7 p.m. Even worse, many employees slept during the day. The resultant reduction in end product caused me to shift more skilled workers from the window-frame operation to the pattern shop in order to catch up to my schedule.

The same failure to meet planned targets held true for the foundry. With the accumulated delays, I estimated it would be six months before any machining of castings could begin. Moreover, after initial patterns were created, I discovered that jigs and fixtures machined to "specifications" did not guarantee interchangeability. I learned to live with the reality that anything might *eventually* be made to fit, but only after careful and patient hand filing and finishing.

Of course, the most serious flaw of all was that none of the parts were interchangeable. This made it impossible to easily mass produce the requisite spare parts needed to operate the factory efficiently; this fact proved a constant source of irritation to me.

My admiration for the machinists who worked for Jardine notwithstanding -- some were truly artists -- was somewhat tempered because not a week went by without a serious problem. Quick-change gear boxes had to be hand-fitted; in order to machine long lathe beds, other tools and dies had to be improvised on the spot, which also affected accuracy.

Taking stock after I had managed the machine tool plant for 18 months of severe frustration, only one very large radial boring machine and several lathes had been completed, though each piece of equipment looked quite impressive in its smooth, gun metal gray paint. I had to admit that the Chinese were first-class artists in covering up defects. The wear surfaces were shiny and protected against rust by heavy oil, and an acceptance inspection tag was affixed to each machine tool. Who could doubt that the equipment was ready for shipment?

134

****

In the meantime, the political situation had changed drastically since my arrival in September, 1940. On the morning of December 8, 1941, the company car was parked outside my residence waiting to bring me to the office as usual. That was the last normal occurrence of the day.

As soon as I had said good morning to the two managers already seated in the car, they asked me if I had heard the explosions during the night. I replied I had not. Well, they said, the Italians scuttled their ships in the harbor, in an effort to block the harbor and preventing the British war ships from leaving Shanghai. The scuttling also deprived the British and French concessionaires in Shanghai of a valuable trading asset, since Japan had entered the European war on Hitler's side by attacking the American fleet at Pearl Harbor.

I sat silently in the car, wondering what these events would bode for the future. My mind was racing with questions about what this would mean to our company and to our private lives, but neither my companions nor I had the remotest idea, since our crystal balls were somewhat murky.

The moment we arrived at headquarters, Mr. Morrison, sounding more than a little agitated, summoned me to come to his office at once. With no preamble he asked if I had my passport with me; surprised, I replied that it was at my apartment. He wasted no time with explanations, but picked up the phone and asked for his chauffeur and car to meet me at the rear entrance. I was to go home without delay, retrieve my passport and return with it to his office forthwith.

At that point, I didn't know what he had in mind, but obviously he believed my German passport would play a role in some plan he had. What could it be? I wondered, but raced to the back entrance where the car was already waiting, without asking questions.

Someone at headquarters had apparently alerted my house staff that I was on my way home because all of them were

135

standing nervously at the door waiting for me to bring the latest news. I realized they wanted reassurance. With a hurried sentence or two I did my best to convince them that nothing would change in their lives at this point, but my words rang hollow -- how could I be sure that what I said was true?

I quickly retrieved my passport from the desk, dashed to the car, and we sped back to the office. Fortunately, the traffic was light and the return trip was swift. I headed straight for Mr. Morrison's office. Believe it or not, even in those first harried moments of panic, he ordered tea and biscuits. After some initial small talk (which he never omitted) he unveiled a daring plan he'd devised to save Jardine from being swallowed up by the Japanese.

Since the Japanese Navy had been stationed around the perimeter of the International Settlement ever since the fall of Shanghai in the 1937 war, he assumed it would not take them long to march in and occupy the entire area. It might be only a matter of days, possibly only hours.

Because Jardine Engineering Division was a British concern, and Britain was now officially at war with Japan, it was logical to conclude that Jardine would be quickly taken over and administered by the Japanese.

I, however, could provide Jardine with a way out, he said. I was his ace in the hole. "You have a valid German passport," he said, coming to the point. ("Yes," I thought to myself, "with its ugly brown cover, and disgusting black swastika.")

"I can put you in charge of my entire division of Jardine."

I dropped my jaw. Without waiting for my reaction to this startling idea, Mr. Morrison picked up the phone and asked his secretary to step into his office. He dictated the following:

Effective immediately, Mr. H.L. Riess is appointed
Managing Director of Jardine Engineering Division, and
all personnel will report to him. Mr. Riess is
responsible for all activities of this division.

I was thunderstruck. I felt as if an enormous weight had just been placed upon my shoulders, nailing me rigidly to my seat.

Mr. Morrison asked his secretary to type up the directive immediately, then asked me to wait in his office while he assembled his immediate subordinates for a staff meeting. It took about 20 minutes for all of them to arrive, visibly nervous, squirming around on the soft couches, trying to look as though they were at ease.

The secretary brought in the typed directive for Mr. Morrison's signature. He read it over, signed it, and asked her to distribute copies to all department heads and compradores. He then called the meeting to order, and a very serious Mr. Morrison began to soberly explain his plan to the staff.

His guess was that the Japanese Navy would probably occupy the International Settlement within the next few hours, and once they did, would doubtless take charge of all enemy commercial operations, which would certainly include our British-owned firm. So, in order to avoid this eventuality, he was transferring all administrative power and managerial responsibility to Mr. Hans Riess, a German national, who would take charge of Jardine, effective immediately. He and the entire Jardine staff would henceforth report to Mr. Riess. The factory managed by Mr. Wu would continue to report to Mr. Riess, as before.

The assembled staff actually seemed pleased by Mr. Morrison's plan, and somewhat relieved, for they had feared the worst -- a complete Japanese take-over of the company, and the loss of their livelihood. Maybe this unlikely plan might really work!

Mr. Morrison convinced them that there was a chance, however slim, that the Japanese would not disturb their comfortable positions with Jardine or disrupt their personal lives in any way. I was still unable to acknowledge anything that was being said except for an occasional nod of my head when Mr. Morrison looked at me meaningfully as though indicating that I should signify assent.

137

Solemnly we all returned to our offices and waited to see what the next few hours would bring. Mr. Morrison had said we would not have long to wait. He was right.

At approximately 10:30 a.m. a Japanese staff car pulled up at the rear entrance, the main entrance of Jardine Engineering Division. An elderly Japanese gentleman elaborately dressed in a Japanese naval uniform with a long ceremonial dagger dangling on his side emerged after his chauffeur had obsequiously opened the car door. He portentously climbed the ten steps leading to the principal entrance of our building.

As he entered, he looked around as though surveying a new domain, and approached the receptionist on duty in the lobby, asking in perfect British accented English for the person in charge. The receptionist telephoned me at once and said briskly, and quite as though this was an ordinary occurrence "that a Japanese officer requests your presence in the lobby."

I ran downstairs to the lobby with un-managerial haste until I was within view of the Japanese officer, then slowed to a dignified walk. As I approached the officer he gave me a military salute, and very politely asked if I was the person in charge of Jardine Engineering Corporation. With all the aplomb I could muster, I stood as tall as my five-foot-two stature would allow, (heartily wishing I looked a little older than 22) and replied that I certainly was.

He asked to see credentials. With great dignity I removed my German passport from the inside pocket of my suit jacket and handed it to him. He studied every page for a long time without comment, finally handing it back to me. Then he smiled.

In a formal little speech (in English) he made it clear that as an ally I could continue to operate the offices of Jardine without any interference by Japanese occupation forces. Saluting stiffly once again, he turned 180 degrees, and walked out of the building and down the steps to his car. Again the chauffeur opened the door, the naval officer disappeared inside, and the car sped off. My knees melted.

138

Shaking, I raced up the stairs to Mr. Morrison's office and gave him a verbatim report of the meeting. He was so delighted I thought he was going to dance a jig. He certainly had reason to celebrate. His brilliant idea had rescued our company!

He then sent me to the Shanghai Iron Works to inform Mr. Wu of what had just taken place. Along the Bund at Garden Bridge Japanese soldiers stopped our car before we could cross. Between the time I had come to work in the morning, and my current mission, they had obviously set up barriers and checkpoints all around the city.

I handed my passport to a soldier who scowled and took it into a guard house (a pre-fabricated structure no larger than an outhouse.) He returned it after some minutes and gestured that we could cross into Hongkew. As we drove along Broadway, everything was deceptively calm. We saw a few Japanese soldiers patrolling at a leisurely pace, but from all other outward appearances, it was business as usual. Streetcars operated, rickshaws and trolley buses fought their way through the traffic, all the normal confusion prevailed.

Our car stopped in front of the Shanghai Iron Works and an agitated Mr. Wu came out to greet me, visibly upset, his usual oriental calm quite askew, though not so askew that he omitted the green tea ritual.

Mr. Wu was clearly prepared for the worst, but when I told him of Mr. Morrison's strategy his eyes got bigger and bigger. He listened with rapt attention to what had happened between me and the Japanese officer. I explained that as far as the Japanese world was to know, Jardine's total operations were now under my supervision because the Japanese Navy recognized my German nationality, and considered me an ally.

Mr. Wu smiled warmly and nodded silently, and gave me no reason to think he was anything but pleased about what he had heard. He knew that I knew that he would still be running things his own way!

He then asked me a very good question: when our production line was operational, how would completed machines

139

be transported from the plant and to whom would they be shipped? I could not answer these questions right then, but assured him that there would be no interruption in the production cycle.

Mr. Wu then asked me to brief the English-speaking foreman on what I had just related, so that the foreman could call a factory-wide meeting and explain to all employees that their jobs were secure. This accomplished, I left the plant two hours later. Returning to headquarters I was once again stopped at the Garden Bridge. Again I showed my passport and was waved on through the checkpoint into the International Settlement.

Our headquarters was only five blocks from the bridge, so it took only minutes until I was safely back in my office. I phoned Mr. Morrison and reported that Mr. Wu had been apprised, and understood the situation, and that I did not have any problem crossing the Garden Bridge. He was happy to hear it, and to my relief, told me to go home and relax after the day's excitement. I had been running on nervous energy all day. Totally wrung out both emotionally and physically I welcomed the peace and quiet of my apartment.

The house boy was anxious to hear any news I had about the war and I repeated the day's story one more time, assuring him that his situation would remain status quo, all because I was not an enemy alien. He was enormously relieved, as everyone had been all day, that their personal lives would continue undisturbed.

I remember reflecting that it seemed that as long as people's personal lives were not altered, they were not that concerned about the war. To tell you the truth, I was no different from anyone else in that regard.

During the next few days, the Imperial Japanese Navy released special instructions for residents of the International Settlement. The most serious was the order to all enemy aliens (the majority were British, American, Dutch and French) to register with the occupation forces at once. They would be issued red arm bands (to be worn at all times) with a large black

A, B, D or F, each letter representing the alien's nationality. Severe penalties were threatened for non-compliance.

Other than that, enemy aliens were permitted to continue their normal business activities. Within a few days, my friends who shared the company car and Mr. Morrison wore their red arm bands printed with a "B." Other than that outward absurdity, life continued on as before.

At first, no foreigner experienced any food shortages as a result of the expanded war, and the International Settlement continued to handle its own community affairs under the same foreign management. Both situations would change over the passage of time.

For the next three years under Japanese occupation, enemy aliens continued to earn their living as before. Certain goods eventually ran out; milk was replaced by black soy bean milk; coffee beans by ground-up dried figs; the sweet potato eventually became the only type of potato available. Good fresh bread baked daily, could, however, be bought from the bakeries run by impoverished Jewish refugees who lived in the Hongkew area.

One of the ironies of fate was that although I was deemed a German national (because of gaining a passport extension while still in England), the Japanese considered my parents stateless, since their German passports had expired. Stateless persons were not enemy aliens and therefore, were not obliged to wear arm bands. In the lingo of World War II displaced persons, they were non-persons.

My mother continued to care for their little household, and took up cooking and baking, which she seemed to enjoy. Every day, my father continued to go from their apartment in the International Settlement to the downtown office to take care of his dental practice. His patients (primarily British) visited him as before. I went to see them often and met most of their friends.

My own life continued in a pattern best described as a young bachelor's lifestyle abroad. I started to date young women and ate out frequently in restaurants, many of which were located in

141

department stores on Nanking Road, which were also associated with adjacent hotels. Bubblingwell Road was the nightclub area, and many clubs continued to operate throughout the war. I preferred the ones that offered taxi dancing, where one could purchase tickets and select a dance partner. The girls were usually very young and looked extremely sexy in their long mandarin-style (*cheongsam*) dresses -- brightly colored satin brocade sheaths with slits on each side reaching suggestively to their upper thighs. They wore fairly heavy make-up and very high heels, and sat around the bar until a customer brought them a ticket and asked for a dance (customers purchased several tickets in advance when entering the nightclub.)

The clubs were large and beautifully decorated, with soft, indirect lighting and elaborate decor. One club boasted memorable gold chairs upholstered with red velvet. The bands were made up of partly Chinese and partly European instrumentalists, and they played all the popular Western music, imitating the "Big Band" sound like that of Tommy Dorsey and Glen Miller. Spending an evening at a Shanghai club one could forget that there even was a war -- at least for that night.

Evidently Mr. Wu, while dancing with his favorite taxi girl could also forget the war, among other things!

It was during the dark long evenings of my first winter in Shanghai that he was often seen in Ciro's nightclub on Bubblingwell Road, dancing with the same 19-year old taxi girl. She was extremely pretty and apparently a lot of fun to be with. Many nights Mr. Wu would not go home at all but stay in a hotel near the nightclub.

Mr. Wu was a man of ingenuity, intelligence, and good looks. In the prime of life, he was enjoying the perks of his station in life. He looked particularly prosperous during the winter, when he wore a mink-lined long black coat with a huge mink collar, and a Russian-style mink astrakhan hat.

Mr. Wu's wife was an attractive woman in her mid-forties who had raised their two sons and one daughter. The older son was 17 years old, the younger son was 14 and the girl, only seven. Mrs. Wu seemed quite content with her life. The Wu family lived in an apartment above the factory, expensively panelled in fine wood. The windows were framed by elegant draperies; the floors were of fine parquet wood, always polished to a high shine. A large kitchen was maintained by three servants plus a "cookboy" who took care of the meals and food shopping.

Mrs. Wu seemed happy with her role as manager of the Wu household, which included an array of house plants and a small menagerie of cats and dogs. She dressed well and occasionally asked the chauffeur to drive her into the International Settlement for some serious department store shopping. She would come home with a mountain of packages, happily ready to display her purchases to anyone interested. She enjoyed a comfortable life and was content even though she knew that Mr. Wu went to nightclubs and enjoyed himself in the International Settlement.

It was typical of Chinese culture of that day that she was not supposed to mind. And perhaps she did not. The wife of a successful husband was thereby a success herself, and she thanked her ancestors and her lucky stars that this was so. It was right that the wife of such a man should be glad that he could enjoy his evenings after providing her with such a wonderful life. (At least the men thought that was what their wives thought.)

Mr. Wu began to spend more and more nights away from home. On these occasions when he came home the next morning, a little the worse for wear, he was always in an excellent mood. After a bath and change of clothes, he would descend the one flight of stairs to his office in the factory, attend to the most pressing matters and then take a little nap in his comfortable desk chair, the privilege of a Compradore.

Rumors began to spread around the factory that Mr. Wu would soon take a second wife. It was socially acceptable then for a wealthy man to marry more than once. Over the years, the custom of plural marriage had developed into a status symbol for the rich. More than one wife broadcast a man's financial status.

143

It said that he had the wherewithal to support more than one family.

Status and "face" were all important for Chinese. It was good to be overweight; the world would know you could afford more than enough to eat. (Buddhas were always portrayed with big stomachs.) A member of the middle class might aspire to own a gold watch, a fountain pen or gold front teeth.

Nobody with good sense (or much money) kept it in the bank, because the Central Reserve Bank of China (the Central Reserve Bank that regulated banks and banking throughout the country) hardly looked after the interests of depositors; the bank was a tool of the Nanking Puppet government, and therefore indirectly controlled by the Japanese. Its paper bank notes could be devaluated without notice (and frequently were) and they did not have gold backing. Therefore, wealthy Chinese kept their money, consisting of gold and silver bars and coins, at home or in safes in their offices. Mr. Wu was no exception.

One sunny spring day, after a winter spent mostly with the 19-year old taxi dancer in the city, Mr. Wu went to his safe and removed several gold bars. He took them to his wife and told her that he would marry Sue (for that was the girl's name) in the summer and that Mrs. Wu should make the necessary arrangement for his marriage to Number Two wife.

Mrs. Wu was not shocked, nor did she lose face when Mr. Wu showed her a picture of his beautiful, slim girl friend with long black hair, and smooth, light ivory-colored skin. She was instead extremely happy for Mr. Wu that he had found a young woman who could take care of all his sexual needs and bear additional children for him. Mrs. Wu's attitude was "What a wonderful time in the life of my successful husband."

What made this remarkable, she must have thought to herself, was that this could happen in the middle of a war during the Japanese occupation. Most men had a tough time making a living. But not her Mr. Wu. He was on top of the world!

Mr. Wu gave his wife the long list of those who were to be invited to the wedding, which he wanted to take place in Ciro's nightclub. He expected Mrs. Wu to make all the arrangements, and she happily did so.

Together, Mrs. Wu and the maitre d' at Ciro's chose the wedding date, a Saturday in July, expecting that the weather would be warm and clear. After the date was agreed on, Mrs. Wu went to a printer to discuss the invitations. She wanted them printed in gold letters on red paper and enclosed in red envelopes (red being the Chinese color of good luck).

Mrs. Wu gave a guest list of some 300 guests (a number that would easily fit into the nightclub) and the envelopes to one of the Hope-Crittal office clerks, who addressed them in traditional Chinese calligraphy, lettering the characters from top to bottom with a black calligraphic brush.

I was among those who received an invitation, as did all the Jardine department heads, and eagerly anticipated attending my first Chinese wedding. I made discreet inquiries about what present would be appropriate for me to give the couple, and was advised by my co-workers that a silk dressing screen for the second bedroom (next to the Number One bedroom in which Number One wife slept) would be a quite suitable gift.

As hoped, the day of Mr. Wu's second wedding was a warm and sunny Saturday. I dressed in my light shantung silk summer suit, a light yellow tie and a white silk shirt, and felt I was quite elegantly enough turned out for this grand occasion.

I pedalled my bicycle to Bubblingwell Road near the Race Course where Ciro's nightclub was located, locked it onto the bike rack near the entrance of the building, and stopped there for a moment to admire a huge fountain splashing a beautiful water pattern. Almost immediately Mr. Ching, our office and payroll supervisor, came up to me to say hello and to introduce his wife. She did not speak English and as I was greeted by others I realized that English was definitely not the language of choice for this Chinese wedding. Although I understood a good bit of the Shanghai dialect, I remembered the company rule as it related to Europeans. I was not to admit that I understood or spoke Chinese. The truth is, that although I understood a little, having taken a few language classes at one of the clubs, I had been only a desultory student (already overwhelmed by so much to absorb in this new culture), and thus was thankful for the company rule. "Pidgin" Chinese was about my level.

Entering through huge, ornate double doors into an extravagant vestibule, we found hot tea and biscuits set up on tables, but no liquor. Most of the male Chinese guests wore traditional long gray or black Chinese coats and their wives had selected their best summer silk shantung cheongsams or "esangs," colorful, long sheath dresses with standing-band collars, knotted silk "frogs" (silk closures), charmeuse piping, a single kick-pleat in back and long slits up one or both of the sides.

Among the guests were some grandmothers, old enough to have bound feet, who took very careful, small steps while discreetly sizing up the place. Some of the old gentlemen were the vain possessors of excessively long pinky fingernails, a status symbol indicating that they did not have to work, since it was impossible to do so with such a fingernail. Their gray beards grew in sparse strings, quite unevenly. But if the face had a wart, and a very long hair grew out of it, it was left uncut, pristine in its hairiness -- perhaps to confound Westerners. At least it confounded me!

After about an hour, delicacies were brought around on small trays by lovely young waitresses. By this time the guests were becoming impatient to see the bride; they were ready to get on with the ceremony.

In the meantime, Mrs. Wu had arrived with the Wu children. She greeted everybody and then checked with Ciro's manager that everything was in readiness for the ceremony. The children enjoyed themselves and ate everything offered. The girl was well turned out in a handsome red silk Chinese-style dress and the boys in blue Western style suits with shirts and ties.

Finally the bride arrived. More accurately, she made a grand entrance, seated high in an enclosed colorful cedar sedan chair borne by four coolies. The chair had a traditionally ferocious looking dragon design (though denoting beneficience in the Chinese tradition) carved into the wood and was painted in gold, red and blue colors. Attached to it were an assortment of bells and ornaments tinkling gently.

We squinted and peered in vain to see the bride's face because she was not only hidden behind large glass windows, she wore sunglasses! We could tell she wore an elaborate and colorful crown-like headdress, but her hidden face, I was told, was a Chinese tradition.

Her wedding dress was made of a rich red silk with brocaded gold flowers, but while she was seated in the cedar chair, one could not see the style. A bevy of bridesmaids, also wearing sunglasses, accompanied the procession. They too wore elaborate crowns and dresses, intentionally like the bride's, because of a tradition that if the groom was confused about which girl was the bride, it was a good omen for the success of the marriage. And so her bridesmaids all looked identical to the bride.

The guests assembled in the hall where the ceremony would take place and sat down on uncomfortable wooden benches. (Mr. Wu was not a Buddhist, but a Christian, of what denomination I do not remember. I do remember that he considered this religion helpful in increasing his status in life. Since Christians do not embrace plural marriages, the person officiating at the ceremony must have been some kind of civil official, but that I do not remember either.)

Mr. Wu appeared in a dark business suit, white shirt and blue tie, looking prosperous as usual. His face was all smiles as he greeted his guests, shaking hands and saying he was glad we could come. The person officiating entered and the ceremony was about to begin. Mr. Wu faced the official who started to speak in Chinese; I had no idea what he was saying. The bride remained seated in the cedar chair in the back of the room, guarded by her bridesmaids. When the official motioned that he was ready for the bride, Mr.Wu walked to the rear of the hall to fetch her.

147

He opened a small gate in the front of the bride's elevated sedan chair and helped her descend to the floor; she took his arm and together they proceeded down the center aisle, the bridesmaids following along quite formally, until they reached the minister. During this procession, a female singer began a typical Chinese sing-song, which to me, has always sounded like a cross between high-pitch keening and a 12-tone scale played randomly on an untuned lyre.

The official asked the couple to exchange rings and hold each other's hands. He then spoke a bit more and the ceremony ended. Everybody crowded around to congratulate the couple and the whole scene turned into a melee. Mrs. Wu (#1) did her best to direct the crowd to the next room where large round tables were set up for a sit-down dinner.

Moving with the tidal flow of people into the next room, I sat down at the first available table, there being no arranged seating. Friends and relatives jockied for position, sometimes successfully, to sit together. Each table was set with the same number and sort of bowls and chopsticks, as well as soup spoons, and without any tablecloths. There was no head table, either, and Mr. Wu sat with his bride among the guests. Mrs. Wu (#1) and her three children sat with the grandparents.

Soon waiters placed large bowls of soup in the middle of each table, and the eldest person at the table ladled it into the small bowls. I tentatively tried the shark fin soup and found it tasty. Next came steaming rice which was put into the same bowls, followed by a beautifully decorated sweet-sour fish on a platter.

Now the fun really began. Everybody had their chopsticks at the ready, but nobody would start to pick the fish apart. Each person pointed politely to the next one to start first. Of course, there were European counterparts to this type of exaggerated politeness; they were similarly not devoid of their own particular humorous aspects, such as the French with their comic routine about who goes first, Alphonse or Gaston?

148

Finally, the oldest person reached for a piece of fish. Then everybody followed. The fish was also tasty and I liked the sweet-sour preparation. The next course was chicken, which again was brought to the center of the table for each to take pieces and place them on the rice bowl, mixing sauces into the rice and then eating it all together. I passed on the 1,000-year-old eggs, considered a major national delicacy, but not by me. As far as I was concerned they tasted just like what they were -- rotten eggs. Some of the other delicacies I did eat, blissfully ignorant of what they were. Sweet-sour pork was another dish that my palate approved. Quantities of lobster and shrimp were placed on the table. Soon the shells, claws and skeletons took up the rest of the remaining space on the table. I found it quite messy; I had more than a little difficulty getting used to using my handkerchief to wipe my greasy fingers, and napkins not being available. I tried to ignore everyone around me spitting into brass spittoons and cleaning noses with their fingers.

After the guests had eaten steadily for three hours, desserts were finally served -- sweet cakes and pastry as well as more rice, which nobody touched, because it would have meant that one was still hungry, and to be polite, there had to be at least a pretense that one had eaten to the point of bursting. And still the hot tea was being poured!

After the meal was over, I stood around for awhile to see if anything further of interest was going to happen, but the guests had started to trickle out and the bridal party was nowhere to be seen. I slowly pedalled home, too full and too tired to return as quickly as I'd arrived. What an extraordinary day it had been.

****

On Monday morning I headed straight to the Shanghai Iron Works. Nosy young man that I was, I was curious to see what new living arrangements Mr. Wu had set up to accommodate his two wives.

149

Mr. Wu invited me into his office, and my enthusiasm for how marvelous the wedding was pleased him. Without any prompting on my part, he volunteered the juicy information that his new bride, Number Two wife, had a bedroom door marked with a "2." It was next to bedroom Number One. He also said that although Number One wife would ride in the car, he had bought Number Two wife a shiny black, brand new rickshaw. Number One wife would continue the care of the children and the household; Number Two wife was there for "fun."

Mr. Wu was all smiles and I thought this might be a propitious moment to bring up some private business I'd been percolating on for some time.

I had noticed that sales of electric calculators sold by Jardine Matheson under the name of Marchant had fallen off to practically nothing because electricity was increasingly unavailable. I told Mr. Wu that I knew of a mechanical design for a calculator that used a hand crank, and that a market for mechanical calculators might be ready to be tapped. Would Mr. Wu be interested in a joint venture with me to manufacture such an item?

He would indeed be interested, provided that I found the capital to purchase raw materials and pay labor costs. I had an idea for that challenge, too. Through one of my father's patients, I had briefly met a wealthy Chinese lady, the concubine of the British Health Commissioner. (The Commissioner had been my father's patient since my father's arrival in Shanghai.) It was common knowledge that he had a wife in England, but it was also believed that he would never return to Britain -- and no one thought it was the charms of Shanghai that would keep him. But the lady was said to have plenty of business pull on her own account, even without the Health Commissioner.

I went to see the lady, whose name was Miss Chen, and she listened carefully to my proposition for a partnership. As I outlined it, I would be responsible for the design and manufacture of a modern, streamlined, mechanical calculator that operated without electricity, and she would be responsible for the finance of its manufacture and marketing. After a brief discussion, she agreed enthusiastically to my proposal.

Given her many connections to Shanghai business people, she assured me it would be easy to sell these practical alternatives to electric calculators, and she would have her lawyer draw up a contract between us. Being young, naive and trusting, as well as very eager to start the business, I signed the contract without engaging my own lawyer. Big mistake. I learned an important lesson, albeit the hard way.

We agreed that our new venture would be called the *China Calculator Company*. I designed a logo with three C's in a circle, and Miss Chen had stationery printed in English and Chinese listing the two of us as directors, as well as business cards printed in English on one side and in Chinese on the other.

I also received a small, square bamboo block with my name appearing as "Lees" (not Riess, because the Chinese seem unable to say the letter "R" and my name was changed to Lees to accommodate our potential Chinese clients). Lees was carved into the bamboo in low relief in squarish-looking Chinese characters. This personal stamp was required in order to do any banking transactions, since a western signature would not be honored. If a Chinese businessman did not have such a stamp called a "chop," he used his thumb print for all official business. A chop worked very much the way a rubber stamp worked. The business end would be moistened by rolling it over an ink pad, then pressed onto the check.

Miss Chen quickly located office space that could be used for the China Calculator Company in a high-rise office building downtown.

With the small amount of operating funds she provided, I went to Peking Road and purchased a second-hand German-made mechanical calculator. I took it to the Shanghai Iron Works and disassembled it completely. It was a simple design. One main shaft had 13 round, brass plates with ten slots milled on to them, each slot holding a single key. A lever plate pulled out a single key when it moved a notch.

151

When a single turn of the handle was made, the number "1" would appear in a slot in the cover. Adding a group of numbers was achieved by turning the handle clockwise and subtractions by turning counterclockwise. A bottom carriage was moved to the left to obtain multiplication and division results, which could be read in another slot on the lower carriage. These horizontal slots were punched into the black sheet metal cover and the black rubber wheels had white numbers engraved on them.

Since Mr. Wu and I wanted to mass produce the parts, which required interchangeability, I began to prepare detailed drawings of each moveable part as well as assembly drawings which had close tolerances. This kind of assembly line production was unheard of in China at the time.

It meant that jigs and fixtures had to be made for the various machine tools. Patterns had to be made for the cast iron frame and brass drum parts; these had to be cast themselves. I also designed a streamlined cover mold to form a shiny, attractive metal cover.

It took me four long months of preparation to do the preliminary design work; during the same period, Mr. Wu and I placed purchase orders for the various materials needed. The most difficult item for us to find was Swedish steel; it was needed to punch out a progressive die that contained the special tooth shapes for the brass wheels. Each one required hardening and grinding.

We finally located a small quantity of flat spring steel which we could use as a substitute for the Swedish steel, which we never found. We also needed milled racks for transporting the calculator carriage horizontally. Modern looking levers with hard rubber handles had to be machined to clear number wheels in three locations. I also designed a slotted number plate to indicate the lever position for each brass wheel.

Finally, I set up a production flow plan and we began to manufacture the many parts we required. The work would be done at the Shanghai Iron Works which had the equipment we required. Gears were cut, shafts were machined, sheet metal parts punched, and handles were sent out for plating. A list of materials was checked for the completeness of all parts of the machine.

When every item was deemed ready for assembly (all parts inspected for quality), we were ready to assemble our first prototype calculator. The teeth were fitted into the slots, and the lever plate applied to pull out the teeth. The carriage was assembled with all number wheels and fitted onto the guide rack. We then tested adding numbers by setting a lever and making one turn of the handle. This in turn moved the number wheel, and a ratchet stopped it at the correct location.

The machine worked! We were elated, even though a few minor adjustments had to be made before the shiny cover could be put on. A name plate with serial number "1" was riveted on the back of the machine, which I then took proudly to Miss Chen's office in the International Settlement. She was properly impressed when she tried the calculator and saw how accurate it was and how smoothly it functioned.

She immediately picked up the phone and made an appointment to see her first prospect, a vice president of the Shanghai Hong Kong Bank, a good friend of hers. I was invited to go along, and on the way over Miss Chen explained that the bank had originally been part of the British-owned Hong Kong-Shanghai Bank headquartered in Hong Kong, but the war had changed all that.

At the bank we were ushered into a large office with a very high ceiling where the distinguished vice president greeted us politely. We sat, drank tea, and chatted. The bank officer spoke fluent English and after the obligatory small talk, he asked for a demonstration of our mechanical calculator. He liked what he saw, and expressed delight at the prospect of being able to replace the bank's idle electric calculators. He asked the price, then bade his secretary to summon the Bank's purchasing agent to his office.

The young man was shown in, and while he was still standing, the vice president dictated the order in Chinese.

Though I knew only a smattering of "pidgin Chinese," I understood that an order for five mechanical calculators had just been placed. I tried (probably unsuccessfuly) not to look jubilant.

It then being nearly five o'clock, Miss Chen asked the vice president to join us for tea at the Palace Hotel. He accepted, and the three of us walked one short block down the Bund to the hotel. Despite the war, the Palace Hotel was still crowded; except, instead of Europeans, the throng of guests in its lobby and lounges were primarily Japanese gentlemen, some in western suits, some in uniform.

A Chinese hostess ushered us to a small, marble table and the three of us sat down in comfortable arm chairs. We were served the usual hot, green tea in a tall glass and ordered elegant delicacies from the pastry cart. A pianist was playing soft music while we had a conversation about the current state of banking in China. (I was reveling in my new role of "entrepreneur.")

The bank official spoke in a low voice, telling us about his daily problems with the instructions he received from the Nanking Government. As I've already mentioned, the national banking system was then controlled by the Chinese puppet government in Nanking. Central Reserve bank notes were printed without any gold backing or the backing of any other precious metal. Mr. T. V. Sung, a brother of Madame Chang Kai-shek, was the finance minister. The implication was that, from his perspective, he did not find this an ideal situation.

We talked for almost an hour and a half. Finally, the Vice President thanked Miss Chen for the tea, we thanked him for the order (he needn't know it was the first), and he departed.

After the Vice President left, I walked Miss Chen back to her office; on the way she told me to produce the five calculators at once, which she would finance, as agreed. She asked how long it would take but I couldn't answer because I had to consult with Mr. Wu. I retrieved my bicycle, then peddled home in high good humor. Our first order was in hand!

The next morning I phoned Mr. Wu about the order and asked for an estimated completion date for the first five calculators; then we discussed production of not five, but ten machines, optimistically anticipating more orders. He said he needed to check on material deliveries before giving me a realistic delivery time, and would call me back soon.

If I had learned anything at all about Chinese behavior since I'd been in Shanghai, I'd learned that Chinese promises were unreliable to put it most kindly. Mr. Wu's included. After countless calls back and forth, but mostly forth, four days later I finally squeezed a commitment out of him. He said he could produce and deliver the calculators to the customer in 2 1/2 months, "give or take." I groaned silently. It would be "give" for sure.

When I told Miss Chen the estimated delivery date, I could hear the disappointment in her voice; she protested that the date was unacceptably too far in the future (which is what I thought as well), and asked us to try for earlier delivery. Nevertheless she did pass on that estimated delivery date to the bank's vice president.

I visited the plant every week to follow up on the progress. When one week went by without any orders for materials being placed, I decided to take responsibility and personally follow up on all orders. Even after the materials finally arrived, production did not start right away. Castings could have been cast immediately, but that did not happen, either.

"Minsu," said Mr. Wu. Production would begin tomorrow, but tomorrow never seemed to arrive. I insisted that the machining of parts begin at once, otherwise the bank would be waiting for its order to this day.

It actually took three and a half months to get the five calculators assembled. After some adjustments, the final tests were satisfactory, and Mr. Wu delivered the calculators to Miss Chen. Since paperwork was not issued to me, I did not know that he actually delivered more than the five machines. Paper or no paper, I suppose I should have known what was going on

155

anyway, but as I have mentioned, I was still quite young, naive, and inexperienced in business.

So this was how our first bookkeeping problem arose, but of course, the problem involved a little more than bookkeeping. Miss Chen had delivered five machines to the bank as per their purchase order, but she also sold the additional machines that Mr. Wu shipped to her without my knowledge. They simply vanished, and when I inquired, neither she nor anybody else seemed to know anything about them.

After this scenario repeated itself again and again, with me out of the loop, and as Ms. Chen continued to make sales to more banks, I finally sought out the advice of a lawyer, who looked at the one-sided contract and said, "It is very easy to protect your interests before you sign a contract, but almost impossible afterward." I have never forgotten that comment in any dealings throughout my subsequent business career.

The lawyer wrote some strong letters to Miss Chen to remind her of her implicit responsibilities to me as her partner, but he told me privately he doubted that the letters would change the way she was handling things. He explained that filing a lawsuit was also problematic, since virtually all cases in Shanghai were eventually settled out of court, because the entire court system and all the judges were quite corrupt.

He recommended that I try to carry on the best I could, even knowing that Miss Chen would not keep correct books. Although this was hard to swallow, I took his advice and continued to do my best to manufacture quality calculators.

We received many, many orders from banks, since they needed to replace their electric calculators with our manual models, but I was never sure of the total numbers. I more than suspected that a lower quantity appeared on the purchase order than was actually delivered, since Miss Chen would make deals with the purchasing agent and Mr. Wu and the three of them would share the profits. She kept telling me that business in China was conducted quite differently than it was in Europe, and that the success of our business depended on her knowledge of how business was conducted in China.

The situation grew ever worse. Eventually she informed me that our profits had fallen drastically and opened her account books to me, showing that we were losing money. She then asked me to invest my personal funds in the company to pull us out of our cash-flow problem, but I refused. Shortly after that, the company was liquidated, and I was grateful that my first learning experience in business had not turned out to be even more painful than it actually was.

Mr. Wu acted as though he did not know anything about the larger shipments, and I accepted what he said, so our relationship went on as usual.

****

As the war waged on leisure time became harder and harder for this young bachelor to fill. The movie houses ran out of foreign films and showed only Chinese (sing-song) films -- not exactly my glass of tea. (The Chinese speak in very high pitched tones and to my ear, sound like falsetto singing.) The Race Course had ceased operating after the Pacific War started, and the endless garden parties organized by various Jardine managers became less lavish and more subdued as the war progressed. In addition, the number of competitors involved in intra-company tennis tournaments fell off dramatically.

In less than a year after the Japanese occupation, gasoline became practically unobtainable, so taxis and buses converted their carburetors to burn wood, and special blowers were installed inside the trunk areas to start cars. It was a bizarre sight to see buses loaded with wood on their roofs. Stalled cars and buses became a daily occurrence, as engines repeatedly became clogged with charcoal residues and had to be disassembled for cleaning.

Jardine was finally compelled to give up automobiles altogether for bicycles. My luxurious days of being chauffeured around came to an abrupt end. I became expert at navigating a bike through heavy rickshaw traffic in all kinds of weather.

Except for Japanese officials, nobody had gas to run cars. There was one exception. Mr. Wu's shiny green 1937 Mercury seemed always to have plenty of gas. On one of my bicycle visits to the Shanghai Iron Works, I was surprised to see not one but two 1937 Mercury cars in the factory's driveway. I asked Mr. Wu how he could operate two cars since there were no spare parts for repairs, and no gas for civilians anywhere in Shanghai. He grinned and explained that he scavenged spare parts from one Mercury to repair the other.

As far as gas was concerned, he had removed the back seat of the operating car and installed a large oil drum (which served as a jumbo gas tank) in its place, and connected the oil drum to the regular gas tank. Using this system, he said he never ran out of gas while out driving. When I pressed him to reveal his source of gas, he just laughed. He never did tell me.

From time to time, I noticed another car parked in front of our headquarters, a large, late-model, shiny black Mercedes Benz with a swastika in a gold metal frame. This vehicle belonged to Jardine's very own German brew master.

One of Jardine's divisions was a large brewery that operated under the name of "Ewo," which in Chinese meant "Jardine." During the Japanese occupation, this was the only remaining operating brewery in Shanghai. The Japanese loved this beer, and made sure that the German "Braumeister" had enough gasoline for his Mercedes.

The beer was served in the countless bars along the waterfront in Hongkew. The whole area was a kind of "semi-official" Red Light District. The area was always bright and colorful with plenty of neon lights and sexily-clad streetwalkers. Waterfront bars were packed with prostitutes of all races and nationalities, including expensive blondes from Europe, highly prized by the Japanese. These prostitutes were highly paid and lived in the best apartments in the city.

Interspersed between the bars in Hongkew were lower-class brothels whose exteriors resembled storefronts with large plate glass windows. Customers would walk past each front window, look inside where girls (primarily Chinese) sat on display in a semi-circle; customers would select girls by simply pointing at them, and then disappear with them up a staircase to the private rooms.

****

February 18, 1943, was a dreadfully fateful day. Under pressure from the German government, the Japanese Navy established a ghetto in Hongkew for so-called "victims of Hitler in Shanghai." Hongkew, the most scabrous section of Shanghai was notorious for its disgusting smells of decaying fish, rancid garbage, factory smoke, raw sewage and unwashed bodies. The ghetto order excluded Ashkenazic Jews, mostly from Russia, who had settled in China prior to 1937.

Various euphemisms described the intended residents of the ghetto, but everyone knew that the beneficiaries of this largesse bestowed by Hitler's Asian partners were destined to be Jewish refugees. Ultimately 16,000 middle-European Jews were crowded into this very small district (originally inhabited primarily by the poorest Chinese). Hongkew had the additional stigma of having a huge modern prison in the middle of the area -- built by the British well before the arrival of the Japanese.

The news came to all foreigners in the form of a widely disseminated proclamation that as of May 18, 1943 stateless refugees were to restrict both their residence and place of business to a designated area within the Hongkew district. My valid German passport kept me from being directly affected by the edict, but I realized with a heavy heart that my parents were not so lucky. Since they were considered "stateless" because of their expired German passports, they were obliged to comply with the decree, and accordingly, forced to begin preparations to relocate without delay.

159

They had to find both living quarters as well as a place for the dental practice -- all within the boundaries of the specified area. By now their funds, and the number of suitable houses available, were limited; their task was difficult to say the least.

The small pool of possible houses was owned mostly by middle-class Chinese families who had fallen on hard times both as a result of the world-wide depression and the Japanese invasion of China.

After several trips into Hongkew, my parents (with me going along on these unhappy junkets) finally found a single, large upstairs room in an old two-story, poorly constructed house. Access to most houses in Hongkew was obtained by entering a development of houses from the main street through high iron gates, which led to a narrow road within the gates called a "lane." The house in which my parents' future quarters were situated was approximately halfway down one such lane.

A small entrance to the house led into a small open-air courtyard, where a single sink with only cold running water was located. A narrow staircase led up to the second floor room in which both the dental office and my parents' living quarters would be set up. The large room contained a single over-sized window which looked out onto a modest, well-groomed Japanese-style garden and a beautiful house across the way in which a Japanese admiral lived.

Access to running water in the open courtyard one flight below my father's proposed dental office did his practice no good whatsoever, so my father managed somehow to negotiate with the help of a bi-lingual Chinese with the Chinese landlord, who did not speak English, to tap a cold water pipe off from the pipe in the courtyard and have it brought upstairs to the dental office in which a private sink would be installed. In addition, my father wanted the room divided by a window wall and a door. The landlord agreed to this also. The front part of the room would be the dental office and the rear part, living quarters.

Almost none of the houses in Hongkew had bathrooms or toilets, and the one found by my parents was no exception.

160

Therefore, a bit of research was needed to ascertain where the nearest public toilets were located. We discovered that a displaced-persons camp, sardonically called "Heim" (which means "home" in German as well as Yiddish) was located within walking distance, three blocks away. My parents and I walked to the camp, looked around a bit and spoke to some of the occupants. It turned out that this place had the toilet facilities Mutti and Pappi would be using until the war ended.

The camp housed several thousand stateless refugees (mostly Jewish) who lived in large barracks that served as dormitories. None of the occupants had a private room, but each barrack contained a large bathroom and separate toilet facilities for men and women. The camp also boasted a makeshift hospital operated by doctors who were themselves refugees.

The camp had a huge kitchen where meals were prepared for internees as well as other stateless refugees who lived outside the boundary of "Heim," but could not afford to buy their own food; they showed up twice a day at the camp with their pots to collect their meager rations.

The people we spoke to had lived in the camp for some time, and painted a very grim picture of life in this ghetto. All seemed exhausted and depressed, and the truth is my parents and I became quite depressed talking to them; afterwards we tried to comfort one another by expressing the belief that one day all this would come to an end when the Allies won the war. Nobody knew when that day would come, but hope kept us going.

That night we returned to the International Settlement from our house-hunting expedition in a very sad mood. How luxurious my parents' apartment seemed to our eyes now, by comparison with what we'd just seen, and how professional the dental office looked in comparison to what they would have in their newly found quarters in the ghetto. We felt more than dejected.

The process of leaving the International Settlement was not without complications. To get permission from his current landlord to move out, my father had to make arrangements to remove the office partitions, the sink and the water pipes that he

161

had installed when he moved in. Unfortunately, he could not remove his telephones and re-install them in the new location. With the current equipment shortage, the Hongkew ghetto was not highly placed on the Japanese priority list! (The unexplained disappearance of the telephone he left disconnected in the office became a traumatic incident for my parents not too many weeks later.)

Finally, preparations were complete, a moving company was contacted, and an appointment made. On May 15 two plain wooden carts, each with a truck axle and two rubber tires, appeared bright and early at the apartment.

Coolies in straw sandals and torn trousers carried my parents' furniture and belongings out to the street and loaded the carts. It was a woeful sight indeed. Here were our elegant family heirlooms, which had safely made the long journey from Germany to China, now in dire peril on the much shorter trip to the ghetto.

Three coolies per cart started to pull the heavy load along Bubblingwell Road, chanting "Hi-Ha," the rhythm of the chant evidently a help to their team effort. My parents followed along in two separate rickshaws, hoping their presence would intimidate any of the omnipresent Shanghai thieves from making off with their possessions in broad daylight (a not uncommon occurrence about which we had been warned).

It took the coolies an hour to reach the Garden Bridge. As usual, the Navy sentry on duty at the checkpoint asked for identification papers and checked the loaded carts. After a meticulous inspection he signed a transfer form. It took another 45 minutes rolling along Broadway in Hongkew to reach the new address on Paoting Road.

The unloading procedure proved more difficult than the loading, because the stairway to the second landing of the new apartment was extremely steep and narrow; Hongkew shanties had not been designed for massive German furniture.

Later that same day, two more carts arrived at the freight entrance of my father's dental office to collect his equipment and office contents. When all the equipment, partitions, pipes, laboratory sinks, and furniture were tied onto the two carts, my father quietly took a last long look at his spacious, sunny office before closing the door on life as he'd known it.

Looking forward to the immediate future, he had to be wondering how in the world all this equipment would fit into the new location and how he was going to arrange appointments with patients without the use of a telephone.

The sentry at the Garden Bridge gawked unabashedly at the little convoy of coolies, carts, and my father following along behind in a rickshaw. I am sure the guard had never seen such equipment in Shanghai before. Chinese dentists practiced their trade on street corners. Their "offices" were all alike: a wooden chair, an umbrella covering the chair, and extracted teeth strung up all around the umbrella to advertise how much experience the dentist had.

My father had difficulty explaining the nature of the equipment to the Japanese sentry, who of course spoke only Japanese, but finally there was a glimmer of comprehension signified by a toothy Japanese smile, and the signing of transfer papers that indicated the equipment was being moved into Hongkew at the express request of the Japanese High Command.

When the carts reached Paoting Road, and their contents unloaded and brought upstairs, it was all too clear that the one large room was far too small for all the equipment and furniture. My parents worked all night, trying first one arrangement, then another, to determine how best to set up the office, and which pieces to keep and which to sell.

While this was going on, a carpenter and a plumber installed the necessary partition and sink, and another handyman covered the uneven floor with fresh linoleum. The next challenge was to find posts strong enough to hold the dental drill on its pulley contraption, but even that was eventually worked out. My father did the honors in hooking up the blue light over the dental chair. It was that same light not being on back in Berlin that had warned me not to go home on Crystal Night. Finally, the office looked as if it could receive patients. The living quarters were another story. Everything was crammed into the back half of the room, with not a square inch in which to move around. The beds took most of the space, and it was obvious that most of the tables and chairs had to be sold. Only a little round table with a marble top that was formerly in the smoking room in Berlin remained. As far as cooking facilities were concerned, a few shelves with pots and a cabinet underneath with a kerosene burner on it became the kitchen.

It was a pathetic scene, but my father, ever the optimist, tried to put a good face on the situation for my mother's sake. He told her that since he no longer had to travel to his office, he could always be together with her. How wonderful this would be! He smiled encouragingly and tenderly took my mother into his arms. He was a wonderful man. She almost smiled through her tears.

She very shortly recovered her composure, and began to enter into the mainstream of the Hongkew community, helping wherever she could, and took a particular interest in the children of the ghetto.

After word that a dentist had moved into Hongkew, patients started to trickle in to my father's office. Appointments were made in person or on the streets, since everybody lived within walking distance. My father's practice in the ghetto was a far cry from his first Shanghai office. All his new patients were refugees with little or no money. Even so, my father would fix their teeth knowing that one day they would bring some food or whatever they could in return.

Gradually new friendships were made. Everybody helped everyone else. My parents became part of one big (but not happy) family, the stronger helping the weaker, with an active support group being the core of all organized community activity.

Movie houses were rented in lieu of synagogues in which to observe the high holidays. The Jewish Community set up its own secular and religious court systems and their judges and lawyers settled most cases without interference from the

Japanese or Chinese police officials. The ghetto school system was also run by a committee made up of refugee residents who set up classes in the camps, staffed by eminent teachers and scholars who had fled the Nazi purges.

Sadly, life ended badly in Hongkew for many. They died from the effects of malnutrition, bad sanitation, and lack of proper medical attention, although the sick were pushed through Hongknew in covered white carts (no ambulances existed) to the camp hospital, the source of what scant medical attention was available. More than a few committed suicide, despairing that the dismal life in the ghetto would ever end.

A Jewish cemetery was established, for which there was all too frequently a need. A covered cart being pushed to the cemetery by a Rabbi and members of his flock was a common sight.

But for most of the 16,000 Hongkew refugees, life went on. As long as kerosene was available for stoves, the winters were almost bearable. (Shanghai weather was notorious for the extremes of bitter cold and tropical heat, to say nothing of the plague of insects in the summer.)

Friends would invite others for homemade cake and ersatz coffee, and exchange the latest gossip. Second-hand German books were available in a rental library; even a community newspaper was printed in the ghetto. No matter what their background, or how prestigious their former profession, all of the refugee families looked for ways to provide a service, however menial, that would provide each family with some income, even if a pittance. For example, a hausfrau learned how to repair typewriters, a professional historian sold second and third-hand clothes through the district and a young lad who would someday become Treasurer of the United States hawked sausages in the streets. The ingenuity of the desperate was remarkable.

Small cafes and Viennese restaurants sprang up featuring pastry and mock Wiener Schnitzel and Goulash, dishes improvised by resourceful use of ersatz products. They were

165

remarkably close to the traditional European fare, considering the food shortages. The tables looked appealingly clean and were covered with colorful paper tablecloths. A talented violinist or pianist (who might once have been a famous musician in Vienna) would play soft waltzes and *Lieder von dem Wiener Wald*. Former food processors produced ersatz honey and jam, delivered on pedicycles. Delicatessen stores offered such delicacies as sausages, brown sugar and pickles.

****

The war years passed slowly and I focused on my work. As for entertainment, there was very little except for an occasional movie. Because of my German passport I was allowed to continue living in my apartment with the house staff assigned to me. The Shanghai Iron Works was in the Hongkew area, only 4 blocks away from the ghetto and that enabled me to visit my parents frequently, passing in an out of the ghetto area freely because of my business connection.

I got plenty of exercise during those years. With the limo service gone, bicycling from my apartment to Jardine and to the Shanghai Iron Works on a daily basis kept me in shape. Needless to say, I did not go home every day for lunch, but carried it with me instead.

Because arrangements had been made for my salary to be paid by the Shanghai Iron Works, I continued to be paid throughout the war, even though Jardine was a British company. This enabled me to help my family financially. (I still have the letter from Mr. Wu which states that from November, 1943 to October 31, 1945, I was in charge of the Technical Management of Shanghai Iron Works.)

One memorable occasion took place on my parents 30th wedding anniversary. I invited them to celebrate with me at a ghetto Viennese restaurant, where I presented them with a pair of gold wedding rings, as near like the ones confiscated by the Nazis as I was able to describe to the jeweler who made them. I cannot put in words what pleasure it gave me to be able to do that.

Hans Riess

Shanghai - Part Two

In the spring of 1943, the Japanese navy began to intern selected enemy aliens; by 1944, all British nationals employed by Jardine Matheson and Jardine Engineering Corporation were interned on the island of Pootung, just outside Shanghai. I was the only member of the original pre-war home management left.

With only a skeleton staff, I carried on as best I could. Our capable white-Russian engineers were of enormous help to Mr. Wu in keeping the Shanghai Iron Works going, but it became more and more difficult to get electric power from 7 a.m. to 7 p.m. so the work at the factory was frequently halted and the whole operation seemed on the verge of shutting down permanently.

Mr. Wu was afraid that the Japanese would curtail the availability of electric power completely with no warning. After all, they took no direct benefit from its production. All of us at Jardine, however, had a great interest in keeping the plant alive since somehow our entire output of machine tools found its way to market inside free China. Mr. Wu would never explain to me how this was so, but Mr. Wu assured me that it was true, and knowing how ingenious he could be, I believed him.

As the threat from the Japanese to cut off power to the plant grew, Mr. Wu came up with a scheme that was pure inspiration. Since we could not continue to rely solely on the power the Japanese doled out in increasingly small quantities, he asked me to design a system that would make the factory energy-self-sufficient, regardless of what the Japanese did to interrupt our utilities.

Accordingly, I set to work designing a special two-compartment boiler for burning acetylene. The design was fairly straightforward. A copper pipe directed water drops to the acetylene which produced a gas stored in the boiler. Valves

169

Hans Riess

controlled the gas feed into a special carburetor of the V-8 Ford engine that Mr. Wu had used as a spare for fixing his Mercury.

When the design process neared completion, I solicited the assistance of a Russian engineer to prepare the drawings for the boiler; with his help, it did not take long. Mr. Wu actually beamed when I handed him the completed drawings; he thanked me and the engineer profusely, and ordered his machinists to begin to build the boiler at once; in only one week it was ready. No *minsu minsu minsu* this time!

The Ford V-8 engine was mounted on a cement foundation and fitted with a special pulley next to its clutch. The counterdrive belt was disconnected from the electric motor that normally powered the factory and reconnected to the V-8 pulley. The water connections on the boiler were tightened and the acetylene was loaded manually into each compartment. Mr. Wu placed a young boy in front of the boiler to regulate the flow of water into the first boiler compartment containing the acetylene. Before long, the resultant methane-like gases could be smelled all through the factory.

Mr. Wu then opened the gas valve to the V-8 carburetor and tried to start the engine. After several adjustments, the engine finally began to chug. With the clutch in neutral, the engine gradually warmed up. Everybody stood around watching and wondering how this single automobile engine could possibly drive all the machine tools in the plant.

After about ten minutes of idling the engine in neutral, Mr. Wu was ready to engage the clutch. He carefully moved the clutch lever and as the clutch began to engage, the pulley slowly started to move the belt and drive the countershaft. It may have been "jerry-rigged," and it may have resembled a Rube Goldberg contraption more than it should have, but it worked! In another minute or two, as the rpms of the drive shaft increased, the belts were driving all of the factory's machines at the desired speed.

The workers returned to their lathes, drill presses, planers, boring and milling machines grinning in disbelief that the factory could run without electricity, but they had seen it with their own eyes, hadn't they?

A few months after we had put together that acetylene boiler and Ford engine power generator, as Mr. Wu had foreseen, the Japanese government severely restricted our use of electricity to the point that if Jardine had possessed no back-up power supply, it would have definitely been out of business completely. Instead, all Mr. Wu had to do was obtain a large supply of candles (to light the factory) and we were back in business.

A short time after this, a Japanese delegation visited the factory. They had heard that Jardine's factory was making a lot of noise and they were curious to learn the source. It did not occur to them that we could operate our machines without their electricity.

They requested a tour of the factory; when taken to the heart of the power source, they were puzzled -- why was a small boy sitting on a low stool in front of the boiler? I explained that he was regulating the flow of water and filling the two boiler compartments with acetylene. It took an interval of one-half hour to empty one compartment, and then the water flow was re-directed into the second compartment while the first one was being loaded with acetylene rock. I explained that this method of alternating from one boiler compartment to the other assured an uninterrupted flow of power to the pulleys.

The Japanese naval officer in charge of the delegation spoke briefly with his men, politely saluted, thanked us for the demonstration and the still amazed delegation departed, shaking their heads.

That night Mr. Wu held a big party for everybody who worked in the factory. Special fish dishes were served and Ewo beer flowed freely. Everybody was happy. Once again, their jobs had been saved.

******

In the meantime, my parents had been coping bravely with their diminished lifestyle within the Hongkew Ghetto, or the "Designated Area" as the Japanese euphemistically called it. Coping, that is, until an ominous postcard arrived from the Bureau for Stateless Refugees Affairs regarding an investigation. It demanded the presence at once of Dr. Walter Riess in Mr. Ghoya's office. Shivers of anxiety ran through both of my parents, for Mr. Ghoya's name was anathema throughout the community, and with good reason. I was also quite worried. Mr. Ghoya's manic volatility had made life miserable for a great many ghetto residents, and he seemed to take sadistic pleasure in playing hot and cold with his victims, giving permission for certain dispensations one day, and changing his mind for no reason the next.

The Japanese military had given the responsibility for carrying out all Bureau matters to a former Japanese naval officer named Tsutomu Kubota, who was to reign supreme over the refugees, as head of the Bureau of Stateless Refugee Affairs. He, however, downloaded the job and left his "dirty work," the personal contact with the refugees, to two subordinates, men named Ghoya and Okura. Ghoya was a tiny man with jet black hair, slicked to the back of his head. He was a more than slightly crazed self-styled dictator, and was dubbed with black humor "King of the Jews" by the refugees. Ghoya unabashedly reveled in the title, ignoring the intended ill will and even proudly allowed a photograph of himself to be made in front of a placard bearing his title.

On the fateful Monday morning of my father's command appearance in front of the King, my mother insisted that she accompany my father to the interview. By the time they had arrived at his office, Mr. Ghoya had already worked himself into a frenzy of fury, accusing my father of having sold his office telephone in the International Settlement, which he, he shrieked, property of the Japanese. My father was surprised at the accusation, and insisted repeatedly that he had never in fact sold his telephone. What he had done was to simply leave it behind in the office when he moved.

Since the Japanese found no telephone when they took over the office, Mr. Ghoya screamed that he did not believe my father at all, his shock of thick black hair practically stood on end as he ranted. Exhausted from his tantrum, and since no proof existed that the telephone had indeed been sold by my father after it was removed, Mr. Ghoya, who could on occasion return to the world of the rational, suddenly closed the case. With a rude flip of his hand he dismissed them. My parents returned home extremely shaken by the experience and in a near state of shock.

This was the only bad experience they had with the Japanese Navy while living in the ghetto, but having heard tales of horror from others, they had expected the worst.

There is an old adage that says that human beings can adapt to almost anything, and as far as my parents' life in the ghetto was concerned, this saying proved to be true. By the time my parents had lived in Hongkew for two and a half years, they had become largely innured to its numerous indignities. Hongkew had also changed during that interval. Chusan Road was lined with so many European-style shops and restaurants, it resembled a street in a typical European city; as a matter of fact, the area was called little Vienna.

My parents went out every Saturday night either for a full course dinner or for drinks and coffee and cake. They could usually be found at either the White Horse Inn or the Roof Garden, their two favorite cafes, where they met their many friends.

On Sunday mornings they would go to the Wayside Park, which was located at the edge of the ghetto. Wayside was a well-kept park maintained by the city, which had lovely flowers in the spring. Before their removal to Hongkew, my parents had spent Sunday mornings at Jessfield Park, located at the edge of the International Settlement. But Jessfield was no longer an option, since ghetto residents required a special pass to enter the

173

Settlement. (Ghoya issued such passes as though giving out the gold from his own front teeth.)

My father had such a pass because all foreign doctors and dentists were issued passes by the Japanese forces in the event they themselves had to call on foreign doctors because of an emergency.

Now and then, my father would go into the International Settlement to buy items not available in Hongkew. But like most inhabitants of the ghetto, my mother had no pass and was obliged to restrict her shopping within the boundaries of Hongkew. One day she ventured out to buy a loaf of long French bread; as she left the store (the bread tucked loosely under her arm) a Chinese boy suddenly, from out of nowhere, ran up from behind and grabbed her bread. She tried to snatch it back before he fled, but he was too fast for her.

A Chinese policeman standing nearby saw the whole incident, and chased the boy, catching up with him at the next intersection. Upon being questioned right on the spot, the boy pleaded that extreme hunger drove him to steal the bread, and he had in fact taken a bite of the bread before he was caught. This was reason enough, according to Chinese law, for the policeman to let him go, which is what he did. My mother could well believe the reality of the boy's hunger -- so many in the ghetto were *always* hungry.

On occasion, my father also had experiences that underscored the extraordinary difference between Asian and European ways. My father was well acquainted with their Chinese landlord and his wife. Their baby became ill and had a very high fever. Disdaining any kind of medication, the parents hoped to drive the devil causing the illness out of the baby by banging pots and pans together and causing a terrific din. All night they danced around the baby making this terrible noise. Not too surprisingly, the baby's recovery was not enhanced thereby; as a matter of fact, he only grew worse.

The next day my father pleaded with the parents to allow him to give the child a penicillin injection to save his life, but the

174

parents did not believe in drugs. Illness, they said, came from being possessed by the devil; health was achieved by driving the devil out. They danced around the baby the second night as well, and if anything, made a more terrible noise than before. The following day the baby died. The parents were sad, but moved on, as custom bade them, to the next step, which was to prepare a traditional funeral.

A proper Chinese funeral involved sending the deceased into his next life with many possessions which he would need in his subsequent incarnation. Accordingly, the father bought small models of many things made from colored paper: a paper rickshaw, paper furniture, a complete paper kitchen, and a bundle of fake paper money.

A funeral dinner was arranged for relatives and friends. Tables were set up in the lane outside the entrance to their home. A separate table was set up with candles and incense; it held all the paper items. The dead child was placed in a small coffin on the ground in front of the table with the paper goods. A Buddhist monk prepared the religious symbols on the table for an offering to Buddha. Relatives and friends then picked up pots and covers and danced around the coffin, making as much noise as they could.

The monk then began the religious part of the service. He burned the incense and all the paper goods, signifying the conveyance of all the material goods to the next life. When black smoke rose into the blue sky, the mourners were happy, because they knew the baby was now rich and no longer suffering. The devil had been banished. When the ceremony was over, the assembled party sat down to a large meal, the more sumptuous the better, that lasted several hours.

After dinner, the men and women proceeded to play mah-jongg, a game for those who love gambling, played by matching bamboo tiles on which symbols are engraved. They played for very high stakes. The game finally ended the next morning, and everybody left. The father then took the coffin and brought it to an open field nearby. He placed it on the ground and built a hill of earth and rocks around it and covered the top as well. Because of the area's high water table, burials were always above ground. After the burial, the simple life of the parents continued as before.

****

Summertime was monsoon and typhoon season; the sky poured down such a profusion of rain that the lanes and streets of Hongkew became quickly flooded, since drainage sewers were non-existent. During this season, transportation was limited either to wading ankle-deep through the flooded streets or hopping aboard a rickshaw. In the winter, the same options applied, except one could freeze in the rickshaw (protected only by a flea-infested blanket), or one could walk on one's own steam and get closer to the sights of the homeless, the starving, the diseased, and the already dead.

When families had no money to bury their own family members, the corpses were left on the streets to rot. The unwritten law was that if anybody touched them, they were responsible for the burial costs. I will never forget the horrible sight, when I once walked to my parents' house, I passed a dog gnawing on a dead child's head.

****

The ghetto consisted of some forty square blocks, an area small enough to be strictly controlled. The exits were checked either by Japanese soldiers or the "Pao Chia," the Jewish ghetto auxiliary police. The closest analogue to this group was the *Ordnungs Dienst*, the cadre of Jewish capos that assisted the Nazi guards in controlling Jewish prisoners in the European death camps.

About 3,500 men between 20 and 45 years of age were obliged to serve in the Pao Chia several hours a week. Refusing to serve was not an option. This auxiliary police group was

176

supervised by the Japanese Chief Inspector of the Wayside police station.

Only refugees with occupations needed in the International Settlement were issued special passes (by the infamous Mr. Ghoya) to cross the guarded checkpoints. These passes were issued for a period of three months maximum, and were called seasonal passes, or temporary passes.

Life in the ghetto was not without many other problems as well. Since electricity was strictly rationed, only 15-watt light bulbs could be used for two hours a day. For cooking food, my mother had to use a small Japanese charcoal stove that resembled a flower pot. Charcoal briquettes made from compressed coal dust, ashes, straw, and cinders that had been moistened, compressed by hand, and dried on the pavement were sold on street-corners by Chinese children.

My mother had difficulty starting up a coal fire and keeping it going. She once became ill as a result of the excessive smoke and fumes generated from the burning fuel. She had tried to use a coal fire to help warm up their room during the memorably cold winter of 1943, but found out that an open window was required to vent the fumes. So much for her idea.

The war progressed and life plodded on in Shanghai. The United States Air Force intensified bombing raids covering the Shanghai-Nanking salient. Mysterious sky writing appeared over Shanghai about one hour before each bombing raid, but what it signified I never found out.

When the raids began, explosions were heard all over the city. The local grapevine had it that the U.S. objective was to bomb docks, supply depots, oil tanks and ammunition storage facilities, and that residential areas like Hongkew would not be bombed. This was the same logic that convinced the Japanese to store ammunition inside the ghetto and construct a radio transmitter there as well, in order to help control Japanese naval traffic in coastal shipping lanes.

Unfortunately, an American air raid on July 17, 1945 targeted the Hongkew radio station, and as a consequence many

177

residential houses in the refugee district were destroyed. I was terrified about the safety of my parents and biked as fast as I could out of the International Settlement down Broadway along the docks. Many areas were damaged and I was forced to make several detours.

Wherever I rode, a sickening stench of decay and putrefaction seemed to float above the ground like a terrible miasma. Volunteers were everywhere, wearing surgical masks, digging in the rubble for survivors as well as for the dead. No one can really describe the horror of war, nor can one imagine it without having seen it first hand.

Arriving at Paoting Road, with relief I found my parents' block undamaged, although bombs had fallen just half a block away. Some houses nearby had completely collapsed and other were smoldering from small fires. People were digging in the rubble to rescue people trapped in the debris. Many bodies lying in the street were already covered with white sheets. During that raid, two hundred and fifty people were killed in Hongkew, of which thirty were refugees. Five hundred were wounded and seven hundred refugees were made homeless. Jewish doctors and nurses attended all those in need of help, refugees and Chinese alike, free of charge.

It was quite a different story at the Ward Road Prison, which was opened as a shelter to house the new homeless created by the raids. It was the only well-constructed building in the district. It boasted a hospital with the best of German equipment and a good staff. But neither the Chinese wounded nor any refugees could receive medical treatment until a fee was paid in advance.

Assured that my parents were alive, my next concern was to see if my current girlfriend, Armgardt, and her parents were unharmed. By the time of the raid, I had been dating her for about a year. Armgardt had come from Berlin with her parents at about the same time as my parents had. Her father was a dentist and a good friend of my father's.

At first I was hesitant to approach the house, fearing the worst, for I knew that bombs had hit their block. As I took the corner with my bike, I cautiously sized up the situation. My girlfriend's house with its little roof garden was not damaged, although two buildings to its left were totally destroyed. With a flood of relief I knocked at the front door, and rushed up the stairs. All three of them were standing there with open arms to welcome me -- though only Armgardt gave me a kiss with her hug.

I first got to know Armgardt socially at a music seminar, even though I had met her earlier, because of our fathers' friendship, and I had also seen her at Chinese language classes we both attended. I had simply not looked at her as "girlfriend material." Out of the blue one day I received a little card from her saying that she would like to know me better. She had included in the envelope two tickets for a musical evening in the nicest theater in the ghetto, and asked me to meet her in front of the theater if I cared to join her. Having nothing better to do that evening, and flattered that she had so assertively sought my company, I went.

When I arrived at the theater on the Saturday night she specified, I looked at her with new eyes. I saw a tall, blonde girl with a lovely face and fair complexion, standing at the entrance to the theater, smiling at me. This was Armgardt. She was beautiful, but quite a bit taller than I, which was not surprising to me, since very few people were as short as I was, namely 5'2". Nevertheless, I saw no reason not to enjoy the company of this pretty girl. We chatted for a few minutes outside the theatre before finding our seats, and it turned out that she knew a lot about me, though I knew nothing about her.

The curtain went up at 8 pm and the orchestra played the overture to *The Merry Widow*, a Franz Lehar operetta, one of my favorites. The entire cast was made up of ghetto refugees, many of whom had sung professionally with the Vienna Opera. The principal conductor was a Berliner named Rosenstock, who had been the conductor of the Jewish Cultural Bund. Prior to enactment of the Nurenberg laws he had conducted the Charlottenburger Opera.

179

Armgardt could not have thought of anything more likely to engage my attention than that evening of light-hearted music. The production was superb, and the lighting particularly good. It was truly amazing that in the middle of the war, inside the ghetto, *The Merry Widow* could be staged and performed so professionally.

During intermission, we walked around the entrance area and ran into people one or the other of us knew. She was quite an extremely gregarious extrovert, but between her chattering with others in the audience, I learned a little bit about her. Coincidentally she had lived only two blocks away from us in Berlin. (When I told my father about this, he smiled and said he and Armgardt's father had been friends in Berlin long before they got to Shanghai. Armgardt's father was the president of the dental association in Shanghai.)

After the show, I suggested we go up to the theatre's roof garden for coffee and cake, and Armgardt thought this was a splendid idea. Since other theater-goers had the same idea, we had to wait on line nearly 20 minutes for a table, giving us a chance to get even better acquainted.

We were finally seated at a round table with an umbrella in the center. The whole roof garden was lively and colorful with spotlights directed at an array of flowering plants. A piano player and a violinist played romantic songs from *The Merry Widow*, and for a short time it was easy to forget we were in the ghetto. Finally a waiter came for our order of crunchy *Nussahnen Torte* and espresso coffee. While waiting, we became so deeply involved in a conversation about politics and life in general, we didn't notice how long it was taking for the coffee and cake to arrive. We had become so engrossed in each other, we forgot about everything, even where we were. Armgardt began to touch my hand with hers, her knee gently rubbing against mine. I found I was enjoying her closeness and these small intimacies immensely.

At midnight, Armgardt said she was feeling "a little tired," so I walked her home, only five blocks from the theater. The house had an entrance from the street and a rear entrance from the customary lane. She suggested that we walk to the lane entrance, where she opened the rear door to her house and invited me into the hall. Evidently no longer so tired, she threw her arms around me and kissed me passionately, and I was returning her kisses with equal fervor. After some time and many more kisses, I prudently said good night before something serious happened. I told her that I would see her soon again and reluctantly left.

I walked through the dark lane to the street, then tried to find a rickshaw to take me home. Since it was quite late, not many were around. I started to walk towards the Garden Bridge, and it felt good -- the air was crisp and fresh and my mood upbeat. Suddenly out of nowhere, a rickshaw coolie chirped, "Wanchee rickshaw master?" I told him my destination, he gave me a price, and we began to negotiate as I kept on walking while he followed me. Finally he agreed to accept my original offer, and I jumped in. It took him 45 minutes to get me home, running all the way. To this day, I am amazed at the endurance of all rickshaw coolies.

The next morning at about 10 a.m. my office phone rang and it was Armgardt at the other end inviting me to dinner with her parents at their home for the following evening. I accepted with pleasure. The next evening I arrived with a bouquet of fresh-cut flowers in my hand for her mother. Armgardt met me at the front door and we climbed up the stairs to meet her parents, a pleasant couple about the same age as my parents. Her father offered me a drink, and together we sat down in the living room while Armgardt and her mother prepared the dinner. It was all very *gemütlich*. I didn't realize that things could easily get more serious than I could handle!

Compared to that of my parents, their house was spacious, and from its size one could easily deduce that they were better off than most people living in the ghetto. The dental chair was situated in one room with all the other dental equipment crammed into it; a small waiting room was adjacent to it. A short

181

flight of steps led to the upstairs floor where two bedrooms were located. Additional steps led up to a skylight opening on to a roof garden.

Like my parents, they had brought many pieces of furniture with them from Germany. Her father and I chatted on about my job at Jardine Engineering, and life in wartime Shanghai. Much of this was small talk, but I got the idea that he was sizing me up to see if I were suitable marriage material. Armgardt and her mother had set the table with the finest Rosenthal china and crystal water glasses, sterling silver knives and forks were arranged formally on the white linen table cloth. There was no doubt in my mind that I was the guest of honor. I hadn't seen such finery since I had left Berlin.

Dinner was soon served and we took our places around the table. I sat opposite Armgardt. The meal tasted just like my mother's German home-style cooking and I was an enthusiastic audience. Armgardt's mother was more than usually curious about my position in Shanghai and peppered me with many questions about my job, some of which I felt were a bit intrusive, so I didn't answer them directly or fully. Coffee and biscuits ended the meal.

Armgardt helped her mother clear the table and wash the dishes, then suggested (with a ladylike leer) that I join her on the roof garden where we could be alone. It was a lovely evening; the stars were sparkling, and a full moon illuminated the roof garden. I couldn't have chosen a more romantic setting, if I had designed it myself. We sat down on deck chairs adjacent to one another and relaxed.

I welcomed the respite after the modified grilling by Armgardt's parents over dinner. It wasn't until Armgardt left her chair that the kissing began. As before, she initiated the advance; I not only didn't resist, I reciprocated. She lay down on top of me and after a while I felt myself getting hard. She must have felt it too, since her hand started to rummage around the outside of my trousers. Her skirt had slid up easily allowing my hand to find her warm body underneath her bloomers.

182

As I touched her, I could tell she was becoming quite excited. She skillfully opened my zipper and began to massage my penis, and when she whispered that she wanted to have intercourse, I told her I was concerned that her parents might surprise us suddenly. Armgardt assured me that her parents went to bed early, and we would have complete privacy, so we gave free rein to our youthful passion. Delicacy permits me to say nothing further except, perhaps, that the interlude was all that I expected and more.

Three hours later, we tiptoed down the two flights of stairs to the back door. We kissed good night and I was on my way home, once again trying to find a rickshaw.

On my way home I ruminated about the contrived dinner invitation; while Armgardt wanted sex, it was clear that her parents had marriage in mind. I felt too young for such a commitment, especially just at the start of my career, in the middle of a war we had no way of knowing then when or how it would end. But, I rationalized in the moonlight, since Armgardt offered her company to me, and I enjoyed being with her (she was highly intelligent in addition to being sexually hungry), what could be wrong with playing the dating game?

After this first experience turned out so well, Armgardt wanted to see me constantly; I did my best to slow down the affair by making up excuses not to meet with her every day. I did indeed enjoy her company, but I was not in love. I made it clear to her that I just wanted friendship. Nevertheless, she bought me presents, regularly said that she loved me and, as an additional sales point, (though it didn't carry much weight with me) that her parents liked me a lot. It was clear they would have liked it very much if we had married.

A typical date with Armgardt went like this: she would meet me at the ghetto movie theater, and as soon as the room was dark, she would try to find my penis. We sat through many Chinese films, without understanding a word, not that it mattered! I would touch her body and we would moan, then come, half lying, half sitting in our seats.

183

After walking her home from the movie, taking the lane entrance to her house, she would suggest sex with me standing up in her hallway, and from time to time we did just that. She always assured me that her parents were sound asleep, which I found amusing as it may or may not have been true.

She wanted to please me so much, and since I seemed to please her, the absence of a marriage proposal notwithstanding, I kept seeing her to the very end of my stay in Shanghai.

Meanwhile, her parents tried every ploy to get us to make a marriage commitment, including working on my parents, who were invited to their home for dinner many times. Armgardt made it clear that I was her "intended." On my birthday at a restaurant where she had invited me, she presented me with a small box, hardly able to contain her excitement until I opened it. I slowly unwrapped the package to find a cultured pearl with a sterling silver pin resting on a blue velvet cushion. It was really quite a beautiful tie-pin, which she had made to order at a jeweler's. She spoiled me too much, and I loved every minute of it. But not enough to propose marriage.

Around the same time that April we heard a short-wave radio report (a few ghetto residents had hidden radios) from TASS News Service that the Nazis had suffered great losses of manpower and materiel at the siege of Stalingrad and that the Axis powers were experiencing severe problems in a number of other campaigns. This news encouraged us all to think that soon the war would be over and the allies would emerge victorious. Perhaps soon we would be able to contact our family in Berlin, from whom we had been out of touch since 1941. Tante Lillie's letters had been very cautious, bland to the point of supplying no information at all, though Mutti gathered that money was very tight, and sent food packages from Shanghai. We never knew whether she received them, and after March, 1941, we heard nothing.

In the meantime food shortages and higher prices of coal made life in Shanghai increasingly problematic. When electric power was rationed even further, acetylene lamps took the place of 15 watt bulbs.

The American Joint Distribution Committee, an American relief agency, tried to help the Jewish refugees in Shanghai financially, but money transfers, even though sent through the Red Cross into Shanghai, which was considered a war zone, required the approval of Henry Morgenthau, Jr., Secretary of the Treasury, and thus, were not easily facilitated. It was an approval Morgenthau withheld until well into 1944, since a particular provision of the "Trading with the Enemy Act" had to be amended by the U.S. Congress; only then did money begin to be legally transferred from America to Shanghai via Switzerland. It was not the Japanese who had prohibited these money transfers into Shanghai; it was the U.S. government which had caused the delay.

By April 1944, over 7,000 refugees living in Shanghai had received financial aid from American Jews through the Joint Distribution Committee. By that time, approximately 15,000 Jewish refugees were living in Shanghai, and by June, 1945, about 11,000 were in serious need of financial help. Although my parents were never destitute, they did reach the point of having to sell personal effects to make ends meet. I remember particularly my father going to the street with his handsome wooden coat hangars borne so carefully from Berlin, to be traded for food. As for me, I carried on as usual at Jardine Engineering Corporation, and was never harassed by the Japanese officials.

We heard about D-Day on June 6, 1944, again through the shortwave radios hidden throughout the ghetto, and knew with confidence that the war in Europe would soon be over. That day happened to also be my father's birthday, and we celebrated happily (but quietly.)

The Japanese knew that things were not going well in the Far East and started to replace their stern Navy personnel with more reasonable people. For example, the loathed Mr. Ghoya was replaced by a Mr. Harada, a much more rational administrator of the ghetto community.

185

Germany finally surrendered to the Allies on May 8, 1945, and shortly thereafter, reports of Nazi atrocities committed in Europe began to surface in Shanghai, but they were too monstrous to be believed by anybody. In the two years prior to V-E day, we received no communication from Germany whatsoever, but were sure the reports of gas chambers and crematoria were untrue. We still had no idea of the magnitude of the Holocaust.

In the meantime, American air raids over Shanghai increased in July 1945. During the summer, the rumor mill was working overtime throughout Shanghai. We heard that Russia had entered the Pacific war on the side of America, and that a new breed of devastating bombs had been dropped over Japan the first week in August. Both rumors of course turned out to be true.

An odd incident, still inexplicable to me, occurred the day President Roosevelt died. The Japanese surprisingly seemed to feel a sense of loss, and Japanese imperial flags were temporarily flown at half mast throughout the city.

When the war in the Pacific finally came to an end on August 10, 1945, Allied flags were suddenly raised on some public buildings, such as the Custom House, the Bank of China and the Shanghai-HongKong Bank. There was dancing in the streets, and Europeans and Chinese freely mingled together showing a rare solidarity. The Japanese might have surrendered to the Allies, but they were still very much in control as occupiers of Shanghai. They immediately removed the Allied flags, even though the Japanese Navy had been advised by the Allies to maintain law and order until they arrived.

A day or so after, we found this out when a huge number of B-25's (an airplane aptly nicknamed "the Liberator") flew over Shanghai, dropping leaflets printed in Japanese, Chinese and English, informing the population that the Japanese would be temporarily responsible for maintaining public order. I was amazed at the size of these planes. All I knew of, first hand, were DC-3's, which were very small compared to those that dropped the leaflets.

I was also amazed at the extraordinary self-discipline of the Japanese soldiers who stood stoically, even dispassionately, on the street at major intersections, maintaining public order, knowing that they had lost the war.

The Japanese Navy maintained order until August 22, 1945. The morning of August 23 found them gone; they had totally vanished during the night. On September 3, 1945, two very large planes were seen flying over Shanghai, even bigger than the B-25's. Later that day, I heard a rumor that the large planes (called B-29's) had landed with GIs to help the Chinese Army under Generalissimo Chiang Kai-shek liberate Shanghai.

This rumor was confirmed when I looked out my window and saw an amazing sight of huge American soldiers travelling in open, square-looking vehicles. I found out later that these cars were called "Jeeps" and that they were brought in the B-29 planes. It was hard for me to believe that cars could be transported in planes. We had been completely cut off during the war and had no idea of the technical advances made by the Allies.

Later that afternoon, I walked around Nanking Road and saw a huge crowd gathered in front of the Cathay Hotel. When I inquired, I was told the Hotel was being established as American Military Headquarters.

An American Rescue and Goodwill Mission had also arrived on B-29's, and a delegation from this Mission went across the Garden Bridge to inspect the so-called "designated area." They declared the ghetto officially open and many refugees expressed their joy by dancing in the streets. Signs at various checkpoints surrounding the perimeter of the ghetto were ecstatically torn down by the refugees, and that day I heard many outpourings of thanksgiving in addition to devout hope that Shanghai would return to its former status as an open port.

One of the very biggest surprises for me occurred when I took a walk along Bund and Nanking Roads, and saw giant negroes dressed in the uniforms of U.S. paratroopers strolling along. I stood agape, mouth open in amazement. I had never seen black people before, nor for that matter, had the Chinese. Little children trailed along behind them in delighted curiosity. The GIs wore jumpsuits, heavy boots, and colorful parachute insignias on their shirtsleeves. An American flag with Chinese writing was imprinted on the back of each jumpsuit.

These paratroopers belonged to the Flying Tiger squadron, which had acquired quite a bit of fame, I learned later, as a result of participating in General Doolittle's bombing raid on Tokyo. These first GIs who arrived in Shanghai were so happy that the war was over they basically went wild. They had a lot of money saved up, had not seen a cosmopolitan city for many years, and were ready for some serious recreation. They sang, they danced, they ran in and out of shops, buying everything in sight, and having an absolutely marvelous time. Hordes of curious Chinese children trailed after them.

On the black market, a single U.S. dollar was worth 1,000 Chinese dollars, so these soldiers found themselves instantly wealthy. The black market trade in dollars took place right on the street or in small, so-called "bank stores," which had iron bars above their counters instead of store windows. These stores made it easy and convenient for soldiers to exchange U.S. dollars for Chinese money.

These bank stores had a wonderful security system to discourage hold-ups. Not only was the store caged in, but money was not kept on the ground floor. When a clerk shouted a signal, a basket was lowered through a hole in the ceiling; the clerk placed the currency to be changed into the basket, and somebody on the next floor pulled it up and returned the requested currency. The GIs kept the money stores working merrily around the clock.

The Shanghai Chinese were accustomed to well-behaved "foreigners," like British and Italian sailors prior to the war. The GIs made the Chinese modify their concept of foreigners from that point forward. The American service men ran after double car trams, got a grip of the hand rail, and leaped on board like gymnasts. In high spirits they would push the Chinese driver

188

aside and actually take the wooden knob of the steel crank and drive the streetcar themselves. This rowdy behavior provoked a negative reaction from the normally reserved Shanghai populace, but a typical Chinese passenger was helpless to modify the GI's behavior in any way; he did not speak English and he certainly couldn't challenge him physically, because the GI was far too large and strong.

It did not take very long for the Americans to lose all the respect the Chinese had had for Westerners that the British had enjoyed before the war. Unhappily, the Americans also offended the British, their closest ally, by suggesting that the British should return Hong Kong to Chinese sovereignty as a good will gesture roughly fifty years before the British 99-year lease expired. The British did not take kindly to this unsolicited advice.

Popularity for the Americans was also waning, for they were only too eager to help the cause of Chiang Kai-shek. From the perspective of those of us who lived there, the Chiang Kai-shek regime seemed corrupt from the very beginning, and nepotism was rife. For example, Mme. Chiang Kai-shek, who controlled all licensing, refused the Kodak company a license to do business; instead, she imported their film herself via her office in San Francisco. Perhaps the most reprehensible act was secretly advising their friends and supporters to buy gold before the Finance Minister (Mme. Chiang Kai-shek's brother, T.V. Sung) devalued the Chinese currency by 50%.

General George Marshall arrived in person at the Cathay Hotel to negotiate a relief plan for China similar to the Marshall Plan that was already successfully working in Europe. As his delegation checked into the hotel, preparing to occupy an entire floor, they discovered that all their luggage was stolen. The Chinese left in charge of the luggage were questioned, but claimed complete ignorance of what had happened, which was not surprising. The Chinese would never admit to any wrong doing where foreigners were involved, and that went double for Americans.

189

My boss, Mr. Morrison, and all the other British, American and other Allies were soon released from the internment camp. Private life and commercial life in the International Settlement and in the French sector slowly returned to normal. One day Mr. Morrison simply re-materialized in his office, ready to take charge again. He immediately called me into his office and I was overjoyed to welcome him back. We could hardly stop grinning, shaking hands and slapping each other's back.

I commented on how surprised I was about how good he looked, considering his long internment. He was a little thinner, but seemed to be in good health. We talked about his internment for a while, which, except for the severe lack of food, he said was not too bad. He was eager to hear my status report and to get back to work. I gave him a full de-briefing; I told him how Mr. Wu and I had managed to manufacture machine tools all through the war, tools that had gone to Chungking. He was very pleased at the report, and asked me to carry on with Mr. Wu as before, except that I was no longer the "Big Boss." I would once again be reporting to Mr. Morrison. We both grinned. I told him it was a happy demotion for me, and I meant it.

Mr. Morrison told me he would contact London for instructions about whether or not to continue manufacturing machine tools or perhaps return to the production of windows; he would let me know if changes were necessary. He planned to recommend that London approve the continued manufacture of machine tools. Working together, we set up a new production schedule for the factory, and invited Mr. Wu to discuss it with us the next day in Mr. Morrison's office.

Mr. Wu arrived at promptly 10 a.m. the next morning, and I was already seated in Mr. Morrison's office. Mr. Wu put his arms around Mr. Morrison and was full of smiles. Mr. Morrison congratulated him for his good work during the war and told him that we would continue as before. Mr. Wu expressed delight at the arrangement, then we all turned to review the production schedule. As we worked, a boy entered the office carrying a tray with hot green tea and biscuits as if Mr. Morrison had never left;

it was a strange feeling to pick up where we had stopped when he was first interned, two and a half years earlier, but that is what we did.

Hans Riess

Shanghai - Part Three

Life in Shanghai took on several new twists after the occupation ended, and I noted them all with my usual curiosity and attention to detail.

It took some little time after the war's end for automobiles to make their reappearance in the streets, since gasoline was still largely unavailable. Those who had functioning bicycles counted themselves lucky. They were still in great demand. Fairly soon after the war ended, a brisk trade opened up between Shanghai and Canadian ports that involved the importing of Canadian-made bicycles, nylon stockings, and plastic goods. Generally speaking, everything the Canadians brought in sold like ricecakes, and the traders made a fortune. Going the other way, traders found the export of cultured pearls a lucrative and fast moving business, and they were constantly on the lookout for whatever else of value they could export, such as used cameras of the departing Japanese, used gold watches, silk fabrics and jade.

I quickly got rid of my heavy, Chinese-made bike, and replaced it with a lightweight Canadian import. Daily I lugged it one flight up to my office at Jardine, since it was not safe to leave even locked bikes on the street. As if by magic, the streets were once again congested with rickshaws, bicycles and streetcars and impenetrable phalanxes of pedestrians on the sidewalks and in the streets. Post-war Shanghai was once again a bustling city of commerce, as it had been before the war, except now the black market had more or less replaced the legitimate marketplace, and vendors did a brisk business in goods like GI rations, Parker 51 fountain pens, and Swiss watches. These items could by no means be considered necessities, but that did not prevent the eager Chinese from letting necessities take care of themselves, preferring the status that ownership of these prized luxuries bestowed on them.

193

Hans Riess

I myself was not above the lure of these particular items, though not interested in them for "face" or status. Always interested in photography, I bought a German Zeiss camera from a Japanese naval officer just before he was repatriated to Japan. (I still have it today.) I also bought a gold chronometer watch from someone who had brought it into Shanghai from Switzerland, and last but not least, I purchased a handsome Parker 51 fountain pen on the black market.

Most of the black-market goods were sold on the sidewalks near prosperous offices on busy Nanking Road. Coming out of my office at lunchtime one day, and hearing a click near my ear, I reached reflexively to my breast pocket to feel if my Parker 51 fountain pen was still there. It was not. I was so outraged that a pickpocket had lifted my pen, for which I had paid the monumental sum of $25 American dollars, I could feel my adrenalin spurting like Vesuvius. Without thinking, I grabbed the Chinese man walking just in front of me by the neck. He had been walking with two companions, but after I grabbed the one, the two other men kept on walking without even turning their heads, abandoning their friend to my wrath. They knew the jig was up.

I had grabbed the man at an intersection just as the traffic light changed to red. When I loudly and forcibly demanded (in my pidgin Chinese) the return of my pen, he widened his eyes in fake innocence. "No have," he protested, but I could tell he was lying.

I forced him to empty his pockets, which he did, and showed me that the pen was not there. Still I did not believe him, since I had heard that pickpockets had double pockets. My anger reached a boil, and I threatened to drag him to the traffic policeman by the nape of his neck and have him arrested if he did not return my pen. My seemingly uncontrollable rage and this threat of arrest did the job. He quickly reached into a hidden pocket of his baggy pants and produced my nice black pen with the silver cap. I snatched it from his hand, then let him go.

I still have that pen today.

194

Shortly after the war, as the GIs brought in American cigarettes, these too were traded on the black market. Chinese children could be seen collecting cigarette butts and discarded cigarette packs all day long. They would then sit on the tiered entrance steps outside large office buildings, carefully sorting out butts and cigarette packages. They would take loose tobacco from butts and with new cigarette paper, roll "new" cigarettes, which they artfully repackaged into the now neatened packs that had been discarded. When the packages were re-sealed, they looked almost like new American cigarettes to the uninitiated. They were sold either in cartons or as individual packs on the black market. This had to be the most labor-intensive black-marketeering enterprise in all of Shanghai.

A short time after the incident with the pickpocket, I was the victim of another post-war "irregular" business that I also did not find at all amusing. One day as I was bicycling from the Shanghai Iron Works in Hongkew into the International Settlement, I crossed a small but very high bridge and noticed a lot of youngsters shouting and running towards me. By the time that I realized what was going on, I had two flat tires. When I got off my bike, several young boys competed like the dickens with each other to get me as their customer to repair my tires which they themselves had flattened by throwing small nails on the street and which I had run over with my bike.

The boys came totally prepared either to repair tires or to make a fast getaway from the police. They carried their tools in wooden boxes with carrying straps, so they could make a quick disappearance if policemen would try to catch them. They targeted foreigners primarily, and since the cards were stacked against the rider of any bike unlucky enough to make their acquaintance (how else would he be able to continue his journey?), the young brigands were quite adept in negotiating a deal to fix the damage they themselves caused -- a splendid Chinese example of street crime masquerading as business.

I have to admit that the price they charged -- (400 CRB dollars) -- was ridiculously low, since the rate of exchange was

195

4000 Chinese Reserve Bank dollars to U.S. $1. To give an idea of the buying power of the U.S. dollar, a rickshaw coolie would pull a person through the entire International Settlement -- a trip that normally took about an hour -- for a fare of one U.S. dime. That was the going rate, and they would have starved if foreigners had not supported their trade. Price structures began to change quickly, though, because the GIs would pay the rickshaw coolie one U.S. dollar instead of the dime, which made it difficult for their regular clientele to maintain the original rate.

The lowliest member of the Chinese caste system believed that any oriental could outsmart any European or American and when it came to GIs, they weren't far wrong. A case in point was another street scene. Chinese boys were selling canaries in small individual bird cages made of bamboo. The GIs were told that the canaries were great singers, but given the horrendous street noise, they were too frightened to sing. The gullible GIs believed the boys and bought the canaries for one U.S. dollar each.

When they arrived back at their billets with their purchases, closer examination revealed that they had actually purchased sparrows painted yellow, not canaries at all. This was Shanghai at its commercial best during the day.

The city operated differently at night. Adult crime replaced child crime. Neon lights in variegated bright colors painted a beautiful picture along Nanking and Bubblingwell Roads. Pretty girls lined up on every downtown block with their "mothers." The mothers negotiated the price with passersby for their "daughters." Every type of sexual pleasure was offered for ready cash. The least expensive was French without intercourse. The next was the missionary position, then 69, and finally, anal intercourse, the most expensive. This last activity cost the grand amount of CRB $4,000, or U.S. $1.00, but this was still quite inexpensive as foreign prices went. It was not cheap for the average Chinese, however, since the cost of renting a basic no-frills room for a month was about U.S. $2.00.

Nightclubs employing taxi girls did tremendous business, since ships with American and British sailors began to arrive often and regularly. American sailors drank a lot of beer, and when they felt really good, would sit at tables with taxi girls on their laps. Sometimes they would have condoms hanging out of their shirt pockets. If they had a little too much to drink, they might blow up a condom, like a little party balloon, fasten a knot at the end so that the air could not escape, and let the balloon fly above the dancers. This was harmless amusement for the sailors, but they would sometimes get so drunk they got into drunken brawls with each other or with other patrons, breaking chairs, tables, bottles, anything that came to hand. The Shore Police who regularly patrolled the bars and nightclubs usually arrived on the scene too late to prevent the damage.

Without any advance hoopla, the Wing-On department store suddenly re-opened and in no time at all was back in full swing. This was where American officers would buy their Chinese girlfriends gifts, dine at the Wing-On restaurant (in the same building as the store), then wind up spending the night in the adjacent Wing-On Hotel. One stop shopping, Shanghai style.

As gasoline gradually became more available, the provisional Shanghai city government converted surplus army trucks into municipal buses. Wooden benches were built for passengers in the van section of the bus, and the truck bed enclosed with a wooden roof and windows. A step ladder attached to the back of the truck allowed able-bodied passengers to climb on and off. These vehicles were not suitable for the halt, the lame or the elderly. The converted trucks were painted green and. nicknamed "Chicken boxes" by the locals. This ingenious mode of transport finally disappeared when city-wide mass transit began to normalize.

German-speaking refugees had the luxury of being able to read a German-Jewish newspaper called *Aufbau* (meaning "Reconstruction"). The paper was printed in New York City and air-mailed to Shanghai every week. Readers used the personal columns to advertise for information about the whereabouts of friends and relatives dislocated by the Holocaust. Other personal

197

ads sought companionship or marriage. The paper also reported general-interest news about Palestine and the United States.

Within a few short months after the war, virtually all the foreign nationals returned to their respective homes and offices they occupied before the occupation. For a while it seemed that Shanghai would revert to the same life-style as before the war, but that was not to be. The era of British colonialism in Asia was over. The changing political and economic realities in mainland China would soon change Shanghai forever.

Many "demobbed" (British slang for demobilized) GIs would return to China as civilian traders, importing American goods and exporting silk, cultured pearls, and jade. As they became more and more knowledgeable, they started to form trading companies. A few were excellent businessmen. How the market in used cars was manipulated is illustrative.

Officially, the quota for the import of American cars was limited to 500 per year, but in 1946, there were easily several thousand shiny De Sotos tooling around Shanghai. Used De Soto cars were purchased by traders in America, then shipped via American President Line ships on which they were passengers, and finally re-sold in Shanghai. As the traders boarded ship in San Francisco, they claimed they were transporting their own cars to China so they could drive around the country as tourists.

The cars were off-loaded from the ship onto sampans in the river outside the harbor a day or so before the ship was due in Shanghai Harbor, though a single De Soto could barely fit on one of these tiny boats. The following day the liner would dock as if nothing unusual had occurred, and custom officials would not find a single car on board. These cars were sold on the black market for U.S. $15,000 to rich Chinese bankers and compradores, who paid with gold bars. Everyone associated with this business was well paid for his efforts: The American captain and his crew, who anchored the ship outside the harbor to facilitate off-loading; the British and Chinese custom officials who closed their eyes to the remarkable disappearing act; the motor vehicle department which issued the license plates; and

198

the former GIs who had purchased and then sold the cars. They made the most of all.

It was interesting to observe how the corrupt Chinese government (which the foreign community supported) operated. The rumors of corruption were plentiful. It was well known that Madame Chiang was the power behind her husband's "throne." It was she who controlled all import licenses. Kodak had applied to the Kuomintang government for a license to import its film into China, but an import license was denied. It was rumored that Madame Chiang then set up an export company in San Francisco and imported the film into China herself.

Even more egregious was the tale of her brother, T.V. Sung, the finance minister, who devalued the Chinese Central Reserve Bank dollar by about 50%, but only after he and his friends and relatives had "gone long" on gold bars; by converting their cash to gold, they literally doubled their net worth. Somehow for me, this tale has always literally personified the very essence of corruption.

Over a short period of time, general conditions worsened severely, and although we still supported the regime, it was gradually becoming clearer and clearer that almost any other form of government, including a Communist dictatorship would be better for China than the Kuomintang. As I indicated earlier, the black market was so pervasive it had practically replaced the normal market.

The foreign community became increasingly concerned with the growing chaos in Shanghai. Except for the utilities, which were again run by foreign companies such as AT & T, all other municipal services -- public transportation, law enforcement, garbage collection, etc. -- were rapidly going downhill. Various reports on the radio suggested that although Western governments tried to exercise influence on Chiang Kai-shek to urge the reform of his corrupt regime, and the granting of more rights to his citizens, their efforts met with no success.

One day, about a year after the end of the Pacific war Mr. Morrison called me into his office and advised me that the

British consulate had heard that the Kuomintang regime would soon be replaced by a Communist regime. It was just a matter of time, he said, and suggested that I speak to an officer in the British Consulate (located in the same building as Jardine) about the possibility of my returning to England. I did have a conversation with him and learned that England was in dreadful shape, like the rest of Europe. This dampened whatever enthusiasm I had (which wasn't much to begin with) for returning to England. Mr. Morrison himself, as well as most of the other British in Shanghai were also thinking it was time to return to England, or perhaps move to Hong Kong, for the same reason -- Communism would soon overtake Shanghai.

The United States was where I wanted to go, the one country undamaged by the war. I loved the idea of its tradition of freedom and I persuaded my parents we could all get into the U.S. under its German quota. However, since the American Consulate in Shanghai had not yet re-opened for business, we couldn't make an application to immigrate. Seeking to speed things I wrote to the State Department in Washington, requesting registration numbers for my parents and me.

Three months later the good news came: registration numbers had been recorded for all three of us and we would be contacted by the Shanghai Consul as soon as that consulate was re-opened. When that would be, they didn't say.

It was by now the end of 1946, and the prospect of facing yet another bleak winter in Shanghai would have been daunting except that with the war over, the availability of electricity and gas was plentiful. Offices and houses were comfortably warm again, and there were plenty of activities to entertain restless bachelors like me. Hotels and restaurants were once more serving first rate food, and the city's sole American bakery had all the good breads, rolls and cookies as before the war.

The "good life" in Shanghai notwithstanding, I became preoccupied with thoughts of life in the United States. Professionally, I was a capable mechanical engineer with Chinese experience, but I knew I should have American experience under my belt before reaching the U.S. All too aware of the lack; I became obsessed with finding a way to fill the void in my training. Jardine was willing to pay my passage to any place in the world, but could be of no help in placing me with an American firm in Shanghai. As a matter of fact, all of the foreign companies in Shanghai had initiated a hiring freeze. Gaining practical experience with an American firm in Shanghai seemed totally blocked.

Research being a way of life with me, I headed to the office of the U.S. Information Agency and scoured the trade magazines in its reading room. An ad in *Machine Design* about the International Correspondence School in Scranton, Pennsylvania, offering a course called "Machine Design and Jigs and Fixtures" caught my eye. The tuition for this course was U.S. $150, for which ICS would furnish lesson books and instructions on how to mail papers for grading. If I could successfully complete the 12-month course and pass the final examination, I would receive a diploma from an American school -- all accomplished through the mail. My salvation was at hand! I mailed the reply card back to America, and waited impatiently for the response, which came by air-mail in only two weeks; by return mail I sent my bank check for tuition and my filled out questionnaire to Scranton, Pennsylvania, the home of my first American University.

In February, 1946, two neatly sealed packages arrived with labels from ICS, and I tore them open. Inside were orange-covered books: Some dealt with design, some with dimensions and calculations, some with materials, and others with presentation of drawings. I was sure I was on the right track to learn the American system.

After starting the book on design, I saw that a book called *Machinery Handbook* would be necessary. I found a copy in an English language book store, a very thick volume, but amazingly inexpensive. When I examined the book more closely, I saw that the paper was coarse and acidic and the printing so small one almost needed a magnifying glass. It was, however, the only edition available. I subsequently discovered that it was a pirated edition; no royalties were ever paid to authors or publishers for any books sold in Shanghai. The Chinese had no respect for copyrights; indeed, their court system seemed to have no concept of intellectual property rights. (To a certain extent, this problem still exists to this day.) Patents were also useless in China, since the rights of patent holders were regularly trampled upon as a matter of common practice, and civil cases against infringement rarely went to court at all.

In any event, pirated or not, I diligently studied the different subjects of the course one after the other, and mailed papers and other completed assignments back to Scranton for grading on a monthly basis. My goal was to have the diploma by the time the American Consulate re-opened in Shanghai, which I hoped would be sometime before the end of 1946. ICS did its part and returned graded papers to me quite rapidly.

In a second-hand store on Peking Road, I bought a little red portable typewriter when I signed up for the ICS course but it did not have a carrying case or handle to carry it around. Once again Mr. Wu's ingenuity came to the rescue. He had a brass case with a steel handle made for me at the Shanghai Iron Works. The typewriter helped not only with my papers for ICS, but with all of my correspondence, which steadily increased as we prepared to leave Shanghai for America.

The studies were demanding, but it was invaluable for me to learn the differences between European and American systems of machine tool design and manufacture, of drafting length, width, and height, as well as computing tolerances. I earned mostly A's on my papers, which not only delighted me, but gave me confidence that I could "make it" in the States.

My winter nights were occupied with study and a little with Armgardt. I was spared the pain of actually breaking up with Armgardt, since she was already in Australia. Sometime during the summer of 1946, her father made arrangements for the entire family to emigrate to Melbourne where he planned to resume his practice of dentistry. His arrangements included Armgardt, who wanted me to come with them, but I told her as gently as possible that I could not. She was depressed for a while, but the excitement of going to a new continent alleviated her sadness. We saw each other less frequently, but I respected her and never forgot the difficult war years, made easier for me by her company. We remained friends until she left.

When I slept, I dreamed about America. I completed the course in December as scheduled, and received my diploma the following month, January, 1947. I was very proud of myself, and wanted to celebrate my good news so I invited my parents out to dinner at the Palace Hotel restaurant, which had once again regained its reputation as the fanciest restaurant in Shanghai.

It was good to sit in the elegant dining room again; it brought back many memories, most of them happy ones. Over dinner, while discussing what the future might bring us in America, we finally focused on the issue of my father's dental practice and American licensing requirements for foreign dentists. My father had heard that German credentials were not recognized in the U.S., and therefore he would have to spend some (perhaps considerable) time as a student in an American university before he could become qualified to practice. He was dubious. At his age, (he was in his fifties by now) he was concerned that he couldn't cut the mustard. (We'd heard that "cut the mustard" was an American expression.) Though I tried to get more information for him about certification, I heard nothing before we left for America. Nevertheless, my parents could see that I was determined to leave for the United States, and that sealed their decision to come too. They did not want an ocean between us ever again.

Earlier in the year, we had made contact with my cousin Werner. He had been living in Buenos Aires before the war, and my parents had his address there. However, someone in Argentina forwarded the information that he was now living in Wilmington, Delaware, and sent us his address as well.

Werner had had his own struggles just before and during the war. He had left Berlin in 1934 with his musician friend Alfred Knopf (who later became a conductor) to study music in

203

Munich. After a year they had gone on to Paris to study music, and earned money taking pictures of tourists on ski slopes. When his friend left Paris to return to his home in the United States, Werner went to Buenos Aires where he worked in a photo lab for a while, but sometime during the war, Alfred was able to get Werner into the United States via Cuba. Again, Werner was able to support himself working in a photo lab, and best of all, became an American citizen.

Werner responded at once to our letter and wrote my father that he would do anything to help us to come to the States. He offered to provide an affidavit in support of our application attesting to our good character, the fact that he was a relative who knew us well and swearing that he would help us financially if necessary. He was sure all this would carry weight in our favor with the immigration authorities.

My parents felt that Werner (who had been emotionally closer to Pappi than to his own father) would indeed do what he could to help us. They knew he was heartbroken because of his failure to get his parents out of Germany in time. Guilt for being alive when his parents were not had been gnawing at him for years. Only later would we know the details of how and where Tante Lillie and Uncle Kurt died.

The tragedy was that Uncle Kurt had given money to a friend in Berlin to spirit out of Germany somehow to Werner in America (who at that point did not have any money of his own). This money was intended to get necessary affidavits from someone in the United States for Kurt and Lillie. Werner never received the money, and very soon it was too late anyhow.

Werner's initial help came to us in a very practical form -- fabric. My father and I had worn our suits to shreds during the war and we needed new ones. It was near impossible to buy suits in Shanghai right after the war, because fabric was in short supply. Werner sent us "previously owned" suits which an excellent Chinese tailor turned into handsome new-looking suits for my father and me.

As the situation in Shanghai worsened, I wrote to my cousin urgently to hurry up those affidavits he'd promised. Finally he had good news: Werner had succeeded in obtaining the financial backing of the husband of his wife's best friend to support his own affidavits. This well-to-do benefactor was the president of Kohner's Toy factory, and his financial backing would be more than sufficient to validate affidavits for the three of us. He wrote that he was working very hard to make sure nothing would go wrong this time around. We could tell from his letters that his parents' fate was ever on his mind.

The day finally came when Werner told us the affidavits had been approved by the proper authorities in Washington and were ready to be forwarded to us when needed. The American Consulate in Shanghai opened for business at the beginning of 1947, and I was Johnny-on-the-spot. I contacted them immediately, by telephone, mentioning our registration numbers issued from Washington. The consulate made an appointment to see all three of us in early February, 1947 to review our immigration application. The speed with which we obtained an appointment astonished us and all our friends. The only earlier exit from Shanghai by any of our friends had been Armgardt and her family to Australia in 1946.

The American consulate was located in the Hamilton Building, a modest skyscraper located only two blocks away from the American Express building where my father began his first Shanghai dental practice. When we arrived for our appointment, the receptionist told us we would be interviewed by Vice Consul Elizabeth L. Engdahl. We sat down on a comfortable brown leather sofa and waited nervously, like actors before an audition. After about 20 minutes, a secretary ushered us into the presence of the Vice Consul, an attractive middle-aged lady who was polite, but very businesslike.

The original affidavit Werner sent to Washington had been forwarded to her and she now examined it in front of us. She asked probing questions and was particularly interested in our place of birth and our relatives, which she duly recorded in our

205

dossiers. After the interview she sent us to the consulate's medical department for a complete physical examination and X-rays, saying that if we were in good health and did not have any proscribed diseases which excluded immigrants, she saw no reason why our visa would be delayed more than a month. Our next appointment was made for March 13, 1947.

Up early that fateful morning, we were excited and hopeful that our visa would be granted that day. Though we arrived at the consulate a half hour ahead of time, we were preceded by a long line of anxious refugees queued up outside the building, hoping to receive registration numbers. How glad I was to have written the State Department in Washington the year before to obtain those precious numbers!

For this important occasion, my father and I wore our "new" suits and my mother wore her new dress, all courtesy of Werner. While we waited for the Vice Consul to see us, several well-dressed Chinese, talking loudly in Chinese and carrying briefcases, emerged from the elevator. Instead of sitting quietly and waiting, they paced back and forth nervously. From what we could gather, these were parents who wanted to send their children to the United States on student visas.

It was common knowledge that the U.S. had no Chinese quota of any kind and we wondered how these parents would fare. We didn't have long to wonder. A consular employee soon appeared, greeted the Chinese, then whispered something we couldn't hear; the Chinese promptly opened their briefcases and removed several packages of American hundred dollar bills, neatly tied together by a string, openly handing the money over to the consulate employee. The mystery was solved, and I cynically observed to myself, "money does buy happiness."

Shortly thereafter we were ushered into the Vice Consul's office, who asked each of us separately to raise our right hand and swear that the information we had provided was true; she then asked us to sign separate documents, to which our respective photographs were attached, then bound the documents together with a red ribbon and affixed a U.S. consular seal to the cover page. Finally she stood, shook our hands, congratulated each of us and handed us our official visas.

She warned, however, that the visas were valid for one month only, which meant that we had to reach America no later than April 13. We dashed to the offices of the American President Line, found a vessel sailing on March 20 that would reach the United States before the visas expired and immediately booked passage.

I wrote Werner at once, informing him of the date of our arrival; he responded by return mail with alarming information: As soon as I stepped off the ship, I would be drafted into the U.S. Army, since, under the Selective Service Act, even as an immigrant I was eligible until my 26th birthday. I would not be 26 until April 10. He therefore strongly advised us to request a one month extension on our visa, giving as a reason our need for additional time to liquidate our assets in Shanghai.

My parents and I agreed to follow his advice, so accordingly, I called for an immediate appointment with the Vice Consul. Two days later the three of us found ourselves sitting once more in Elizabeth L. Engdahl's office. She listened politely to my request for a visa extension, using Werner's "liquidating assets" as the reason.

She examined the papers a few moments, then with a big grin, saying, "I give you just one month's extension, do not come back again." She obviously knew that I would be 27 by that time, understanding the real reason for my request without saying a word. We thanked her profusely and rushed again to the offices of the American President Line, where we exchanged our tickets and booked passage on a ship departing Shanghai April 14, arriving in San Francisco May 2, 1947.

Relieved at the outcome of the morning meeting, at that point my parents and I parted company. I walked the short five blocks to my office at Jardine and called Mr. Morrison immediately to ask to see him as soon as he was free. Thirty minutes later I entered Mr. Morrison's office, and as usual, he offered me a seat on his comfortable couch and rang for the ritual hot tea and biscuits.

Mr. Morrison had anticipated my resignation and departure from Shanghai; he had been extremely helpful in planning my exit from Jardine Engineering Corporation. Now he reminded me that two-thirds of my salary for six years was waiting safely for me at the Bank of England in London, and that as promised before, he would assist me in any way he could. I told him my departure date, and he reinforced the rightness of my choice to go to the United States.

Before we got down to Jardine business he first called in one of his new young assistants, a Mr. McDonald, who would be my replacement. We made plans for me to introduce this gentleman to Mr. Wu at the Shanghai Iron Works the following day.

At 9 a.m. the next morning, Mr. McDonald and I took off in the new company car, an Austin with a chauffeur (just like the good old days) and arrived to find Mr. Wu standing outside to greet us. It was a sunny March day, almost too nice to walk inside, and I had a moment of nostalgia, thinking about my own first day on the job, meeting Mr. Wu, with him waiting outside to welcome me, followed by the hot tea served almost immediately. After a reasonable amount of small talk, Mr. Wu suggested we take Mr. McDonald on a tour of the plant. The only substantive change in the factory since the Japanese left was that instead of the Ford engine, an electric motor once again turned the pulley and belt, driving the overhead pulley to each machine.

After a go-through of the pattern shop, foundry and machine shop, we returned to Mr. Wu's office to discuss my plans for leaving Shanghai and a schedule of transferring or winding up my work in the company.

Just before we left, Mr. Wu called in his young son and asked if he would be interested in my Canadian bicycle, since it wasn't going to the States with me. The boy's eyes lit up. It was a major honor to possess a bike once owned by a foreigner. Then a small discussion ensued. Mr. Wu would only accept the bike if he could pay the full price of US $50. I insisted that he not pay anything, he was a friend. It ended with me accepting the proffered $50, after I realized he would lose face if I did not.

His son timidly asked if I would sell my little red typewriter to him as well, but I told him that I couldn't part with it, and that newer and better models than mine were now available in Shanghai (though I knew he wanted mine for the prestige factor.)

As we returned to Jardine, and Mr. McDonald and I discussed the transfer of responsibilities in greater detail, I felt satisfied that I was leaving things in good order, well under control, with no loose ends.

My impatience to be on my way to the United States was reaching a new level. I tried to visualize what being an American was all about, and how I could prepare for it; because I had no real information, my thoughts were more daydreams than reality. I had read somewhere that cars were an important part of American life, and so my dream was to purchase one as soon as possible. Dream on I might, but I was also pragmatic. I had never driven a car; therefore this deficiency must be remedied at once, I decided, so I called a driving school and made an appointment. I couldn't wait to get behind the wheel.

Two days later, the instructor picked me up at home, and after some brief instruction on "theory," I started to drive along a quiet street. His car had a manual transmission which required shifting gears, and it took me some time to get a feel for the clutch engagement. At first the mechanical brakes were also difficult for me to operate, but eventually I got the hang of it. Steering the car was the easiest part of the lesson. After an hour, the instructor drove me home in heavy traffic and we made another appointment.

After five practical driving lessons, the instructor proclaimed me ready to pass a driving test for a license in the States. That was all I wanted. I was now ready to be an American.

Meanwhile, my parents were busy with preparations to leave Shanghai. My father sold all of the furniture in his dental office, plus the large wardrobe, chairs, and tables. My task was easier; I just had my old clothes to sort, Shanghai worn-outs soon to be replaced with brand new American fashion.

Two weeks prior to departure, my mother and I joined forces for a shopping foray in the International Settlement. We could take so little in the way of cash out of the country, it seemed wise to spend what we had before we left.

We went first to the cruise wear department of Whiteaway, Laidlaw, the British department store. How odd it felt, but exciting, to buy bathing suits and sport shirts after the grim war years. In a few hours, fatigued by non-stop shopping, I suggested afternoon tea on the new restaurant-boat docked along the Bund only two blocks away from the department store. We sat at a table overlooking the harbor; Mutti had always loved being near the water.

It felt like old times in Berlin as we sipped coffee and savored eclairs, as the water danced and flickered in the late afternoon sun. Was it nostalgia for our old life mixed with trepidation about the new that made us both a little sad that afternoon? We spoke wistfully for a long time, recalling, sometimes with laughter, sometimes with tears, the events that had brought us to that day. Late in the day as my mother tried to light a cigarette, the wind on the terrace extinguished her match. After several unsuccessful tries, she burned her finger. Suddenly, we both knew our day together was over. Her burn was painful and I brought her down to the street, found a rickshaw to take her home, and set off on foot in the opposite direction toward my apartment. It had been a bittersweet day.

****

Our last event was the festive farewell party my parents threw for themselves in their Hongkew apartment the day before departure and to which they invited all their friends, who poured in with homemade cakes and desserts. As they wished us well, many shared the news that they would also try to go to the

United States. Everybody had plans in the hopper to leave China soon.

I will never forget the morning of our departure. My parents' best friends, the Blumbergs, came to my parents' house to help with the hand luggage. We had called for a large De Soto taxi and when it arrived all five of us crowded in for the last Riess trip along Chusan Road through Hongkew to our ship, the *General Meigs.*

We were to sail on a 25,000 ton former troop carrier the American President Line had converted to a passenger liner, relying on it to get normal passenger traffic going again. The ship was to stop at Hong Kong, Kobe, Yokohama, and Honolulu, reaching San Francisco after 16 days at sea.

The wharf where the *General Meigs* was docked was not more than 15 minutes away. As we drove down Broadway, we could already see the huge ship with its two tall smokestack chimneys in the distance. Large blue eagles were painted on a white background, and the rest of the smokestack was painted red. Our hearts beat faster; we were finally leaving the war years behind.

The wharf itself was a muddy area with a broken cement super-structure, and we teetered across a path covered by rickety bamboo flooring in order to reach the gangway. We happily waved our tickets in the direction of the purser, who examined them and invited us aboard. (The Blumbergs, with temporary boarding passes, were allowed on board too.) We climbed steps and walked along decks until we finally found two large dormitories, one for men, the other for women.

The wartime sleeping arrangements for troops -- row after row of vertical bunks, one on top of the other, with just enough space to climb in -- were still in place. With only 1,500 passengers booked on this voyage, just the lowest and highest bunks were assigned. The three middle bunks in each vertical tier of five were folded up.

My father and I took our hand luggage and disappeared into the men's dormitory. Coming in from the bright sunshine, it seemed inordinately dark inside and I got a quick impression of a seemingly endless row of hanging bunks connected by chains. A sailor helped us to find our bunk numbers. My father took the lower and I took the upper bunk. The ventilation in the dormitory was pretty poor, but the sailor assured us that once we were underway, the air would circulate and it would be better (and it was.) Leaving the hand luggage on our bunks, we rejoined the Blumbergs and my mother, who reported that her quarters were no better than ours.

We wanted to find a public lounge where we could visit with the Blumbergs until departure but learned that the only public room on board was the cafeteria. We opted instead to sit on deck, but deck chairs on a former troop ship were non-existent so we perched on packing material we found nearby. I was sure of one thing. The *General Meigs* was not the *Haruna Maru*.

I sat quietly while conversation swirled about me, caught up in my own thoughts. I felt a touch of sadness leaving Shanghai after almost six and a half years. I had learned a great deal professionally, and had more memorable experiences than I could possibly have foretold; I had enjoyed working for Jardine, Matheson, especially in the beginning before Pearl Harbor. Now, the world was a vastly different place from the way it was in 1940. Life in China was more uncertain than ever. A strong, Chinese Communist movement had developed. "China for the Chinese"-- without foreign influence -- was its xenophobic motto of the day. I already knew too much about racial hatred from life in Berlin, so I was not questioning the wisdom of leaving the Far East, only indulging a moment of nostalgia.

Once more I was sailing into the unknown; this time, the unknown was the United States of America, a land long reputed to be a land of freedom and opportunity, and historically, a haven for refugees. But the only American I knew was my cousin in New York. And I did not have a job. Those were the negatives. On the positive side, I was young, intelligent, and educated; surely it wouldn't be hard to find a job. Surely my father could again pick up his dental practice. Life could be

212

wonderful for us in America. All my fears and hopes swirled together through my mind as I looked at the Shanghai skyline for the last time.

While we chatted with the Blumbergs, more and more refugees boarded the ship, many of whom we knew. By two that afternoon everybody was on board, and the public address system announced that visitors should leave the ship; we would sail in one-half hour. We bid the Blumbergs a mixed happy-sad farewell, but with every expectation of seeing them again when they arrived in the United States, soon to join relatives in Denver.

As the visitors left the *General Meigs*, we leaned over the ship's railing to watch our friends as long as we could. They carefully threaded their way along the unstable bamboo walk until they left the muddy wharf, frequently turning around to wave to us.

Finally the ship's deep bass foghorn blew three times, signalling coolies on the wharf to withdraw the gangways and then the heavy mooring lines; only then did the tug boats begin to slowly pull the ship away from the pier and into the Whangpoo River. The yellowish, muddy water of the Whangpoo was not a pleasant sight.

Sampans and junks filled the water around the ship by the hundreds, their brown sails visible everywhere, weighed down with entire families living on them. This was our last impression of Shanghai as the skyline slowly grew tiny and finally disappeared. Soon the tugboats left the *General Meigs* and we sailed down the Whangpoo River to the sea under our own power.

We walked around the various decks exploring, and found a canteen and a barber shop. We were told that the cafeteria was on one of the lower decks, but so far we hadn't found it. Somewhat later my father and I returned to the dormitory to unpack, but since we found no storage space, we wisely gave up on the idea of unpacking at all.

213

We located the bathroom, on the same deck as the dormitory; it consisted of a long row of urinals on one side, and an even longer row of open toilet stalls on the other side. Adjacent to the toilets was another room that had a row of showers opposite a row of sinks. No doubt this was a far cry from a typical peacetime passenger ship on the American President Line, but it was the only civilian transportation between China and the United States available at the time. Who cared? We were on the way to a new life.

At 6:30 p.m., loudspeakers throughout the ship announced dinner. When we finally reached the cafeteria several decks below, a long line of passengers moving at a snail's pace was already waiting at the entrance. Finally inside, we were handed stainless steel trays with partitions. We helped ourselves to silverware and waited some more. The line moved slowly along a glass counter laden with steaming trays of food. Behind the counter, white-garbed kitchen helpers dished up meat, vegetables, potatoes and gravy on each tray as best they could; service was sloppy but practical. At the end of the line, we helped ourselves to coffee and on wobbly legs (the ship was already rolling) bore our trays to the nearest long table.

We sat on the backless benches and helped ourselves to paper napkins pried from odd-looking containers we had never seen before. Another novelty for us was to find sugar on each table housed in a glass jar with a screwed-on metal top with a hole in the middle for pouring. The fare was hot, filling, moderately palatable, and I for one was grateful for it. As we ate, we introduced ourselves to other passengers at the same table, their stories, not too surprisingly, very much like our own.

We lined up for breakfast early the next morning, eagerly anticipating the ship's arrival in Hong Kong, downing with gusto ham and eggs, juice and coffee. It was all palatable except for the coffee, so weak it looked like tea. Afterwards, we climbed to the top deck in time to watch our slow entry into the harbor, and the magnificent sight of skyscrapers ringed with high mountains.

We docked at 9:00 a.m. and shortly thereafter went ashore to look around, the treat I had been denied in 1940. The city's similarities to Shanghai were obvious: the Chinese population, the coolies, the boat people, and so on. The presence of London-style double deck buses and traffic policemen made the city look like colonial British Shanghai prior to the war. It gave us a good feeling about Hong Kong.

We couldn't afford to waste our meager resources, the U.S. $10 with which we had each been allowed to emigrate, so we only window-shopped on our tour. I was still mentally thanking my good fortune that two-thirds of six years of Jardine salary was safely deposited in my name at the Bank of England in London. I could visit any British bank in the world and withdraw funds from my account in London. (With the Chinese ruling against taking money out of the country, I had done exactly what they probably wanted me to do: spent everything I had in Shanghai.)

After enjoying a day in Hong Kong, we sailed out of the harbor that night. Standing at the stern, we watched the city slowly recede from sight, the colorful lights of the downtown area still glittering when all other images blurred. We sailed out into the sea of Japan and headed towards Kobe.

In the morning we rose early once again to witness our arrival in Kobe. Kobe harbor had suffered some destruction during the war, and had not yet recovered; there was very little visible activity. I wondered how my ministerial cabin-mate on the *Haruna Maru* had fared during the war, but there was no time and no way to find out.

We remained in Kobe only a few hours, then left for Yokohama, a port which had been a major military port during the war; many buildings were still camouflaged and several bore signs of heavy damage. The dock workers wore military caps and odds and ends of uniforms, and were endlessly cleaning their equipment with rags hanging out of their rear trouser pockets when not polishing something. They went about their business

215

quietly and with extreme care. We remained in port only long enough to unload some cargo.

We settled down now for our longest ocean run, crossing the vast Pacific to Hawaii. The challenge on board was to find some kind of diversion with which to occupy our time, and in this we succeeded. The ship had no swimming pool or gym, but it had a full-fledged smoke-filled gambling casino located on the lowest desk. It was always crowded and bustled with activity. Passengers and crew alike would stand five rows deep around a large, gaming table. The game was dominoes. A single heavy-set Chinese ran the table with one assistant who collected the player's money.

I did not understand the game, but managed to participate anyway. One of the casino's employees said if I would risk betting one US dollar I could win an additional dollar. Risking one-tenth of my entire shipboard resources, I gave him one dollar. In a few minutes, he returned with two dollars and asked if I wanted to try again. I put the original dollar back in my pocket, and gave him the dollar just won to make another wager. Soon he returned with another two dollars, and asked the same question as before. Why not? I thought, as he melted into the crowd again. I kept playing that one dollar until I was ten dollars ahead, at which point, I stopped. Quit while ahead, I thought, not having the soul of a true gambler. Ten dollars was a lot of money in 1947, as I happily found out later in Honolulu.

As the evening progressed, the game became hotter and hotter, with passengers and crew members shouting back and forth, some angrily. Losers would rush out to the barber shop to pawn a valuable, and quickly return to play. I learned it was common knowledge that the barber kept a running account on the crew members who gambled, and who frequently arrived in San Francisco with just the clothes on their backs, having lost everything else, but were nevertheless ready to sign up for the next trip back to Shanghai. It was rumored that the Chinese who operated the casino never left the ship, but that was somewhat hard to believe. The casino did operate 24 hours a day, however.

216

Since I was not a gambler at heart, I was on the lookout for other ways to spend my time. Luckily, the next day I noticed a good-looking girl with dark hair and a lovely figure, leaning over the railing; I could tell she noticed me too. After a while we started to talk. The girl's name was Ruth; she, too, had been a German Jewish refugee, and we had a lot in common to talk about.

Ruth had married a GI in Shanghai, and was on her way to join him in San Francisco. Now she was having trepidations (she hadn't known him long before they married.) Uncertain that she had done the right thing, she didn't want to think about the reason for her journey, but intended to enjoy the trip without letting waves of anxiety overwhelm her. I knew I was a handy distraction.

At the very next meal we started to eat together while my parents ate with their friends, both those they'd known in Hongkew, and those whom they'd just met on board.

I also enjoyed the company of a Marion Freundlich. Like me, she was born in Berlin, and my parents knew her parents from Germany. I found her attractive and very intelligent. She was on her way to New York to live with her aunt in Flushing. Between the two girls, time passed fairly quickly. Marion and I sunbathed, acquired a bit of a tan, exchanged books, and speculated on what America was like. We wondered aloud whether living in California would be more enjoyable than living in New York, an issue which we obviously could not resolve.

Of the two girls, I was far more friendly with Ruth, the GI's wife, who was more outgoing than Marion. Or perhaps it was because she was unavailable, and therefore more tantalizing. After all, wasn't forbidden fruit more seductive?

As the ship drew closer to Hawaii, the weather became sunny and warm and the water bluer than I had ever seen it. My parents and I were actually beginning to relax and enjoy the trip as if it were a vacation -- and in a way it was precisely that, our first "vacation" together since 1939. I would lean over the railing and contentedly watch the wake from our ship in the calm ocean

217

and spot all sorts of fish I couldn't identify. I loved the gentle sound that the water made; I was happy to be alive.

Ruth and I looked forward to going ashore and sightseeing together in Honolulu; the closer we came to Hawaii, the more excited we grew. Suddenly, 24 hours prior to our scheduled arrival in Hawaii, the loudspeakers blared out a stern message: *"Stay where you are and do not move!"* I was on the third deck at the stern end of the ship leaning over the railing. Quite abruptly, a uniformed U.S. Customs official appeared before me and asked my name. He carried a clipboard and checked his passenger list for my name. When he found it, he directed me to follow him to my bunk. The same angst that had been part of my life leaving Berlin washed over me once again.

At my bunk he asked for the papers that the U.S. Consulate had given me. I feverishly pawed through my luggage and retrieved the papers. He then asked me to follow him into the cafeteria, where a team of U.S. Immigration officials were sitting behind the tables interviewing passengers one by one. I sat down in front of one Immigration official and handed him my documents, the ones the Vice Consul had sealed with a red ribbon.

He examined my picture affixed to the document, which served as my official photo I.D. in lieu of passport, then carefully compared my face with the photo; apparently satisfied that they matched, he asked me to sign my name on a piece of paper, and cross-checked that too with the signature on the picture. He asked if I was born in Berlin, Germany, and after I replied "yes," he scrutinized the visa I was issued in Shanghai. He next asked what my plans were in the States, and I told of my hope to find work as an engineer. He nodded as if satisfied with my responses, affixed some stamps on my visa and handed the documents back. Only then did he unbend a little and welcomed me to the United States. Needless to say, I felt enormous relief that I had hurdled this last barrier, and left the cafeteria looking for my parents to give them the good news. When I found them, they reported undergoing the same kind of scrutiny, and they also had been admitted to the United States. We had all passed muster!

There was a lot of curiosity about how these Customs and Immigration personnel had suddenly appeared on board. Some passengers speculated that they had boarded in Hong Kong, but the fact was they had arrived secretly via something called a helicopter in the middle of the night. (I, for one, had never seen a helicopter.) Though no one actually knew for sure, rumors flew around the ship about why they appeared at the time they did; the consensus was they were looking for 16 illegal stowaways from Shanghai who were planning to leave the ship in Honolulu.

It took several hours before the official count was completed, and the grapevine yielded up the news that the stowaways had been found, to be returned to Shanghai as soon as the ship docked. I felt a sense of sadness for them.

The Customs and Immigration officials stayed on board and mingled with the passengers until we docked in Honolulu. I, however, was not among the minglers but kept a discreet distance between me and them -- I had not yet overcome my distrust of any officials, whatever their nationality!

The next morning, I was topside by 6 a.m. along with the other eager-beaver passengers already there. As the sun rose magnificently on the eastern horizon, we watched the land come up slowly in the dark blue water. Gradually, the rich, green coastline became clearer in its details. After a while the famous large volcanic mountain called Diamond Head rose into view in the background. The ship was still far away from docking, so I skipped below deck for a quick breakfast. By 7:30 a.m., I was back on deck with Ruth and my parents to watch our entry into Honolulu. Soon well camouflaged buildings came into view, grim reminders of the war.

As four tug boats slowly brought the liner to the pier, we heard faint strains of music coming from a band standing on the dock in the middle of a raised platform decorated with red, white and blue banners stamped with big block letters saying "WELCOME." A large reception committee was awaiting our arrival, along with a group of Hawaiian girls holding leis to be offered us.

Surprised by all the fuss, I asked a crewman the reason, and he said this was only the second ship to bring refugees from Shanghai to the United States, and that in Hawaii we were all considered quite special.

As soon as the gangway was attached to the ship, the reception committee boarded, representing the Jewish community of Honolulu, to invite all refugees from Shanghai to lunch at the Jewish Center. My parents accepted with great pleasure, but I had other plans. It was a clear, beautiful, warm April day with very little wind; Ruth and I wanted to discover Honolulu by ourselves.

As we stepped off the ship, two pretty Hawaiian girls put leis woven with fresh white carnations around our necks; the strong floral aroma almost made us dizzy, as if excitement hadn't already done that to us.

A short walk brought us out of the dock area and into the heart of the city where silver-colored trolley buses moved quietly along the streets. As we strolled the clean, wide sidewalks, women dressed in long, colorful Hawaiian muu muus and men in white pants and colorful shirts passed us. The streets were lined with palm trees and every building was painted white, except for a large double-domed hotel, painted a pastel pink. This was the Royal Hawaiian Hotel, its plush grounds surrounded by lush tropical gardens dominated by bougainvillea.

We decided to venture inside just to look around. The lobby was refreshingly cool, thanks to huge ceiling fans, and we welcomed a brief reprieve from the Honolulu heat which had sneaked up on us quickly. A large doorway at the back of the hotel led us out to the beach and ocean where we found parasol-topped tables, but having barely begun to explore the city, we didn't even sit down for a drink.

I enjoyed Ruth's oohs and aahs as we window-shopped, but when we passed a shop marked "Drug Store," we were both puzzled, seeing a counter with stools just inside the front door.

Curiosity led us inside, where we took seats at what appeared to be a food counter. Why would a drug store sell food? In England and Germany, shops that sold only drugs were called *Chemists* or *Apotheken*.

The counter girl tried to be helpful to these two green tourists and suggested one of the store's specialties, something she called "Sundays." We were at a loss to know what "Sundays" had to do with either food or drugs. The girl was amused that we had never seen such a drug store, and grinning, explained that a "sundae is a delicious concoction of various flavors of ice cream, topped with mountains of whipped cream, a syrup of choice (either chocolate or butterscotch) and nuts." She said they were expensive, though. In Honolulu they cost 25 cents, but we would find them much cheaper on the mainland.

The distinction she made between the "mainland" and Honolulu, Hawaii was also puzzling. "Were we in Honolulu or in the United States?" we asked. She patiently explained that we were already in the United States, but Hawaii was an island located off the coast of the mainland. She said that the local Hawaiian population was very sensitive about this terminology and cautioned us to use the words correctly.

We were less interested in the linguistics lesson than in watching greedily as she put together the two enormous sundaes we ordered, barely able to keep from salivating as she topped each piece of her artistry with a maraschino cherry. We had never tasted anything quite as marvelous before, so this definitely counted as my first peak experience in America.

Continuing our walk, a few blocks away we came to a large movie house which had palm trees growing right through the top of where the roof would ordinarily have been. We soon discovered that though it rained a few minutes off and on every day in Honolulu, the climate being tropical, everything dried immediately. Moviegoers didn't seem to mind sitting roofless through a short shower.

We walked on. The sidewalk came to an end abruptly and a small beach began, with a sign saying "Waikiki Beach." The

221

sand was fine and white, and we could see surfers in the distance. The water looked irresistibly clear and blue. Enticed, we bought tickets to use the beach, and rented bathing suits from the outdoor cabana desk.

As we returned from our respective lockers, I was very aware as I walked toward her that Ruth was lovely in a plain blue bathing suit, which accentuated her slim waist and full bosom. I was also properly appreciative of her long dark hair tossing lightly in the Hawaiian breeze.

We found a spot not too crowded on the white sandy beach, spread out our towels and lay down in the scorching sun. With coconut suntan lotion I'd bought in the men's locker room, I swabbed Ruth's back and shoulders and she did the same for me. At her gentle touch, I couldn't help feeling somewhat aroused. "Her husband is waiting for her in San Francisco," I reminded myself and vowed to confine my explorations to Honolulu, whatever my feelings towards her might be.

We distracted ourselves from the sensual moment by watching and eavesdropping on our fellow beach visitors, who seemed to be a mixture of Japanese, Chinese and Caucasian, though most of them spoke English. We admired their beautiful dark skin, black hair and mostly almond-shaped dark Oriental eyes.

At noon we ventured into the water which, though warm, was refreshing because of the powerful surf. The tidal flat was so shallow we had to walk far off shore before we could begin to swim. Paddling in the sea with our faces towards the city, we found the view magnificent. Hotels and apartment houses ringed the crescent-shaped beach, and looming in the background was Diamond Head.

Next to the beach was another hotel with a large outdoor terrace on which lunch was being served. We swam and walked back to shore, and headed there to have lunch, still in our bathing suits. It proved to be a delightful choice, and we were not the only ones in swimming attire.

As I examined the menu and checked out the prices, I realized that I had spent only $1.50 so far that day, and thus had $8.50 left of my $10 gambling loot to spend. The waiter highly recommended that we try a fresh fruit salad served in half of a pineapple topped by vanilla ice cream. He also recommended a typical Hawaiian pre-lunch cocktail consisting of rum mixed with various fruit juices, all of which cost less than $2.00, well within range of my pocketbook. Though I was in a holiday mood, Shanghai had taught me not to be profligate, and I was not about to dig into my original $10.00.

When the waiter brought our order, we could not believe our eyes. Two tall glasses with fruit on top were put in front of us, followed by two large plates, each with a half pineapple stuffed with a mountain of different fruits and topped with a huge mound of ice cream. America was certainly the land of plenty! We took our time, and lazed through a two-hour lunch.

After changing into our own clothes, we walked back to the street in front of the hotel where I negotiated with the driver of a horse-drawn carriage for a two-hour afternoon tour.

The tour was like a dream. The driver showed us the city's historical sites, going slowly along wildly colorful streets so full of blooms they could have been botanical gardens. From our spectator's coach we viewed several exquisite homes and huge plantations. The driver explained that wealthy Hawaiians could take the islands for only about 18 months at a single stretch, then they wanted to get away to the mainland for a vacation. We could not understand ever wanting to leave Hawaii since the weather was so perfect. That was exactly the reason, the driver explained: Because the warm season never changed, because the climate was so consistently the same, with the sun strong all year long without any deviation, many of the wealthy (who could afford boredom) indulged their craving for change.

We passed the Jewish Community Building where my parents were having lunch, and as we turned the corner, we saw many of our fellow passengers dining in the gardens at the rear of the building, but neither Ruth nor I wanted to stop and be sociable -- we would be with them on the ship all the way to San Francisco.

The driver dropped us off in front of the roofless movie house we had passed earlier. On a lark, we purchased tickets and quickly found seats in the center of the theatre; an American film had already begun. Palm trees were illuminated by colored lights, creating a romantic, and to us, exotic effect; suddenly, it started to rain, but no one moved. The rain was gentle and warm, strangely refreshing. It stopped after a few minutes, and soon we were dry again. This happened several times throughout the movie, but nobody seemed to mind, least of all us. This relaxed, laid-back response to wet weather was apparently normal in Honolulu.

By the time we left the theater the sun was sinking low in the sky and the lights of the city were beginning to gradually come on, making a beautiful, dream-like picture. The view filled our souls, but our stomachs were hungry again. Ruth wanted to try Honolulu seafood, and along the wide main street in the opposite direction of the movie-house, we soon found a nice-looking seafood restaurant, which looked casual but expensive.

We walked into the place through an open area that served as the entrance -- there was no door. We were seated amid decorative sea nets and fish tanks with brilliantly colored tropical fish, but we soon turned our attention to what was advertised as a blue plate special of fish and chips for 90 cents. We now had only $4.50 left from my nest egg, so fortunately the blue plate seemed appealing to us both. Though the enormous plates were filled with huge servings of fish, french fried potatoes, cole slaw and fresh bread, we both cleaned our plates. Incidentally, neither of us could get over the fact that our meal was actually served on blue plates. What an astonishing country America was!

There being no stomach room left for dessert, we ordered iced coffee to polish off our elegant feast, the blue plate special.

It was nine o'clock when we finished dinner, and the night was still young, so we strolled very slowly back to the *General Meigs*, where we learned that we would sail at 10 a.m. the next morning. Since we had not yet taken a tour of Diamond Head, something we both had our hearts set on, we made a pact to rise very early for an 8 a.m. tour bus.

When we returned to our deck, we ran into my parents who were eager to tell us how enthusiastically they had been welcomed by virtually the entire Jewish community of Honolulu. They said the hostesses had served a festive lunch in a beautiful garden, they had enjoyed every single morsel, and most of all, found the company *gemütlich*. Ruth and I tacitly agreed not to take the glitter of their day away to tell them about our amazing first day in America; there would be plenty of time after we left port.

Wanting to be rested when we rose early for the next morning's junket, we bid an early good night to my parents and left them chatting with friends on the deck; I reluctantly parted from Ruth as well, as we headed to our respective dormitories, heady from the beauty of the day's excursion.

As I prepared for bed that night, I noted gleefully that I still had one dollar left from my casino winnings. All that fun, and money left over! What a great way to begin life in my new country.

****

The road up to the peak of Diamond Head wound like one of the ocean's spiral conch shells. The view from the top was worth the tortuous mountain climb, for it was magnificent, and we congratulated ourselves for having made the extra effort to get there. The same bus brought us back to the ship, and we boarded at 9:30 a.m., where our absence had been noticed by friends from Shanghai.

As the harbor crew prepared for departure, the mooring lines loosened and the tugboats slowly pushed the ship away from the pier, the band played again, bidding us farewell. Everywhere I looked, people were waving -- everywhere on the dock and from

225

every deck of the ship. It looked as if the entire Jewish community had come to see us off.

The view of Diamond Head growing smaller and smaller as we pulled away from Honolulu is a memory never to be forgotten. The blue, clear water all around us was a wonderful good-bye to the island, our first taste of America the beautiful.

We settled down for the five-day cruise to San Francisco, the last leg of our voyage. As we got closer to San Francisco, I deliberately saw less and less of Ruth. I knew that she must have some private time to set her mind on the reunion with her husband.

I sought out the company of a group of young adults, which included Marion Freundlich. We had never been interested in each other romantically but we had a good time being together for the next few days. There really was nothing to do on the ship, except watch rehearsals of a hula dance company which was on its way to the mainland for a tour. This was at first interesting but after a while seemed endlessly repetitive and boring. The dance group offered to teach passengers the hula, and some took lessons. Not for me, thank you.

Serious conversation was more my style, and I spent long hours discussing our ideas for the future with Marion who was also planning to live in New York. We had been told that a Jewish committee in San Francisco would help us with lodging and job applications, so we had those issues and plenty of other common concerns to discuss.

The five day voyage from Honolulu to San Francisco was uneventful. On the beautiful night of May 1, 1947 at around ten o'clock we sailed into San Francisco Bay. The stars were visible in a clear sky, a gentle breeze blowing across our faces. A thrill ran through us as we recognized the huge Golden Gate Bridge. There was a large, well-lit island in the bay nearby, which we learned was Alcatraz, the infamous prison. The skyline of the city was visible in the distance.

Disembarking was to begin at 8 o'clock the next morning. For the very last time, most passengers rose early to witness the ship's passage under the Golden Gate Bridge and its berthing at the pier near Fisherman's Wharf. There was no need to say good-bye to anyone because all the Jewish refugees were heading for the same hotel. Only Ruth and I bade each other farewell, before she left to find her husband. I have never learned what became of her.

We finally left the ship at 10:00 a.m. Without much hubbub, we patiently joined the line walking down the gangway to the covered pier, where the next challenge was finding our luggage. Large letters on banners hanging from the ceiling lessened the mass confusion. My parents and I eventually reached the letter "R" and squeezed through the mass of passengers blocking our way. We located our luggage, made a pile out of all the pieces, counted them all and were ready finally to get on line for the customs inspectors in an area just a short distance from where we were.

When our turn came, the customs inspector asked us to open all our luggage, and then poked around in all of our belongings. My father had dental drugs in his wardrobe trunk, (which had been declared earlier on a sheet of paper we were required to fill out). Now the inspector found them and asked about them as though knowing nothing of the declaration list. My father told him that as a dentist he had brought his dentistry tools and chemicals with him, since he intended to practice in America. Either the drugs or my father's explanation caused a problem, because the inspector disappeared, asking us to wait; he did not reappear for two hours, and we waited dejectedly, wondering "What now?"

It was almost noon and we were still at the pier. Most of our friends had left the pier, already on their way to the hotel where rooms had been reserved for us by the American Joint Distribution Committee. By now we were hungry, tired, and worried, not knowing what caused the delay. Finally the customs official reappeared with some of the glass capsules that my father had in his luggage. Without ever explaining the reason for his lengthy disappearance, he continued to check the balance of our luggage, as if nothing had transpired, then marked it all with an OK.

We were the last passengers to leave the pier. A lady from the American Joint helped us off the pier to a taxi, and gave the driver instructions to take us to the Hotel Raford on Taylor Street.

We had finally arrived in mainland America. It was up to us to fulfill its promise to all, the freedom to pursue life, liberty and happiness.

And we did just that.

Epilogue

We didn't stay long in San Francisco, although it was tempting to never leave. The people were wonderful, the weather perfect, and I was almost seduced by the suggestion of our American advisor (supplied by the American Joint Committee) with the idea that I was a perfect candidate to work for California's Hughes Aircraft. Nevertheless, our last close living relative (my cousin Werner) was in New York, so we headed cross-country to New York by train. This was not an entirely a happy experience; we missed re-joining our Pullman train after a "station stretch" in Ogden, Utah because of not understanding about zonal time differences and not changing our watches; thus we had to ride one leg of the trip on a mail train before catching up to our original train.

Werner met us at Pennsylvania station in Manhattan. It was a restrained reunion; I suppose the memories of Tante Lillie and Uncle Kurt were intense for all of us, and seeing their son for the first time since he left Berlin, some thirteen years before caused us all to be strangely subdued. We didn't speak of the unspeakable that night, only later learning the details of how Kurt had died in Dachau. We never knew which camp Lillie died in. My grandmother had died in *Therisienstadt*, another concentration camp, at the age of 89 on May 8, 1945. Ironically enough, her death came just as the war ended.

Werner did all he could to help us get established as Americans, including introducing us the first morning to that remarkably innovative institution, the Horn and Hardart Automat. More importantly, he had found us our first apartment. It was on Cathedral Parkway, one block from Riverside Drive; it was a spacious, furnished apartment close to a subway station, also close to the Hudson River, and we were grateful to Werner. Soon, though, we would have to be on our own, as Werner had his own life to live.

229

Thanks to my father's foresight in choosing an engineering career for me, my own persistence in pursuing potential jobs opportunities, and my penchant for coming up with patentable ideas, my dreams of a good life in the United States came true almost immediately. (I even bought a handsome used 1937 black 2-door Ford while still in my first job, within a few weeks of our arrival in New York. It cost the outrageous sum of $550, and my cautious cousin Werner strongly advised against this extravagance, but I did it anyway.) Not even my citizenship papers made me feel more American than owning that car!

One other form of Americanization took place early on: an employment counsellor advised me to change my given name, because Hans was far too German-sounding. ("It's too soon after the war to get work in this country with a German sounding name like that. How about Hanley?") And so I became "Hanley" Riess on all official documents in this country. (Whether the counsellor was right or not, I do not know, but "Hanley" seemed to pass muster just fine.)

Pappi did not go back into dentistry. He would have had to endure two more years of study to receive certification in New York, and by 1947 the Shanghai years had taken too large a toll for him to face starting all over again. He did establish a dental laboratory at Broadway and 86th Street, but was never happy with it -- primarily because he disagreed with what American dentists were instructing him to do. He had a major project, however, and he devoted himself to it with his old zest. Before he died, after tomes of paper work and massive correspondence with German courts and the help of a lawyer in Germany, he succeeded in obtaining partial reparation from Germany for all Mutti's jewelry and stocks, the money that had been frozen since *Kristallnacht*, as well as a pension she was able to live on after he died in 1955.

Mutti lived until 1973, and maintained her friendship with the Blumbergs who settled in Denver. We were able to visit them at their new home in Colorado. Mutti also made many new friends in New York.

In 1948 I met my first wife, a Jewish girl with a Russian/Austrian background named Rosalin, nicknamed Ronnie, and we were married in 1949. I was attracted by tiny Ronnie's small waist, high cheek bones and slightly slanted eyes. Was it her faint resemblance to the exotic Chinese girls in Shanghai I'd found so beautiful that drew me to her? I cannot say. I can only report that the good part of my first marriage was the birth of my two wonderful sons. Marc, born in 1951, is now a college professor, and Charles, born in 1954, a business consultant, married to Melody, a journalist.

My second marriage to Joyce in 1970 has brought the joy and companionship that my parents' devotion had led me to believe marriage would offer. Joyce's two sons by a previous marriage, Kevin and Kenny, and my own two sons, have provided us with a total of four beautiful, lively grandchildren.

After my second retirement in 1996 at the age of 75 (from New York's Metropolitan Transit Authority where I was Manager of Records), I find myself now with time to reflect on all the events between 1939 and 1947, when I was among the unwanted Jews of Berlin. In my retrospections, I now wonder what has become of that amazing cast of characters who peopled my life in those refugee years.

I kept in touch with the Murrays for a long time, and in 1963 on one of my lecture trips, we had a small reunion at my hotel where I stayed in London. I never knew what happened to little Hannie and her family after they were interned at the Isle of Man.

Beautiful Ann, my shipboard companion on the *Haruna Maru* -- did she come through the war unscathed? How I would love to know. I did learn that our 10,000 ton *Haruna Maru* was sunk during the war on July 7, 1942.

I wonder about Mr. Wu -- and how he coped with the take-over of Shanghai by the Communists in 1949. Much as we all had great distaste for the Nationalist government of Kuomintang, I believe Mme. Chiang Kai Shek's style of operating was closer to Mr. Wu's less-than-Communistic approach to business. I have no doubt, however, that he survived by his wits once again.

Did Jardine bring Mr. Morrison (and the other British managers, for that matter) back to London before the Communist take-over? That, too, I have never learned.

Of Armgardt I have learned. She married and visited me in 1959 at my home in Long Island. Sadly, her father wrote me in the late sixties that she had died.

Perhaps someday I will find out if Ruth lived happily ever after with her American GI husband. Perhaps someday I shall visit Australia and see my only living cousin, Annemarie (Hanna) who changed her name one more time. She is now "Anne" and is living in Australia with her daughter and grandchildren, her husband having died there in 1993.

Werner, who died only recently in Manhattan, lived with his wife Ursula quietly in the Bronx. He had been a professional photographer for many years.

I have been able to return three times to Germany, the first time in 1963, when Adenauer (*der alte*) was Chancellor. My heart was warmed on that visit by the demonstration of 3,000 husky German youths marching to the *Rathaus* to honor President Kennedy, in a city where once only Hitler was revered. In 1971 my wife Joyce and I visited the *Anne Frank House* in Amsterdam, where I was able, dried eyed, to point out on the map in the museum section of the house, the concentration camps where my relatives met their deaths; Joyce wept for all of us.

On one of my return visits in 1987 I called on my cousin Ludwig Riess, Jr., who was living in a Jewish old age home. He had survived the Nazis and lived out his life in Berlin, married to a Christian, and somehow "passing" as something other than a Jew. Recently we have traveled with our sons Marc and Kevin and their wives to Germany to show them the happy places of my childhood.

I believe the fact that I am not bitter has been my salvation. I have looked at my German passport now and again while writing

232

this book. The bold red "J," on the cover stands out bleakly, a solitary memory prod that brings back some of the horror of those last days in Berlin. But it also reminds me that I am a Jew who has "walked on lucky stones" all of his life, and can exclaim with millions of others, "Thank God for America, and the kindness of strangers."

Hans L. Riess
Wesley Hills, New York
July, 2000

ABOUT THE AUTHOR

Hans Ludwig Riess was born in 1921 in Berlin, Germany to Jewish parents. As a child, he saw Hitler's rise to power in 1933. He viewed the damage of Jewish shops and fires of synagogues on "Kristall Nacht" and his father being taken to a concentration camp. Mr. Riess was sent to England on a "Kinder Transport" in March 1939 to study engineering and lived with a British family. He sailed during the war on a Japanese diplomatic ship from England via South Africa to Shanghai, China, where he worked for a British trading company. He witnessed the Japanese occupation and was permitted to continue working since he had a German passport. Mr. Riess arrived in San Francisco, CA in 1947.

Printed in the United States
2510